40+ NEW REVENUE SOURCES
for Libraries and Nonprofits

ALA Editions purchases fund advocacy, awareness, and accreditation programs for library professionals worldwide.

40⁺

NEW REVENUE SOURCES

for

LIBRARIES & NONPROFITS

EDMUND A. ROSSMAN III

ala
editions

An imprint of the American Library Association
Chicago 2016

ED ROSSMAN has been involved with libraries and broadcasting since 1980. He holds master's degrees in Communications from Ohio University and the School of Library and Information Science at Kent State University. Currently he is an adult service librarian in Shaker Heights, Ohio, and is a member of and past chair of the Business Reference in Public Libraries committee of BRASS. He is the author of Castles *Against Ignorance: How to Make Libraries Great Educational Environments* (2006). He has taught courses on the internet and mass media for the Kent State School of Journalism, and is currently teaching online courses on Business Writing for libraries at Kent State University's School of Library and Information Science. As a business manager of radio stations in two major markets, he coordinated dozens of sponsorship campaigns, as well as produced over 200 hours of sponsored specialty programming.

© 2016 by the American Library Association

Extensive effort has gone into ensuring the reliability of the information in this book; however, the publisher makes no warranty, express or implied, with respect to the material contained herein.

ISBN: 978-0-8389-1438-0 (paper)

Library of Congress Cataloging-in-Publication Data
Names: Rossman, Edmund A., III, author.
Title: 40+ new revenue sources for libraries and nonprofits / Edmund A. Rossman III.
Other titles: Forty plus new revenue sources for libraries and nonprofits
Description: Chicago : ALA Editions, an imprint of the American Library Association, 2016. |
    Includes bibliographical references and index.
Identifiers: LCCN 2015050642 | ISBN 9780838914380 (print : alk. paper)
Subjects: LCSH: Library finance—United States. | Library fund raising—United States. |
    Nonprofit organizations—Finance.
Classification: LCC Z683.2.U6 R67 2016 | DDC 025.1/10973—dc23 LC record available at
    https://lccn.loc.gov/2015050642

Book design by Alejandra Diaz in the Adobe Jenson Pro, Interstate, and Bodoni typefaces.

♾ This paper meets the requirements of ANSI/NISO Z39.48–1992 (Permanence of Paper).

Printed in the United States of America
20 19 18 17 16   5 4 3 2 1

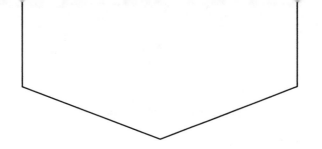

CONTENTS

Books and Materials: General Concepts   119

Naming Rights: General Concepts   157

ACKNOWLEDGMENTS

THANKS TO EVERYONE WHO HELPED DEVELOP THE IDEAS for this book, including my wonderful family, friends, editor, and colleagues. Special thanks to my brother Tom, Vice-President of Sales for MTD Products, who gave me great insights on co-op advertising, corporate sponsorships and building client relationships.

I'm especially grateful for those professionals in the field who helped me pass the torch of knowledge on this critical topic. They include Dr. Charles Clift, professor emeritus, Ohio University; Myles Gallagher, the Superlative Group; Steve Legerski, Metric$ Media; David Holmes, The Foundation Center; George Needham, Delaware County District Library; Diane Jalfon, Memphis Library Foundation; Jan Busa, San Mateo Public Library; Amy Calhoun, Sacramento Public Library; John Trischetti III, Midland County Public Library; Jim Heuer, Ingram Library Group; Linda Hazzan, Toronto Public Library; Mary Housel, Santa Maria Public Library; Brenda Ritenour, Denver Public Library; Erin Christmas, Old Town Newhall Library; Barbara Bishop, Auburn University; and Mary Bear Shannon, Haverford Township Free Library. May you all "live long and prosper."

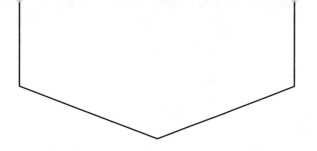

INTRODUCTION

A college visitor paused to admire the new Hemingway Hall campus building.
"It's a pleasure to see a building named for Ernest Hemingway," he said.
"Actually," said his guide, "It's named for Joshua Hemingway, who is no relation."
The visitor was astonished. "Was Joshua Hemingway a writer, too?"
"Yes, indeed," said his guide. "He wrote a check."
—UNKNOWN

THIS LIGHT-HEARTED JOKE UNDERSCORES THE IRONY OF developing revenue streams for nonprofits such as libraries. Yes, we want to pay homage and respect to the knowledge and creativity contained within our walls (and now distributed digitally). But we are challenged in building and maintaining those structures that help us accomplish that. Inspired by Andrew Carnegie, who built many of America's libraries, communities have banded together to build and support these important resources. But for many communities, tax dollars can only do so much, and as we've seen in tight times, many libraries react by cutting expenses. This book runs counter to that strategy. It takes a proactive approach to building multiple revenue sources, or streams that can help maintain and enhance services.

"Revenue stream" is another name for income or sales, and is generally used with a modifier such as "new" or "additional." According to an entry in inc.com's encyclopedia of business terms (inc.com), a quest for new revenue streams is often stimulated by change, for better or worse. Change creates opportunities, and the ability to see and exploit them is what creates new revenue streams. Examples of positive change include the introduction of visual interfaces on computers, which helped to make the Internet accessible to the average consumer. Examples of negative change can be provided by looking at the history of public broadcasting. Once fully funded by the government, cutbacks forced it to develop new sources of funding: membership drives, on-air auctions, and various sponsorships helped public broadcasting survive and thrive. This public broadcasting model will be referred to in this book as one that public libraries and other nonprofits (NPs) can follow.

Certain features of the market come into play when trying to establish revenue streams. In this book we will examine how these general market features apply to the library environment. Some of the features that will be looked at are location, traffic, the right clusters of skills, and technology. And you'll receive guidance developed from practical experience on how to utilize these market features in the most professional and efficient manner to build new revenue streams for your library.

Foremost among the skills needed to capitalize on change is the ability to keep your eyes open to see opportunities, and the discipline and expertise to turn ideas into salable products or services (inc.com). Picking up this book obviously indicates you have an interest in these entrepreneurial skills, which include the ability to analyze community and business needs, creativity in communications, knowledge about negotiation tactics, and the ability to sustain long-term business relationships. You can look forward to learning dozens of revenue-generating methods to use in helping your library's bottom line.

This book was partly inspired by the response my *Public Libraries Briefcase* article from January 2014, "What's in a Name? Naming Rights as Revenue Generators" (Rossman 2014) that drew 500 page views in just a few days. The need for a review of these concepts was further reinforced by the January 2015 ALA webinar, "New Sources of Revenue: Naming Rights, Crowd-Funding, Sponsorships and More," in which more than forty libraries took part. Despite the focus on libraries, NPs of all types can benefit from this book's suggestions on developing supplementary revenue.

In the original *Briefcase* article survey, about 70 percent of the survey respondents planned to use naming rights. Most libraries that have already awarded them have given them permanent status. It's time to rethink that approach to maximize revenue potential. The impact of a onetime gift of even several million can be diluted over fifty years. This book addresses this and other contractual issues, and will:

» Cross-pollinate the broadcasting/advertising method of selling sponsorships to library situations, using familiar examples from media to illustrate existing opportunities in libraries.

» Provide guidelines and examples of how to establish value, write board policies and comprehensive contracts in a toolkit approach that will make the sales process more efficient for libraries of all types and sizes to use.

» Offer examples of rate charts, contracts, and policy statements, as well as answers to questions about naming, sponsorship, and online fund-raising activities. Responses to sensitive questions such as how to handle a sponsor's name changes, unforeseen bankruptcy or "disgraceful" situations with a sponsor, concerns about "selling out," and the use of technology for appeals will be addressed so that your board and management will be fully prepared to respond.

In this book, the topic has been expanded to include many new references, more methods of revenue generation presented on a "Money Matrix," plus exercises designed to guide you along the path of building revenue streams.

HOW TO READ THIS BOOK

Part I includes the foundational chapters. They talk about the context many libraries and nonprofits are finding themselves in these days. A good role model, public broadcasting, is then used to show how it's possible to wean away from traditional government revenue sources. Then come the basics of generating new revenue: establishing value, legalities, contracts, promotions, the use of technology, and how proactive revenue generation can be useful in the grant-seeking process. After this important foundational groundwork is covered, the actual revenue-generating methods are discussed in part II, which you can either read through all at once or go directly to specific sections that interest you.

Part II describes over forty revenue-generating methods. These are divided up into mini-chapters. For each method, I'll describe anticipated revenue, the amount of work and planning involved in contracts and promotions, as well as how to estimate the degree of possible board and government involvement. These are summarized in the Money Matrix table found in Appendix A. Perhaps the most important part of each mini-chapter is its "First Steps" section. For each method, plans and exercises are given to help you begin implementation in an efficient manner. Whether you're running a solo operation or chairing a committee, these steps should guide your thinking as to how to use these methods quickly.

Part II also leads off with an exercise where I ask that you set a "new revenue" goal, maybe 5 to 10 percent of your current revenue, and pick just five of the methods from the Matrix list to research in order to achieve that goal. Calculate the level of success you'll need to reach your goal. How many sponsorships, meeting room rentals, vending machine sales, or passports would you need? This should help you visualize how these methods might easily help you reach your goal. It's strongly recommended to have a goal in mind before reviewing the methods. Hopefully, you'll find you've underestimated your goal once you can see the potential of your chosen methods!

This book is structured as follows:

» Chapter 1 sets the challenging funding context that libraries and NPs face.
» Chapter 2 discusses public broadcasting, an industry with strong analogies to our own, and from which we can learn some very positive lessons on raising money.
» Chapter 3 is a brief education on broadcast sales that draws from both the public and commercial broadcasting fields.
» Chapter 4 talks about the main mistake rookies make: setting proper value for something in which they passionately believe.
» Chapter 5 discusses critical legal and tax considerations.
» Chapter 6 reviews professional contracts and procedures.
» Chapter 7 explains how to get the word out about what you're offering.
» Chapter 8 goes over the use of crowdfunding and other technology-based methods, and reviews a few successful case studies.

» Chapter 9 reviews how all this may affect your ability to get grants and help address important issues in your community.
» Part II details 40+ methods of generating revenue.
» Appendix A contains my Money Matrix, useful for encapsulating key points for group discussions or brainstorming.

Several chapters include suggested exercises that are meant to be done before you approach the next concept. Here's the first one, about keeping current with fund-raising news. This book's topic is also on Facebook. Go to facebook.com/rev4lib to keep current with events, new methods, and cautions. Comment and learn from others concerned about building revenue streams for libraries.

News Retrieval   EXERCISE

Due to the dynamic nature of this field, this book contains concepts that have lasted over time as well as current case studies and methods. To keep up to date on new developments as you read through this book, I recommend creating some Google Alerts. To do this you will need a Google email account or use an email system that utilizes Gmail. Here's how to set one up:

1 Go to www.google.com/alerts (If the URL changes, search "google alerts.")

2 Type in the keywords of your search interest, for example, "public library," "naming rights," "revenue," "sponsorships," "crowdfunding" (with or without hyphens), "partnerships," "book sales" (often an expression used in articles about non-traditional revenue), "fund-raising," "advocacy," "room rental," or whatever method you're considering.

3 Enter an email address that you want alerts sent to and click create Alert.

4 Choose your options:
How often: As it happens, once a day, once a week.
Sources: Automatic, will include web pages, news, blogs, etc.
How many: Only the best, or all the results.

When you begin using the keywords it'll show sample results, so you can change keywords and phrases as needed. Use standard Google syntax for setting up the Boolean searches (a minus sign equals "not," etc.). You can search "google search operators" for a number of help pages.

Whether you consider your organization a learning commons, community center, digital bridge or any other current popular euphemism, you'll always need money to survive. This book will help fast-track you towards achieving your revenue goals no matter what surprises are in store for the future. In chapter 1, we'll briefly look at the past before tackling today's current context regarding funding.

References

Inc.com. "Revenue Streams." *Encyclopedia of Business Terms*. www.inc.com/encyclopedia/revenue-streams.html.

Rossman, E. 2014. "What's in a Name? Naming Rights as Revenue Generators." *Public Libraries Briefcase* 29. www.ala.org/rusa/sections/brass/brasspubs/publibbrief/no291q2014.

PART ONE

FOUNDATIONAL CHAPTERS

CHAPTER ONE

CURRENT CONTEXT OF LIBRARY FUNDING ISSUES AND PROBLEMS

ANDREW CARNEGIE DONATED GENEROUSLY TO THE construction of libraries that contributed significantly to America's development. Thousands of public and academic libraries were built thanks to his generosity. Our challenge 100 years later is how to sustain and grow that gift!

Those of you working in Carnegie Libraries are no doubt familiar with the challenges libraries face today. Despite the increase in the use and the efficiencies of new technology, expenses keep rising, often outpacing funding established through levies and other traditional sources. Aging buildings need expensive repairs. This same dilemma is faced by many nonprofits. Author Ron Mattocks reported that one-third of all nonprofit organizations operate in financial distress, which he calls the "Zone of Insolvency" (Mattocks 2008, xxi).

Studies have shown that 91 percent of funding for libraries comes from the government and local levies. Levies are taxes that need a majority vote in a community to be enacted, often determined by property values. In tough economic times, we've seen how government funding just can't be as predictable and fulfilling as we need it to be. In the federal budget request for 2015, the proposed budget for the Library Services and Technology Act almost chopped 2 million dollars from the 180.9 million enacted for 2014. One million was recovered, but this is a sign of tightening library funding at the federal level (Sheketoff 2014).

Regarding local levies, in 2014 Knutson profiled how six local library funding issues fared. Two out of the six failed. While obviously not statistically significant, the *American Libraries* article does show that the public cannot always be expected to pick up the slack (Knutson 2014).

As this book is being written in the spring of 2015, *Library Hotline* has recently reported that three states were considering major budget cuts in library funding: Missouri, Connecticut, and Vermont (2014, 2015a, 2015b) A wide range of programs and services would be affected. Ironically, a Connecticut consortium created to help libraries save money is threatened. In an excellent editorial in *Library Journal*, Rebecca Miller expresses disdain for state officials who are anxious to cut expenses. They refer to state library funding as "low hanging fruit" instead of using the more positive analogy of seed money to create and foster library initiatives throughout the state, across various communities, wealthy and poor alike. Miller is concerned that libraries will withdraw into local silos and inequities in communities will persist (Miller 2015).

There are other funding villains. Not only do cuts in state funding hurt organizations, but other rising costs do as well. Rising health care costs, as well as increasing book prices (especially for e-media) and aging buildings requiring maintenance have put more pressure on libraries. One library director stated these increasing costs weren't severe enough for libraries to close, but high enough to cut back on hours of operation and new materials budgets. She's taken a proactive step by hiring a philanthropy expert to increase fund-raising efforts to meet her high standards of service (Annarelli 2015).

The table below summarizes the dilemma for many libraries and nonprofits.

Typical Problem	Typical Reaction
Cuts in state funding	Cutting access to services (hours)
Rising health costs	Cutting personnel
Rising material costs (print, video, and digital)	Cutting new material purchases
Rising infrastructure repair costs	Cutting expenses in programming and services

Notice how the typical reaction is to cut. This book will help to alleviate the problems without cutting anything. By learning how to add new revenue streams, you will lessen the library's dependency on government support and protect your library from budget cuts. But learning how to add new revenue streams will also protect your library services when costs rise faster than government support by giving you additional resources to tap when needed. The goal of this book is to teach you how to make money, not excuses, without selling out your patrons or mission.

Leonard Kniffel applauds Abby Johnson's article, "Sponsored by Your Library," in the September/ October 2013 issue of *American Libraries*. It cautions against commercialization in libraries. They should not sell out children or any other patrons. Libraries should reach out to their communities, should have a backbone when negotiating sponsorships and other revenue generators. They need to control the situation, not just back down to the demands of anyone waving money at them. Kniffel suggests setting proper board policies is part of this backbone building (Kniffel 2014).

Another key aspect to responding to these problems is establishing a revenue strategy that utilizes a range of methods. The Aspen Institute has released *Rising to the Challenge: Ensuring Long-Term Sustainability for Public Libraries* (2014), a plan to improve library services. One of their four major platforms is "Ensuring Long Term Sustainability." It cites that only 7 percent of library funding comes from "other sources" and that all libraries must examine alternatives to traditional funding. One such method is examining the current business models to create new revenue streams and profit centers. That would require encouraging entrepreneurship in libraries; in essence, reinventing an institution. More on this study will be discussed in chapter 9, on grants.

Clay and Bangs (2000) discuss the efforts of the Fairfax County Public Library (VA) in creating the Enterprise Group. Their goal was to set up a management committee that would seek out private funding without sacrificing the mission or goals of their nonprofit institution. Teamwork among the various library staff, friends, and foundation was essential for its success, as also stressed throughout this book.

The aforementioned book states that among ways to avoid risk in achieving expanded resources is by associating your mission activities with what it will cost to accomplish them. Any of the 40+ methods reviewed in part II can, and should be considered support mechanisms to the programs and services you want to provide, not just ways to make money on top of what the public provides you. Perhaps this quote from Abraham Lincoln frames the decision to develop new revenue sources best:

> The dogmas of the quiet past, are inadequate to the stormy present. The occasion is piled high with difficulty, and we must rise—with the occasion. As our case is new, so we must think anew, and act anew. We must disenthrall ourselves, and then we shall save our country. (Lincoln, 1862)

Do Your Due Diligence with Sponsors   TIP

Despite the severity of your problems, you really have to be careful with whom you'll be doing business. "Due diligence" is a legal term that can be simply defined as appraising a potential partner's ability to pay you and their past relationships with partnerships and especially the public. The book *Financing Non-Profits: Putting Theory into Practice* cautions that the danger for NPs is sharing their names with an undeserving business, and emphasizes that they must exercise due diligence so they don't hurt their own reputation (Young 2007, 106). The book states that to pursue their mission, NPs must expand their "resource constraints," but warns against going overboard on opportunities for making money. Fallout from an ill-advised partnership could impact your future levy campaigns with the public.

	Funding Shortfall Scenario	**EXERCISE**
	Take a look at your current budget and play a "what if?" game.	

1	Anticipate a reduction in funding by 3 percent, due to state cutbacks, property tax reductions, or whatever. That 3 percent is now your goal for new revenue stream activity.
2	If 7 percent of current library revenue has been from "other sources," now your goal is 10 percent.
3	Aim for a three-year period, as it may take time to gain traction.
4	If your budget is one million, that mean an increase of $30,000 in supplementary revenue will be necessary.
5	As you read this book, use this figure as you consider options in setting fair value and terms for the various revenue stream methods that will be discussed.

This next funding shortfall scenario exercise helps you realistically target what you have to generate to keep up with, or better yet, exceed, your current operations.

No one who went to school for libraries or social work was ever told "you'll make a lot of money doing this type of work." This never dissuaded anyone I've worked with. Now, to do the work you love, you may have to make a lot of money. Just not for yourself.

This era is not unique for nonprofits having tough times. In the 1980s, nonprofits with the mission of providing education and entertainment, which received most of their funding from government sources, also had to deal with a sudden loss of support. The next chapter reviews how public broadcasting not only survived, but thrived.

References

Annarelli, S. 2015. "Schlow Centre Region Library Steps Up Fund-Raising Efforts." *Centre Daily Times*, July 12. www.centredaily.com/2015/07/12/4832687/schlow-centre-region-library-steps.html.

Aspen Institute. 2014. *Rising to the Challenge: Ensuring Long-Term Sustainability for Public Libraries.* http://csreports.aspeninstitute.org/Dialogue-on-Public-Libraries/2014/report.

Clay, E., and P. Bangs, 2000. "Entrepreneurs in the Public Library: Reinventing an Institution." *Library Trends* 48 (3): 606–618.

Johnson, A. 2013. "Sponsored by Your Library." *American Libraries Magazine*, 44 (9/10): 56.

Kniffel, L. 2014. "Letters: Dear Abby." *American Libraries*, 45(1/2): 8–9.

Knutson, B. 2014. "Update: 6 Referenda to Watch." *American Libraries.* November 6. www.americanlibrariesmagazine.org/article/update-6-referenda-watch.

Library Hotline. 2015a. "CT and VT Libraries Await Budget Cut Decisions." *Library Hotline* 44 (18).

———. 2014. "Atlanta-Fulton Library Faces Budget, Hours Cut." *Library Hotline* 43 (8).

———. 2015b. "Missouri Library Funds Restored; FY 2016 in Flux." *Library Hotline* 44 (15).

Lincoln, A. 1862. "Annual Message to Congress—Concluding Remarks." www.abrahamlincolnonline.org/lincoln/speeches/congress.htm.

Mattocks, R. 2008. *Zone of Insolvency: How Nonprofits Avoid Hidden Liabilities and Build Financial Strength.* Hoboken, NJ: John Wiley and Sons.

Miller, R. 2015. "The Budget Dance: State Funding Is Not 'Low-Hanging Fruit.'" *Library Journal,* May 28. http://lj.libraryjournal.com/2015/05/opinion/ editorial/the-budget-dance-state-funding-is-not-low-hanging-fruit-editorial/.

Sheketoff, E. 2014. "Federal Library Funding Cut in Proposed Budget." *District Dispatch,* March 25. www.districtdispatch.org/2014/03/federal-library-funding -cut-proposed-budget/.

Young, D., ed. 2007. *Financing Non-Profits: Putting Theory into Practice.* Lanham, MD: AltaMira Press.

CHAPTER TWO

NONPROFIT LESSONS FROM PUBLIC BROADCASTING

NONPROFITS (NPs) WERE OFTEN STARTED BY ONE enlightened source—an individual, family, organization, or government—to address some problem in the community. Their challenge was that the better the job they did, the more resources they needed as more people in the community looked to them for help! The original funds and general community contributions did eventually plateau, so the NPs had to spread their roots and look for other sources.

NPs have not always been able to expand their revenue base easily. One typical problem encountered by NPs is dissension within their own ranks, centered on the fear of and resistance to commercialization. The book *What Money Can't Buy* offers many examples of this phenomenon. One prominent example detailed in the book is former New York Mayor Bloomberg's administration being criticized for granting a 5-year, 166-million-dollar agreement for exclusive beverage rights in New York City schools and public buildings. Much of the criticism chided him for turning the Big Apple into the Big Snapple (Sandel 2012, 189). Another example from our own profession is when, in 2014, libraries became upset over a publisher's requirement to offer eBooks for sale to their patrons in order to license them. Despite the fears about commercialization, three library networks trying the system reported little actual sales activity and no negative feedback from patrons. Additionally, some library systems are legally restricted from selling books by this method. (The publisher involved did eventually back down from the licensing requirement after pressure by individual libraries and their professional organizations [Ennis 2014]).

Dr. Charles Clift, Professor Emeritus, Ohio University, is an expert in broadcast programming, advertising, and the history of public broadcasting. He recalled that after the government started the public broadcasting system, it pulled the rug out from them. National Public Radio almost went bankrupt in the 1980s, so stations had to learn to be self-supportive. When national funding dried up, stations had to move to state and local funding (personal communication, August 2014).

An effort to supplement non-governmental local funding was spearheaded by the Temporary Commission on Alternative Financing for Public Telecommunications (1983), which delivered its recommendations to Congress on October 1, 1983. The report, "Alternative Funding Options for Public Broadcasting," had in its appendixes a summary of "Most Discussed Options for Alternative and Supplemental Funding." These included many revenue-generating methods applicable to libraries and NPs today, including facility rental and the acceptance of underwriting. It's the inspiration for the Money Matrix in Appendix A.

The Campaign for a Commercial Free Childhood opposes targeted advertising in libraries. It has a noble cause, the protection of children (Association for Library Services for Children 2013). As a major producer of children's programming, public broadcasting had to handle both the transition away from public funding and the issue of proximity in placing ads to achieve the goal of protecting children while still generating revenue. It is a great role model on how to shield children while funding expensive productions.

How did public broadcasting address the challenges of raising money through "commercialism"? Dr. Clift recalls that the professional cadre was exceptionally concerned with the effects of commercialism on a publicly funded entity—far more than the public was. They were strict about "no proximity" of commercials near programming related to the commercials. The perception of bias, and temptation to adopt particular views to retain funding dollars, was and is a legitimate concern at the national level. For instance, a hospital system couldn't be allowed to sponsor a health program nationally. At the local level, stations were sometimes more liberal regarding proximity.

A faction of our profession is strongly opposed to commercialism. For example, in response to one of my promotional announcements for my 2015 BRASS article, one listserv member criticized the idea of naming rights, which he considered a step onto the slippery slope of privatization. However, that same dire prediction did not happen in public broadcasting, and corporate and individual fund-raising efforts are going along well, even in the new competitive media environment. Like nonprofit professionals, library staffs should be wary of commercial relationships, but not so much that they don't take advantage of situations where they can strengthen their organizations.

There are currently a good set of editorial policy guidelines for public broadcasters about accepting underwriting, that is, those brief acknowledgments of a sponsor that take the place of advertisements. I review the specific differences between underwriting and advertising later in this chapter. These guidelines could easily be cross-pollinated into the library landscape, because they deal with the control that broadcasters have over their programming while accepting funds needed for its production (Public Broadcasting Service 2013a).

Every funding arrangement needs to pass a series of three tests to determine if:

1. The underwriter has exercised any editorial control.
2. The public may perceive the underwriter might have done so.
3. The program is broadcast just because it promotes the underwriter's business.

The rules are very specific regarding on-air credits. They address overall appearance, restrictions on placement in children's and how-to programs, and even the order of placement of multiple funder credits. They also include specific rules for on-air announcements promoting program-related goods and services.

These rules have been refined since the launch of public broadcasting in the turbulent 1960s to address modern media's myriad of available channels of communication. They are worth perusing by library staff and boards alike. Currently there are eleven guidelines enacted to guide the stations and producers on what constitutes acceptable content. One of the rules states that "limitations are intended to preserve the noncommercial character of public television and assure that programming decisions are motivated by the public interest rather than considerations of private gain. They are also intended to limit clutter" (Public Broadcasting Service 2013b).

Since moving to a more proactive fund-raising model, many public broadcasters now only depend on much lower percentages of funding from the federal government. The rest is raised through grants and underwriting efforts. Most, if not all, stations

---

Advertising versus Underwriting and Acknowledgments — TIP

The actual content of outsiders' messages was a controversial subject for public broadcasters, and is an important consideration if you're just beginning to expand your revenue streams by building partnerships with businesses. The following characteristics distinguish the difference between ads and underwriting:

ADVERTISING	UNDERWRITING AND ACKNOWLEDGMENTS
Promotional: Distinguishes itself from others: "The best place to shop for . . ."	Informative only
Consideration: You accept money *and* give them a promoted visit (stop in for library bookmarks)	No consideration; accepting money only
A call to action: "Visit us online @ . . ."	No call to action, but are allowed to use "more info @ . . ."
Inducement: "The best place to shop for . . ." or "Between now and then get a free . . ."	No inducement to buy

Please note the subtle differences, and make sure you can emphasize to your prospect the need for a low-key approach, as befits a library or other service-first oriented NPs.

Source: Data from Keeping the Public in Public Radio (2010).

steer underwriting or advertisements away from the children's (daytime) dayparts. (Dayparts are broad periods of a broadcasting day. They vary in value based on ratings and/or content. This and other broadcasting concepts are discussed in the next chapter.) Underwriting by certain foundations is allowed in those times, in the belief that children would not be influenced by knowing Sesame Street was funded in part by the Annenburg Foundation, as opposed to a brief plug for educational products by Toys-R-Us.

NON-GOVERNMENT SOURCES OF REVENUE

For years, public broadcasting has used membership drives to remind viewers watching their favorite shows to support them. The library version of this is, of course, the Friends of the Library concept, sanctioned nonprofit fund-raising organizations that are usually staffed by volunteers. This powerful fund-raising group engages the public through direct Friends membership drives, traditional fundraisers such as book sales of weeded and donated materials, sponsored author book talks (with portions of sales going to the Friends group and then passed onto the library to support specific, visible efforts), and creative events that generate both money and publicity (e.g., Literary Libations, a cocktail party offering drinks named after books).

These activities are similar to what public broadcasting offers; however, a major difference is the frequency of public contact these groups have. A "core audience" public broadcasting viewer or listener may tune in daily. A core library user might only come in every few weeks, making it more of a challenge to get him engaged with fund-raising efforts (Oder 2004). There are ways that are constantly evolving to encourage this engagement, which will be discussed in the chapters ahead.

Besides their viewers and listeners, public broadcasting has three distinct areas of revenue-generating clients:

» Underwriters, or local businesses. These are local people buying mentions, or ads at, for example, $150 for a fifteen-second spot. Public broadcasting stations' ad policies are very specific about not using hyperbole or inducement language. Statements must be neutral—for example, "Support comes from Your Corner Market." An acknowledgment with brief identification language affords both parties tax breaks, which I'll explain in the discussion of legal issues in chapter 5.
» Corporate support from national businesses. These are coordinated with advertising agencies as part of their overall media buys for the client. In these relationships especially, the station has to watch proximity to both programming and competitive advertisers.
» Local and national foundations. They often use Run of Station (ROS) schedules, meaning they can run any time of day.

Many development officers both in public broadcasting as well as other nonprofit organizations have passed through the Indiana School of Philanthropy. A basic fund-raising

FIGURE 2.1
Prospect Moves

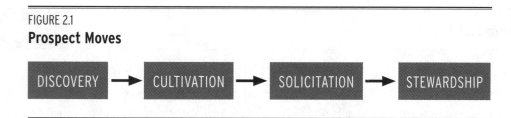

class teaches about "Moves Management," a concept created by former Cornell senior development officer David Dunlop, which is essentially moving through a sales cycle (Prosper Fund-Raising Strategies). It's all about relationship building! You move a prospect toward a point where they want to support you.

For libraries and NPs just embarking on the path of proactively seeking to build revenue streams, the four progressive sections of moves you make are shown in figure 2.1.

1. *Discovery*—Staff brainstorms a list of the top twenty-five businesses that could possibly be sponsors. Ask "does anyone here know someone working at ABC Widgets?" Arrange an introduction meeting, find out about the business and what they know about yours, and build rapport.
2. *Cultivation*—Make a second appointment. Ask if you can come back and talk about what they want to do. Discuss how you can help them.
3. *Solicitation*—Deliver your proposal, or "pitch," which establishes your value and lists specific features and benefits you have to offer: "Thanks for the conversation! You showed interest in doing X at Y cost. *We could do X at Y and throw in Z!*"
4. *Stewardship*—Acknowledge their support and deliver what you promised. Invite them back to see the results of their investment. Stay connected. Try to leverage sponsorship in one area with other events to engage the client, even if they did not financially participate in that specific event. The events may be the introduction of a program, ribbon cutting, personal tours, volunteer participation for your organization's community events (e.g., book sales, spring landscaping cleanup, etc.). Three months before the expiration of their sponsorship, begin renewal talks.

According to research, "time and time again, listeners confirm the value of NPR on-air sponsorship through research demonstrating that listeners prefer to do business with companies that support NPR" (National Public Media, 2016). This should help alleviate the fear persons in the nonprofit sector have that commercialism will have a negative effect on their patrons. The audiences of Diane Rehm and other popular programs don't boycott them, but instead help support them when they can, not only during membership drives but by patronizing the businesses they know support the program as well. This positive ripple effect should also hold true for libraries and other NPs.

Media Audit

To help you start off with the first move, the discovery process, do a media-use audit of your service area:

- Gather a few weeks of local publications (newspapers, entertainment magazines, etc.).

- Set up a recording device for local TV (PBS and commercial) and cable channels that relate to your mission (if time is precious you might skip the Golf Channel and spend time auditing the History Channel).

- Task people to listen to top-rated commercial and NPR radio stations, especially at key times.

- If there are major races or other types of community cause-focused fund-raisers sponsored in part by several companies, review these as well.

- Record the business's names, product category (fast food, car sales), media used, number of units (print or broadcast ads), and frequency.

This environment scan will give you a good prospect list. Who in your community advertises, when, and how? You can then use this information to brainstorm about people who might know someone in those advertising organizations.

The Denver Public Library's sponsorship page (www.denverlibrary.org/sponsors) does a great job of acknowledging corporate sponsors, one of the moves discussed in part 4, Good Stewardship. They even throw special "Happy Hours" for sponsors-only which act as a networking opportunity for everyone.

FIGURE 2.2
Denver Sponsorship Page Screenshot

If you're wondering about how to use your media audit, let's break down Denver's sponsors categorically.

At the time of writing, thirty-seven sponsor logos were on the page. I separated these into three sources:

» Businesses and corporations: 19
» Media: 12
» Foundations or other nonprofits: 6

The nineteen corporations, break down into the following product categories:

» Financial or business-oriented: 9
» Retail: 4
» Food: 4
» Entertainment: 2

Remember the $30,000 that you hoped to achieve? If each of the nineteen businesses, plus just one either of the other two sources, could be brought into a library revenue stream valued at $1,500 (e.g., meeting room name, collection area or program sponsor), that would achieve your goal (20 x $1,500 = $30,000)!

Beginning the Moves Management process is easy and straightforward. You and your team spend some time brainstorming a list, targeting whom within those companies you should approach, and determining if you already have a connection to them. Talk to them, share ideas, and find out what their marketing objectives are.

Since the early days of broadcasting, advisory councils have always been invaluable to learn the needs of the community and promote the broadcaster within it (Quaal and Brown 1976, 157). Key stakeholders, staff, board members, and public support organization (e.g., Library Friends) officers can contribute to not only the discovery process, but all the other moves as well. You can have them confirm your active listening results in the cultivation stage, ask for anticipated possible reactions before your pitch, and have them alongside you as the faces of a grateful public, as you move into the stewardship phase.

Like public broadcasting, libraries have a well-known, positive mission, a good vibe in the community. But other NPs are also hungry and out there looking for

Diversify Your Sources of Revenue

TIP

You have to resist the temptation to accept money from only a few sponsors. Spreading out your efforts will insure that there will be no sudden drop in services if one sponsor is lost or demands too much. It gives you strength to walk away from a bad deal. Proving your service and value to a wide variety of sponsors will insure consistency in revenue and build up your relationships in the community at large.

Be aware of your competition. Keep in mind that by offering sponsorships, naming rights, facility rentals, and so on, you are moving money from one business or NP over to yours. Your goal is to not only raise revenue, but to help your sponsors achieve their goals so they'll stick with you.

support; your most serious competition, commercial media, also wants to package your audience to sponsors. Understanding their methods are crucial to success, as will be reviewed in the next chapter.

References

Association for Library Services for Children. 2013. "An Interview with Susan Linn," June 27. www.commercialfreechildhood.org/blog/interview-susan-linn.

Denver Public Library. 2015. "DPL Partners." www.denverlibrary.org/sponsors.

Ennis, M. 2014. "Librarians React to Simon and Schuster Dropping 'Buy It Now' Requirement." *Library Journal*, November 25. http://lj.libraryjournal.com/2014/11/technology/ebooks/librarians-react-to-simon-schuster-dropping-buy-it-now-requirement/#_.

Keeping the Public in Public Radio. 2010. "Ads vs. Underwriting." http://keeppublic radiopublic.com/2010/07/27/ad-vs-underwriting/.

National Public Media. 2016. "Impact." http://nationalpublicmedia.com/npr/impact/.

Oder, N. 2004. "Can PL Support Be More Like NPR's?" *Library Journal* 129 (12), 22–24.

Prosper Fund-Raising Strategies. nd. "Moves Management: The Science of Fund-Raising." www.prosperfundraising.com/pdf/moves_management.pdf.

Public Broadcasting Service. 2013a. "Editorial and Funding Standards." www.pbs.org/about/editorial-standards/.

————. 2013b. *Guidelines for On-Air Announcements.* www.pbs.org/producers/guidelines/onair_rule3.html.

Quaal, W. L., and J. A. Brown. 1976. *Broadcast Management: Radio-Television.* New York: Hastings House Publishers.

Sandel, M. 2012. *What Money Can't Buy: The Moral Limits of Markets.* New York: Farrer, Strauss and Giroux.

Temporary Commission on Alternative Financing for Public Telecommunications (TCAF). 1983. Recommendations to Congress, October 1. The report, *Alternative Funding Options for Public Broadcasting* has in its appendixes a "Summary of Most Discussed Options for Alternative and Supplemental Funding."

CHAPTER THREE

BORROWING FROM BROADCASTING
Definitions and Concepts for Generating Revenue

THERE WERE TWO SCHOOLS OF THOUGHT IN THE EARLY age of the advertising discipline. The concepts of "real pros" and "uplifters" (Meyers 2014, 56). Real pros took a business and scientific approach to maximize results. A certain amount of messages directed toward a certain type of person would guarantee a certain amount of sales. Uplifters thought the purpose of advertising was for education and public service. Their messages, crafted in the right way, would convince people to buy their product with common sense, and for the common good. Modern commercial broadcasting focuses on real pros, and by using their techniques has been profitable. However, nonprofits and libraries that are trying to make ends meet need to understand and subscribe to both schools of thought.

In order to protect and sustain efforts in the nonprofit realm, we need to siphon off funding from the for-profit area. To accomplish that, we need a good understanding of how for-profit advertising work is done, beginning with the language it uses.

TERMINOLOGY EXPLAINED FOR THE LAYMAN

Radio "remotes" are a good example of value-added promotions. You'll hear DJs say to stop by and see them at Big Ed's Car lot, enter a drawing, take a test drive, etc.

Advertising Terminology

These are advertising terms real pros are familiar with, and you should be as well. I have them broken out into three specific operational areas: product, or what is being sold; measurement, how value is established for the price asked; and contract, the terms and conditions that govern the relationship between the advertiser and the media channel:

1. PRODUCT

ADJACENCY—A position between two programming segments for a commercial, a natural division or border. For our case, this might be equivalent to a sponsor's name on an aisle end-cap.

DAYPART—A broad period of a broadcasting day. They vary in value; morning is higher in radio than mid-day due to more listeners in cars during morning rush hours. An analogy to this would be an entire Dewey or Library of Congress classification areas (e.g., 000s for computers or R for medicine), or fiction genre areas, like romance.

2. MEASUREMENT OF PRODUCT

AUDIENCE ACCUMULATION (OR "CUME")—The total audience, over time, for an advertising campaign; the unduplicated reach of a campaign. Libraries want to make this an easy match between their audience and advertisers' goals.

EXPOSURE/IMPRESSION—The presentation of a single advertisement to a single target; not necessarily read or understood, but there!

FREQUENCY—The number of exposures; using real pro's logic, after X number of exposures a connection is made.

REACH—Total number of individuals exposed to an advertisement; often expressed as the percentage of total population target exposed over a given time period. Per capita usage of the library might reflect this in general terms.

3. CONTRACT

COST PER THOUSAND (OR CPM; THE M IS THE ROMAN NUMERAL FOR 1,000)—A standard advertising metric (explained in the next section).

ENHANCED UNDERWRITING—For public broadcasters, sponsorship of a program that includes mention of the sponsor at the beginning and end of the program, plus positions adjacent to and/or within the program; a method of saturation and capturing late-comers, such as for a long opera broadcast.

EXCLUSIVITY—The purchased right to block out competitors in the sponsor's business category. NOTE: Be careful. If this is done the fee will be subject to Unrelated Business Income Taxation (UBIT) by the IRS (discussed in later chapters).

RATE CARD—A published list of charges for advertising.

RUN OF SCHEDULE/STATION (ROS)—Advertisements sold at a low rate that can be run in any daypart. This can be very handy to counter fears of exclusivity, proximity, and bias.

TRADE—Payment-in-kind for advertising; you should strongly avoid doing one-to-one exchanges. What your sponsor says is valued at one dollar may actually cost them only fifty cents. You would be underselling a revenue source if that were the case. If you can go for a two-for-one value exchange, do that. Straight cash, of course, is always better.

VALUE-ADDED PROMOTION—A promotion whose cost is included in the total advertiser's media buy (Martin 2004, 115).

In libraries, sponsorship of a cookbook collection area combined with a "remote" at a food store or a programming series on nutrition would be a similar value-added promotion. The signage and extra exposure for a sponsor can be included to sweeten the deal or increase its monetary value. Although libraries do not "broadcast," thanks to technological advances librarians can have a table anywhere, for example, at a local Farmers Market, and with an electrical outlet available create a "hot spot" where they can have Wi-Fi capability and connect to library resources. This would be handy to use for signing up people for a sponsored summer reading program onsite at a sponsor's location. Not only does the sponsor get exposures within the library, but people will also be drawn to their location!

Cost per thousand (CPM) is a standard advertising metric designed to allow the sponsor to know how many people will be reached by a certain investment of dollars. Different media have different CPMs. Direct mail pieces, newspaper quarter-page advertisements, thirty-second TV spots, fifteen-second radio announcements: all can have various CPMs, and because each uses a different style of communication, the impact of the exposures on the audience naturally will vary as well.

To use the basic CPM formula to determine the cost of exposing 1,000 audience members to a message, divide the total cost by audience (in thousands). For example, for a $500 monthly sign cost in a traffic area with 30,000 library patrons passing by, 500/30 = 16 CPM. Compare the CPMs of various media to help establish a unique library rate. Use this to avoid overselling or underselling yourself in the marketplace. Real pros look at this metric and you should too. We'll discuss more metrics used in establishing value in later chapters.

A range of options for "adjacencies," special advertising areas next to popular programming (or library resources), are part of every successful broadcasting revenue model. Every bit of time is accounted for in broadcasting, and some time periods have much more value than others.

In a broadcasting schedule, you usually see the commercial areas adjacent to the newscasts being priced higher than all the others, in the belief people know to tune in at those times for the latest news, weather and sports. In libraries, end of shelving displays or other signage methods (bookmarks, screen-savers, etc.) could be used to highlight the sponsorship of an area or book genre. When people are looking for navigational aids for the book shelves, they'll see a sponsor's name. Selling adjacencies, sponsorship or naming rights are all methods of acquiring revenue in exchange for the close association with the libraries products and services. Pricing things higher is, like in broadcasting, based on where and when in time that association is reached. Broadcasting has prime time, Libraries have new Best-sellers.

In libraries, too much is not being utilized now; in radio speak, we have too much Dead Air. For anyone who's ever seen "Talk Radio" (1988) it sometimes adds to the ambiance to have Dead Air if artfully done and you can get away with it. Usually it's perceived, rightfully so, as a mistake.

REAL WORLD: SPONSORED COLLECTIONS

You're probably glazing over a bit right now. Here's a library example using one of the more widely known third-party providers, OverDrive, which distributes e-media to hundreds of libraries.

OverDrive example:

» Libraries can expand their digital collections with content sponsored by a local company, individual, or organization
» There are three ways sponsored content can be highlighted at a library site: in a special collection, with a graphic, or with a "book plate" message

Here's how it works. The library sets a value for the collection, based on various factors including CPM (based on web statistics), circulation figures, customer profiles, etc. Then a cart named after the sponsor is built in Marketplace, OverDrive's buying portal. Some donors like to specify which titles or areas to purchase (day parting = theme or genre) and others won't care (they will take an ROS schedule) This is your call. If you don't want a business involved in your collection, offer them a less-expensive ROS package that you control.

If you want to offer an enhanced program with more bells and whistles, or offer specific high-demand genres, that should cost more. For instance, if they want to

FIGURE 3.1
Screenshot of OverDrive Sponsored Collections Article

sponsor the Romance genre because their marketing calls for targeting women, you can have a higher CPM due to the fact that although they may be seen by fewer patron overall, they'll be the right kind of patrons.

In other words, you're offering them a smaller target, but a bigger bulls-eye!

BROADCASTING AND MOVES MANAGEMENT

Where does this knowledge come into play in the four stages of prospect development using Moves Management? After we get a prospect list together, and we've broken the ice, we move sequentially through Stage 2, cultivation, and Stage 3, solicitation.

Let's revisit the stages of building relationships with businesses for library fund-raising:

1. *Discovery*—Staff brainstorms a list of the top twenty-five businesses that could possibly be sponsors. Look at their use of media, their advertising content, and websites. After that, target the persons within those companies they should approach, and determine if they already have a connection to any of those persons. Talk to them, share ideas, and find out what their marketing objectives are.
2. *Cultivation*—Make a second appointment. Confirm your understanding of their marketing goals. Ask, "Can we come back and talk about what it is you want to do? How we can help? Whom would you like to reach?"
3. *Solicitation*—Deliver the pitch! Give them a proposal detailing the duration of the library campaign, locations they'll be in, type of verbiage and signage, payment details, and any extras. Your closing statements should be: "Thanks for the conversation! You showed interest in doing X at Y cost. *We could do X at Y and throw in Z!*"
4. *Stewardship*—Follow through and show results. Although you don't want to promise exact numbers, you can show the outcomes of their support.

The cultivation and solicitation stages are where you speak the language of the sponsor, or their advertising agency representatives, and deliver your offer in a way they understand. Likewise, you are using and listening for any mentions of the terminology reviewed above so that you can explain how you could help them reach their goals and justify the price asked.

Both profit and nonprofit organizations need the model shown in figure 3.2 to survive and thrive.

FIGURE 3.2
Business Model

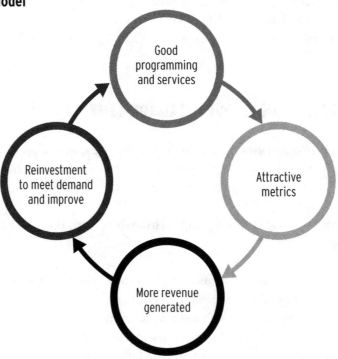

Not all revenue has to be generated through sponsorships or naming rights. There are plenty of opportunities to increase revenue in order to get to the first step above. For instance, a crowdfunding campaign can raise revenue and be a catalyst for new programming and services that then can lead to sustaining sponsorships. All of these methods will be discussed in part II. But first, before using any of the methods, a proper value must be set. Those concepts are next.

References

Cybercollege.com. 2013. "Radio Station Formats". www.cybercollege.com/frtv/frtv022.htm.

Martin, P. 2004. *Made Possible By: Succeeding with Sponsorship*. San Francisco: Jossey-Bass.

Meyers, C. B. 2014. *A Word from Our Sponsor: Admen, Advertising, and the Golden Age of Radio*. New York: Fordham University Press.

OverDrive, Inc. 2014. "Find Funding with Sponsored Collections," June 16. http://blogs.overdrive.com/front-page-library-news/2014/06/16/find-funding-with-sponsored-collections/.

Oliver Stone. *Talk Radio*. 1988. *This is dead air, Barry*. [Video file]. www.youtube.com/watch?v=vZf68MdJC_g.

ESTABLISHING VALUE, STATISTICAL REPORTS, AND TARGETING PROSPECTS

THIS CHAPTER ILLUSTRATES HOW TO JUSTIFY THE PITCH to the sponsor, how to identify high-traffic areas for advertisers, and how to define your patrons into groups that advertisers and vendors want to reach. It will give guidance on how to establish the value of library sponsorships by using statistical reports that many libraries already generate for collection development and weeding. Changing lead into gold! It will also provide an easy-to-use tool to target prospects through the Dewey Decimal or Library of Congress classification systems.

It's important to know how to employ user analytics and material usage statistics to establish value that advertising agencies and marketing people cannot argue. Identifying areas through statistics already collected—door count, circulation, web visits, "friends and followers," could be easily transformed into generating revenue—not just to be used in government reports.

Remember: The biggest rookie mistake is undervaluing what you have to offer!

In the 1970s, prior to the era of the Internet and broadcast consolidation, stations in most markets had their own research personnel. The National Association of Broadcasters emphasized the importance of research in these four ways:

1. It can resolve differences of opinion between equally competent peers as to what the facts are.

2. It can help management assign the proper weight to a set of known factors.
3. It can disclose relationships among what were thought to be unrelated facts.
4. On occasion it can uncover ideas no one had thought of before.

It was strongly suggested to keep the actual administration of this research effort divorced from sales and promotional departments, because a clear eye is needed to look at the effectiveness of past operational patterns and to provide guidelines for the future (Quaal and Brown 1976, 154).

OUTPUTS VERSUS OUTCOMES

A popular trend these days is to focus on outcomes versus outputs. A recent comment from a Gates Foundation director was "We need to stop measuring outputs and start measuring outcomes" (Chant 2013). This makes sense, coming from an issues-oriented foundation member, but not all revenue is raised through foundations. Advertisers still relate to real pros' techniques of business and measurement. The Gates director quoted is right in asking to quantify outcomes. It boils down to the choice of the word "measuring." Outputs are measurable, objective, easily within the understanding of a Real Pro looking to invest money wisely. Outcomes could be quantified by well-designed surveys and focus groups, which can be expensive and provide only snapshots of attitudes at a certain time. These are not impossible to fit into a sales proposal to establish value, but not as automatic or practical as monthly statistical reports.

An example of outcome effectiveness can be as valuable as a high number of outputs. For example, one day the owner of a local barbershop came into the library desperately needing assistance. He had a very large aquarium in his shop that burst, releasing hundreds of gallons of water into his shop, as well as some colorful fish! After contacting his insurance agent, he needed to quickly get some forms that were online, fill them out, and send them in ASAP to get the funds needed to get his barbershop back into shape. He was clueless about computers, but library staff was able to assist him in locating and printing the documents. Then after he filled them out, they helped him scan and send them back to the insurance company. His business had only a minimal amount of downtime, thanks in part to the help and resources available at the library. These may just be a few statistical outputs (two computer sessions and one use of a scanner) but it generated a major positive outcome for a local businessman and the surrounding community.

Outcomes and outputs both need to be tracked. Outputs are usually easier: they can be produced with computers, although they also could be tracked by a diary method. Outcomes can also be quite useful in finding future sponsors. Positive outcomes form the foundations of relationships.

HOW TO CREATE OUR OWN RATINGS

Broadcasters use rating services such as Nielson and Arbitron, as well as other measurement statistics.

Libraries and other NPs already have their own measurement techniques, and need to establish others! Automated traffic counters can be very valuable. Most libraries have them at entrances, and new technology is making closer assessments possible. However, even without hard traffic statistics, you can make observational studies over time, and base estimates on checkouts and program attendance.

Library user profiles and usage analytics are already in annual and government reports, census data, weeding statistics, and a variety of already generated circulation data. With a little work, these can be part of an effective sales package.

Advertisers still relate to the real pros techniques of business and measurement. Collection Analytics software provided by companies like SirsiDynix's Director's Station, Collection HQ, and Envisionware can help raise revenues by pointing out patterns and momentum to determine opportunities.

Location Audit   EXERCISE

Try doing an internal audit of sponsorship availabilities within your facility.

- Pick three areas such as meeting rooms, quiet study areas, or audiovisual collection areas (especially if they have any kind of restricted access), and estimate usage over time: weekly, monthly, annually.

- Establish a revenue goal.

- Divide the goal by usage (in thousands)–remember the CPM formula?

- Dollars/impressions in thousands = CPM translated into: $500/30 = 16 CPM.

Is that CPM *competitive* with other media in your area? If not, adjust accordingly. For revenue methods that include CPM as a determining factor, this is how you can fairly set value, and determine if that method will be worth the effort.

REVENUE BASED ON SQUARE FEET METHODOLOGY

Some real pros partially determine value by the size of ad they use, as well as individual exposures. One advertising agency manager who runs partnership campaigns between nonprofits and advertisers that display banners, bench wraps, and other visual advertising products, uses the following revenue formula:

For a Tier 2 school

$0.75 x 3,000 sq. ft. = $2,250/per month x 12 months = $27,000/per year.

Not bad for a passive program. In this case he used a high school environment, and has divided the size of schools into three tiers:

Tier 1

$1.00 per square foot of Ad Product per month
(approximately 3,000 square feet) for a school with 2,501 students or greater.

Tier 2

$0.75 for 1,001–2,500 students.

Tier 3

$0.50 for 1,000 students or fewer (S. Legerski, President, Metric$ Media,
personal communication, January 12, 2015).

PRODUCT CATEGORIES

Many advertising statistics are analyzed via product categories; for instance, auto sales are often at the top of radio categories, and within that category various national brands are tracked for their expenditures. Broadcasters use these for efficient prospecting. *Advertising Age*, the *Wall Street Journal*, and other sources often give advance notice as to whether a category or individual advertiser plans to increase its expenditures.

Approaches to Multiple Sponsors in One Category   TIP

In the next exercise, notice how many categories might have multiple sponsors? To reduce problems associated with exclusivity and proximity to collection areas, you could have a version of an ROS schedule, rotating all your sponsors at end caps among all of these categories.

If you want to approach businesses for sponsorships without fear of clashes in your physical building, or just want to carefully, slowly enter the sponsorship arena, consider bundling sponsors on a web page that can also be transformed into a poster. One library that followed the ladder approach discussed earlier sent out a wide, targeted sponsorship mailing to businesses. Among other benefits, donors' names were put on a web page, with higher spending businesses at the top of the page (Wyomissing 2015).

Another tactic is to get sponsors of similar types to partner in a joint program. In 2014, King County Public Library system created a "Start to Finish" fitness program in the Seattle area with the help of a number of health-oriented private and nonprofit organizations, as well as media companies to help promote it. A number of activities, including races, classes, and local author presentations were offered. This "cause-marketing" approach can be replicated anywhere you have an oversaturation of potential sponsors and can tie them together in a positive cause. Cause sponsorship spending is on the rise, projected to be 1.92 billion dollars in the US in 2015, an increase of 3.7 percent from 2014 (Cause Marketing Forum 2015).

Product Prospecting

This product category table can be used in Stage 1 of the Moves Management prospect development process, the discovery, or brainstorming, phase. This is by no means an exhaustive list, but these are some of the most common product categories advertised today. The ones marked with asterisks were among the top ten advertising categories from January‡June 2014, as determined by Kantar Media reports (Kantar Media 2014)

Potential advertisers' product categories arranged by Dewey Decimal and Library of Congress classifications

LIBRARY CLASSIFICATIONS	ADVERTISER PRODUCT CATEGORY
Dewey: 000 LC: A, Q, P, Z	Computers, telecommunication services,* communications
Dewey: 100 LC: B, H	Novelty gifts; counseling services for grief, addiction, and depression; cemeteries and memorial services
Dewey: 200; LC: B	Religious activities, charities, religious bookstores
Dewey: 300 LC: H, K, L	Financial and legal services,* insurance,* schools
Dewey: 400 LC: P	Language instruction
Dewey: 500 LC: Q, T	Automobile*; museums 2005
Dewey: 600 LC: H, K, R, S, T	Medical services, diet and nutrition, food services* (fast food; convenience and grocery stores); restaurants,* accounting and business services, personal care products and services,* home repair services; home construction and landscaping services*
Dewey: 700 LC: A, G, M, N, T	Media, arts and crafts, sports
Dewey: 800 LC: P	Books stores, office supplies
Dewey: 900 LC: D, G	Travel services*

Align this table's classification area with circulation figures and metrics from the location audit, and develop individual CPMs.

1. Keep separate figures, and then merge the CPMs for an average.
2. You'll see the various strengths and weaknesses in terms of CPM for your advertising locations. Depending on your goals, you can start sponsorship sales slowly, only going after specific ones in strong areas.
3. If your area is sponsor-rich and you want to start using ROS, you know your average CPM.

If proximity of an advertiser is of concern to you, you can offer an ROS schedule whereby every month their sponsorship signage is rotated to another area. They can REACH their immediate target audience occasionally, and could still have a fair amount of EXPOSURES to the CUMULATIVE audience they wanted to achieve. (Capitalized words above relate back to the advertising terminology list in chapter 3.)

Sponsorship.com is a web-based portal into the world of sponsorships, for profit and nonprofit businesses alike. They offer reports, training, and a variety of services. Registration is free and it's great for notifications and insightful articles. A recent webinar (which did require a registration fee) was on the topic of targeting emerging sponsorship product categories, everything from cannabis dispensaries to wearable technology. Another free report recently gave a seven-page breakdown on the rise of supermarket sponsorships. It discussed how establishing relationships with Kroger or Publix can also uncover money available from consumer packaged-goods dealers like Frito-Lay. (IEG 2015). More on co-op advertising will be discussed in chapter 9, on partnerships for grants.

USING STATISTICS TO ESTABLISH AND INCREASE YOUR VALUE

When using metrics, remember that good retail methods can draw traffic and increase usage.

A great resource in understanding retail marketing techniques is Paco Underhill's "Why We Buy" (Underhill 2009). Very useful in talking to potential sponsors of areas within your library. It will not only help strengthen your own understanding of retail environments, but also help you speak the language of Real Pro's without compromising your role as a community uplifter. It's useful in increasing your circulation, program attendance, and any other public usage metric.

An *American Libraries* article from 2010 entitled "How to Thrive by Design in Tough Times" discussed how one library used retail techniques to handle a crush of users during recession years. The author of the article, Lisa Rosenblum, now the Chief Librarian of the Brooklyn Public Library, discussed a number of Underhill's topics, including decompression zones:

> Often used in retail environments, decompression zones are areas of transition, usually at a store entrance, that allows customers to acclimate after entering. When done right, such a zone houses little clutter or distraction, such as flyers or giveaways. The area should reflect the library brand, as customers form their first and lasting viewpoint of the library there. (Rosenblum 2009)

These are clearly important areas, and the less clutter there is, the more attention can be paid to whatever messages are there, including important sponsors of the library.

In the library field, most statistical packages have dealt with circulation, as for inventory control. Reports can be run on how many books, DVDs, and other material are circulated, moved between libraries, are in higher demand than others, and are lost, stolen, or damaged. All of these statistics are highly relevant to proper business operations and responsible stewardship of the public's resources. Arguably though, good stewardship in lean financial times also requires analyzing a bit more about the patrons who are using this material, and as public broadcasting has done, leveraging them to acquire more funding to sustain their operations.

Public broadcasting uses statistics to describe both NPR's and PBS's programming, platforms, audience, and performance. They combine demographic data, mostly on income and employment status, and qualitative data, such as disposition to be business leaders or supportive of green services. Each page has a subdued, yet highly visible link for potential sponsors to learn more, become sponsors themselves or to contact them. In other words, they encourage prospects along the lines of Moves Management, helping them find out about the opportunities public media has to offer (National Public Media 2014).

The better you can describe your patrons, in terms of their interests and attitudes, the better you will match them to potential sponsors' needs. In the reference above, substitute NPR with your entity's name and strive to achieve even better percentages!

Product's like Cengage's Analytics On Demand (AOD) not only helps data-driven decision-making by analyzing who uses and who does not use the library, but it also gives grant writers an easy to use tool to help describe their community to potential funders. If a foundation requires in their Request for Proposals (RFP) that a grant must be based on a certain demographic served, as well as what issues are addressed, AOD can be used in conjunction with library barcode information to form a very detailed picture. This data merges census tract data as well as information from other accessible databases to describe a library's users, as well as the non-users in the community. This helps in tactical decision-making, collection and programming decisions, as well as strategic decisions such as where to build or expand branches or bookmobile routes (Cengage Learning, Inc. 2014).

FIGURE 4.1
Screenshot of Cengage Scatter Gram

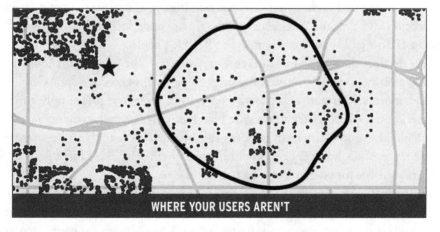

Portion of map taken from *Analytics on Demand* Patron Profile Report from Gale, a part on Cengage Learning. *Analytics on Demand* is a series of web-based apps that enable libraries to quickly blend data from their existing library systems with external demographic data, creating powerful insights.

This scatter gram shows the library as the starred location, with heavy usage to the northwest quadrant above it, but significant gaps to the east.

The data needed for this type of map could be gained by asking Friends of the Library (arguably your core audience) via opt-in research questions, about their address and demographic information, which wouldn't require purchasing any special software package. You could also develop one by analyzing voting information from past library levies.

REAL WORLD: SACRAMENTO PUBLIC LIBRARY'S USE OF ANALYTICS IN SPOTLIGHTING LIFESTYLES AND WINNING GRANTS

At the 2015 ALA Annual convention Amy Calhoun, Communications and Virtual Services Manager for the Sacramento Public Library presented in a forum about revenue streams, on how insightful the Cengage Analytics on Demand software was. She praised the software for being easy to use, and for how it gave a good breakout of her service area's demographics, overview, patron analysis, and specific mosaic/lifestyle portraits. These portraits creatively describe segments of the population based on unique features, for example the "Aging of Aquarius" mosaic cluster draws from the old song and phrase "Age of Aquarius" to describe aging baby-boomers who were hippies in the 60's. They discovered one of their major patron clusters could be labeled as "Cul de Sac Diversity" through matching various demographic and industry survey characteristics.

They then ran reports that showed the vital lifestyle characteristics that they could use to truly profile that group, involving both quantitative and qualitative information (see figure 4.2).

The Sacramento Public Library has used this information to modify their messaging to their community and promote themselves in new ways. They even won a grant to develop a program on the environment and gardening, because they could prove their area had higher than average numbers in the gardening and farming publication and product categories and a large proportion of the demographics were in a "Rooted Flower Power" mosaic/lifestyle profile.

This new product has some amazing capabilities. The biggest challenge from libraries already using this software has been the transfer of barcode data. Only basic age and address information is transferred, nothing else, and it is simply a matter of shoehorning whatever data fields are being used by the inventory management system into the proprietary fields for Cengage software. Once that hurdle is resolved, a wide range of analytic reports, useful for reinforcing the case you're making for value, is available for your conversations with the real pros.

Some may be squeamish about sharing patron data. In a 2015 ALA session on data mining, an ethics discussion reviewed the concept of value exchange; that is, what would patrons get in exchange for their data. Various examples were given, such as Spotify and Pandora, the music services that make "advisory" (sound familiar?) suggestions on music you might like based on past downloads. Or that Google uses

FIGURE 4.2

AOD Cul de Sac Lifestyle Characteristics

MESSAGING	Pro-kids activities and education-oriented messaging via web, email	Ads intrusive; best are value-related, with messages about conservative values, safety, or focus on grandkids	Product-centric messaging, DIY, hobby research	Messaging directed towards kids; Spanish language preferred	Product or news-centric messaging, activities, DIY	Adverse to ads in home (TV), especially targeted to kids; okay with coupons, bus ads, outdoor	Product-centric messaging, DIY, hobby research
POTENTIAL LIBRARY INTERESTS	Family activities, school resources, common core, e-books, electronics, web content ("10 Best Books for...")	Programs for gardening, saving money; traditional library offerings like books, magazines, and newspapers	e-books, electronics, videos, media, DIY programs, web content ("10 Best Books for...")	Spanish language materials, language learning, music, COHS, continuing education, streaming media, kid-centric	Adult education classes, health, fitness, food programs, web content, e-books, media	Family activities, museum passes, education-related, gaming, consumer electronics	Travel info, hobbies and crafts programs, electronics, e-books, online content, consumer reports
PATRON HOUSEHOLDS	2,488	2,648	2,528	1,812	1,818	1,335	718
TOTAL DEMOGRAPHIC HOUSEHOLDS	20,474	24,819	22,027	15,141	15,302	8,126	13,949
IMPROVEMENT POTENTIAL	88%	89%	89%	88%	88%	84%	95%

31

and shows data relevant to you based on previous searches and what you've clicked through. A long-time advocate of using technology in libraries was quoted as saying "You are not your patrons," that is, patrons by and large are not as concerned with restrictive privacy measures as are librarians.

In the data-mining session, it was generally agreed that using some barcode information can be a win-win situation when you:

1. Use data for library marketing.
2. Use data to add value for the user experience.

The consensus was that if you can use data to further the mission of the library, it's a positive thing.

QUALITATIVE METHODS TO ESTABLISH VALUE

Various "guerilla" methods can be used to show the value of the library and qualitative aspects of it to advertisers. At the ALA annual convention there's always a PR Exchange that shows some of the best available methods. In 2014, there was information about a library in Champaign, Illinois, which used a photo-booth at various community events that invited people to take humorous pictures and then share personal, positive library quotes as they posted the pictures on a board next to the booth, and eventually online. Sacramento Library's Edgar Allan Poe project combined the library self-publishing an anthology they created about Poe's work, and other creative Poe projects, including brewing a special Edgar Allan porter that demonstrated not only the intellectual vibrancy of the area, but the fact that the library's patrons would spend cash on food and drink in support of the library's cause—a successful John Cotton Dana award-winning passive project that was a win-win for everyone involved (Schwartz 2014).

The preceding subjective, qualitative outcome generators, plus objective ways to measuring audience are the keys to successfully working with real pros.

The library field has many resources to help campaigns to advocate for levies and urge lawmakers to award more funding. Use these same methods when cultivating sponsors. The Citizens Save Libraries campaign distributes a Power guide for advocacy—free! It contains examples of talking points, flyers, petitions, and more (United for Libraries 2014). A NYLA 2010 presentation entitled "Positioning Your Library as an Essential Service: Marketing, PR and Advocacy" (Post 2010) promoted the use of branding, marketing and strategic communication to successfully advocate for the library. It not only includes using statistics, but also covers how emotions can be triggered in discussing what the library has to offer. Exercises demonstrated that many of the concepts could be cross-pollinated from the process of winning elections to the Moves Management prospect development process, Stage 2: cultivation, where you make a second appointment. Ask, "Can we come back and talk about what it is you want to do? How we can help? Who would you like to reach?"

TRUMPETING YOUR VALUE THROUGH CASE STATEMENTS

Case statements combine outputs and outcomes to lay out a strategic statement as to why your organization is needed and valued in the community. Sharing that case is one of the moves you make in Stage 2, cultivation of your prospects. Does your library have a case statement (as opposed to mission statement) that spells out why it should be supported?

In 2004, Lewis Kennedy and Associates, a firm with a background in fund-raising for both public broadcasting and public libraries, issued a report on ways for libraries to supplement and diversify their revenue (Lewis 2004, 18). One important element was the development of case statements. They offered a five-step structure, which can expand from a quick elevator speech to a large document:

1. The organization's history.
2. Whom it serves and what it does today.
3. The problem to be solved *now*.
4. How the problem will be addressed.
5. What success will mean to the donor in recognition and satisfaction.

The University of Washington's Impact Study on Libraries and their technology offerings to the public demonstrates the influence libraries have in this area. They have an important role in educating about technology, helping people cross the digital divide in terms of accessing vital government programs and financial aid applications only accessible online, as well as providing platforms for budding business owners (University of Washington Information School 2014).

The University of Washington survey is geared toward helping to clarify the concept of outputs and outcomes. When you are establishing value you need to be able to do both. Outputs are the objective, measurable statistics every library uses for descriptive and operational purposes: door counts, circulation statistics, etc., for example, "We had 20,000 individual computer sessions in our library in 2014." Outcomes are the subjective human-interest stories of what those statistics mean: "A technically-challenged patron came in during an emergency for Internet access to file an insurance claim necessary to help keep his business open, and the staff helped him to use a scanner and flash drive, and taught him how to email an attachment." This would then be supported with a testimonial.

The online Library Value Calculator (www.ala.org/advocacy/advleg/advocacy university/toolkit/makingthecase/library_calculator) has been used for years to demonstrate the monetary value of what a library provides. If you check out five books and five DVDs per year, it shows how much you save! It's often used in campaigns where the voter is faced with making a decision on increasing his taxes for library services. If the tax increase is $100 a year and you can demonstrate a high return on investment, chances are you'll win. Your approach to a sponsor in using this can be their association with a respected institution that saves consumers money (American Library Association 2015a).

After you show a prospective sponsor outputs and outcomes and present your case statement, you would then inquire "Would it fit your marketing objectives to

---

Frame Things with Graphics

An ALA annual poster session on infographics from Auburn University demonstrated the value of making sterile statistics more accessible with pictures. They've been using this approach to train non-library development officers to present the best possible cases for funding. In an interview, one of the lead librarians offered that

> It's how you frame things. I think the hardest thing for librarians to learn is that the story may be more important than the statistics. For instance, justifying the expense of article backfiles or a STEM database, because Prof. X's research team working on a vaccine for a potentially pandemic inducing disease outbreak was able to find the article that at 2am on a Sunday morning allowed for a crucial breakthrough for their research. Another would be a student receiving a prestigious scholarship because the libraries' collections in their discipline supported their thesis. Librarians are good at the numbers, and perhaps not so good at conveying the story. (Bishop 2015)

---

be recognized in the Computer Center? Would you like people to see that resources here are 'made possible by' you, Mr. Prospect?"

If there's an indication of interest, you move to Stage 3, and offer them a more specific opportunity.

Before your pitch, set your goals. As a former radio business manager, I've learned you need to meet the realities of your market. The book *Mission-Based Marketing* discusses the competition even nonprofits face amongst themselves. The book presents the first three parts of the strategy below (Brinckerhoff 2010). I've added the fourth.

1. Estimate cost recovery of providing a service.
2. Add a profit.
3. Compare to the market (your objective measures to other media).
4. Beware of the "halo effect" (i.e., our own perception that the library is wonderful ... doesn't everyone think so?).

In dealing with prospects for naming rights or sponsorships, you need to listen to them to determine what they value. Would a children's clothing store find value in sponsoring a Parenting Collection, by paying a fair advertising rate for a few years to supply the area with better resources and staff hours? Would an office supply store find value for its brand name by securing a Quiet Study area sponsorship? Knowing what the prospective sponsor values and having solid statistics will provide a good synergy between a library and new funding partners. And, not "giving the store away" for a one-time infusion of funds, but arranging a contract for a specific time period contract, will help a library to have a steady income stream over time. Be very judicious about using the phrase "in perpetuity," which pretty much means forever, or at least as long as whatever is named continues to exist. The memorializing method of naming rights is traditional and well-accepted, but permanent memorials can be a problem if they inhibit a revenue generator from further growth. Especially in times of tragedy, emotion should be balanced with sound business reasoning.

One of the pre-webinar survey respondents was rightfully appreciative that a family memorial of a "hot" book title collection generated funds from people in and outside their community, thanks to informal word-of-mouth techniques. Distant relatives contributed to the ongoing fund. The special area it funds is in a high-traffic location with about 30,000 people passing by each month, and each collection item on its shelves has the family name branded on a special sticker for the time it's on the shelf. The area has generated $10,000 over fifteen years from donations that total under $700 a year. Enough to buy maybe thirty books a year, each averaging thirty circulations? All well and good, but in our library's area, $700 would be a fair ad price in a small monthly local magazine that provides less exposure than a copy of a title like Grisham's *Sycamore Row* will over the course of its run on the hot shelf.

COMPARISON OF NAMING RIGHTS VERSUS SPONSORSHIPS

A more modern marketing method does not have to replace memorialization/ naming rights, but any library serious about raising funds should consider sponsorships. These take the form of short-term, high-value-oriented contracts based on justifiable statistics as an approach to maximizing current library assets and popularity. "Mission-based marketing" emphasizes seeking a fair value in offering anything public for sale (Brinckerhoff 2010, 85).

Looking at CPMs, getting a firm grasp of outcomes and what it is your potential sponsor wants, will help you overcome the halo effect.

People working in nonprofits are sometimes so close to their cause that they aren't realistic, they give it that halo effect. To paraphrase a line from *The Godfather*, you might hear no because, "it's nothing personal, it's just business." Businesses can choose from a plethora of advertising channels. Your goal is to establish your unique value for them in ways they understand and that will be of benefit to both parties. Be positive toward the other channels, but advise them that your organization will be a good supplement to their advertising mix.

USE OTHER RESEARCH AVENUES

CollectionHQ (www.collectionhq.com) has an experimental reporting function to track circulation of donor-supported collections to see if they earn their keep. They have more than thirty libraries providing data now, with new services forthcoming (M. Robertson, personal communication. 2015). The idea is simple, instead of naming a location with a genre like "Mysteries," add the sponsor's name (e.g., Mystery-ABC Widgets).

The *Library Journal Index*'s Star Libraries are selected based on a variety of metrics (Lyons 2014). If you can make those metrics justify a sponsor's attention, so be it! Likewise, ALA's Office of Research and Statistics is also a good resource for constantly updated research (American Library Association 2015b).

PROSPECT MANAGEMENT TOOLS

We've discussed customer analytics, but there are also tools to use for prospect analytics. Some may be tools that libraries already subscribe to, like ReferenceUSA (www.referenceusa.com/), that help you find companies that fit a specific profile, such as car dealers, within a 25-mile range. Or they can be more sophisticated tools that help you manage all the phases of Moves Management.

Customer relationship management (CRM) is a term that refers to practices, strategies, and technologies that companies use to manage and analyze customer interactions and data throughout the customer lifecycle, with the goal of improving business relationships with customers, assisting in customer retention, and driving sales growth (TechTarget 2015).

There are companies that are geared toward both the profit and nonprofit sectors, in terms of helping discover prospects, cultivate your relationships with them, and help follow up and maintain contact after their campaign with you ends. All have strong online presences, short introductory presentations on YouTube, and offer free trials. Salesforce.com is one of the better-known leaders in this field. It integrates contact management tools as well as social media platforms to keep your relationship momentum moving (Salesforce.com). Salesgenie (www.salesgenie.com) is also useful not only in managing contacts, but in helping you organize campaigns to reach out to prospects as well as the general public (Infogroup 2015).

Blackbaud (www.blackbaud.com) is the leading vendor in this field for NPs. They use the word "constituent" instead of "customer," but their tools and methodology are basically the same. Their services are used by all sorts of NPs, from animal welfare to public broadcasting organizations (Blackbaud, Inc. 2015). Donorperfect (www .donorperfect.com) is geared toward streamlining the relationship between donors and your organization. Like the other services, they'll save you administrative costs as well as help keep donors in the loop with you! (Software Inc. 2015).

Proper valuation and well-organized prospect management are aspects of good stewardship. Stewardship of library assets is a challenge, and sometimes is challenged. You need proper legal grounding, which is what's covered in the next chapter.

References

American Library Association. 2015a. "Library Value Calculator." www.ala.org/
    advocacy/advleg/advocacyuniversity/toolkit/makingthecase/library_calculator.
    ———. 2015b. *Research and Statistics Resources.* www.ala.org/research/home.
Blackbaud, Inc. 2015. "Non-Profit CRM, Fund-Raising Challenges." www.blackbaud
    .com/fundraising-crm/blackbaud-nonprofit-crm.
Brinckerhoff, P. C. 2010. *Mission-Based Marketing: Positioning Your Not-for-Profit in an
    Increasingly Competitive World,* 3rd edition. Hoboken, NJ: John Wiley and Sons, Inc.

Cengage Learning, Inc. 2014. "Analytics on Demand." http://solutions.cengage.com/ analytics/.

Chant, I. 2013. "Reinventing Libraries Keynote Panel Looks into Industry's Future." *The Digital Shift 2013*, October 21. www.thedigitalshift.com/2013/10/public -services/reinventing-libraries-keynote-panel-looks-into-industrys-future-the -digital-shift-2013/.

Cause Marketing Forum. 2015. "Statistics Every Cause Marketer Should Know." www.causemarketingforum.com/site/c.bkLUKcOTLkK4E/b.6448131/ k.262B/Statistics_Every_Cause_Marketer_Should_Know.htm.

IEG. 2015. *Sponsorship.com*. www.sponsorship.com.

Infogroup. 2015. *Salesgenie—Sales Leads, Email, Marketing Tools*. www.salesgenie.com.

Kantar Media. 2014. "Top Advertising Categories". http://kantarmedia.us/press/ us-advertising-expenditure-q2-2014.

Lewis Kennedy Associates. 2004. *Saving America's Libraries: Changing the Model for Library Funds Development*. www.pluralfunding.org/sal.pdf.

Lyons, R. and Lance, K. 2014. "LJ Index 2014: The Star Libraries." *Library Journal*, November 3. http://lj.libraryjournal.com/2014/11/managing-libraries/ lj-index/class-of-2014/the-star-libraries-2014/.

National Public Media. 2014. "Public Radio Audience Demographics." http:// nationalpublicmedia.com/npr/audience/.

Post, L. 2010. *Positioning Your Library as an Essential Service: Marketing, PR and Advocacy*, May 28. www.ala.org/united/sites/ala.org.united/files/content/ powerguide/positioning-powerpoint.pdf.

Quaal, W. L., and J. A. Brown. 1976. *Broadcast Management: Radio-Television*. New York: Hastings House Publishers, Inc.

Rosenblum, L. 2009. "How to Thrive by Design in Tough Times." *Library Journal*. December 15. http://americanlibrariesmagazine.org/2009/12/15/how-to -thrive-by-design-in-tough-times/.

Salesforce.com. 2015. "CRM and Cloud Computing to Grow Your Business." www.salesforce.com.

Schwartz, M. 2014. "DIY One Book at Sacramento PL—One Cool Thing." *Library Journal*, March 9. http://lj.libraryjournal.com/2014/03/opinion/one-cool -thing/diy-one-book-at-sacramento-pl-one-cool-thing/#_.

Software Inc. 2015. "Fundraising Software for Non-Profits—Donor Perfect." www.donorperfect.com.

TechTarget. 2015. "What is Customer Relationship Management (CRM)?" http:// searchcrm.techtarget.com/definition/CRM.

Underhill, P. 2009. *Why We Buy: The Science of Shopping*. New York: Simon and Schuster.

United for Libraries. 2014. *Citizens-Save-Libraries Power Guide*. www.ala.org/united/ powerguide.

University of Toledo. 2015. "Mulford Library Virtual Floor Plan." www.utoledo.edu/ library/mulford/education/tutorials/mfp5colors.GIF.

University of Washington Information School. 2014. "US Impact Study," http:// impact.ischool.uw.edu.

Wyomissing Public Library. 2015. "Corporate Sponsors." http://wyopublib.org/ support_sponsors.shtml.

CHAPTER FIVE

LEGAL AND BOARD POLICY CONSIDERATIONS

THIS CHAPTER INVOLVES THE IMPORTANT TOPIC OF setting correct policies to develop revenue streams. With a little planning and examination of previous nonprofit efforts, policies appropriate to your own governing structure should be able to be put into place. This chapter lays the groundwork for the actual implementation of contracts, covered in the next chapter, and the development of the many new revenue sources discussed in part II.

GIVING YOURSELF WIGGLE ROOM

Careful planning for "wiggle room," the ability to make changes to a plan or contract, is obviously necessary. One library years ago sold naming rights on benches outside of it. As times changed with the surrounding community, the homeless started sleeping on them, and through the years weathering on the benches made them less attractive (Cervantes 2013). It was decided to replace them with wrought metal chairs and move the benches to a staff area.

The question arose, what to do with the old nameplates? Does it violate the spirit of the gift to take them out of the public eye? The library director in this case below, Mary Housel, found an agreeable solution with two-thirds of the original donors that they could actually find, using a "Naming Plaque" overlooking the area. She also shares some thoughts on naming rights in general:

A CAUTIONARY TALE—THE DIRECTOR'S STORY

In regards to the three families that donated the benches in our outside entry plaza, I contacted two of the three and asked for their approval for us to either place the original donor plates on the new chairs, or to redo the memorial plaque altogether and relocate it to the same general vicinity (library entry plaza). One of the three original donors had moved out of state. It was difficult to track that one down. Of the two donors remaining, both were still in the area and easy to locate. One was fine with anything we needed to do, and the other happened to be the President of my Library Board of Trustees. She and her husband became active partners in helping figure out if the original plaques could even be mounted on the new chairs or not. We decided they were not suitable for the new chairs. Because their plaque was in memory of a relative, they were very interested and concerned that the plaque wording was kept and the plaque be placed in an honorable location in keeping with the original gift's intent.

Our Director of Recreation and Parks suggested we redo the three plaques onto one new one, and mount it somewhere in the area. With my Board President and her husband, we found a spot that they liked in front of the library, and the City Manager approved it. With outside plaques, keep in mind that they weather and, at some point, need budget allocation to clean them or redo them.

We added some wording that says "Seating in the plaza donated by . . ." with the original wording that was on the original plaques. Because most of the naming rights for the library were for rooms, I doubt they would ever change to the point that we would have to re-determine plaque locations, etc. With smaller items that could deteriorate and that had less expensive naming rights compared to the more permanent rooms (such as display cases, benches, outdoor statuary, etc.), it could be more crucial to establish a time limit for the rights because they may not be as permanent as an item like a room or an area of the library. However, establishing a time limit for the naming rights up front may cause donors to be turned off. Definitely more to consider than anyone at the time probably thought of (M. Housel, personal communication, January 3, 2014).

POLICY MAKING

Policies are often not properly communicated internally and externally. They are confused with procedural guidelines.

Various state and local library associations also have sets of rules on developing policies on various topics, including fund-raising, naming rights, and dealing with outside vendors, which you'll need to research. You would want to connect your revenue policies to your own mission statement or charter, and insure they do not contradict, but rather enhance and support, other internal or external policies.

The public broadcasting guidelines for producing on-air credits mentioned in chapter 2 could easily be adopted as policies to justify whether or not to accept certain types of advertisers, language, or placement within the library, to avoid controversy and challenges. It's advisable to go through "what-if" scenarios and get consensus on what your organization's stance should be in each case. You should vision out tricky situations and work backwards as to how you could've fixed them.

For example, could you have protests over Planned Parenthood sponsoring a program on or collection area for sex education? How could you have a policy that minimizes controversy but doesn't turn away money?

The best recourse is simplicity. Use the model employed by many museums and orchestras—no advocacy, but a simple but very visible plaque thanking them for their sponsorship. You could also use the ROS concept mentioned earlier to never give a "one on one," which may suggest a perceived ownership by an advertiser to an area of the library.

Other Policy Questions   TIP

- Will the sponsor be able to use your organization's logo on anything?
- Would you make your databases of Friends, etc., available to the sponsor, and under what restrictions?
- Will you collaborate on program or event content?
- Are there business categories that will be off-limits, such as firearms, tobacco, or alcohol? (Martin 2004, 20)

Policies, as I mentioned earlier, are distinguished from *procedures.* They are

- » Statements that guide decisions and actions
- » Answers to "what" and "why" questions
- » General principles
- » Reflect needs
- » Have legal implications

When carefully crafted, policies can be used as

- » Communications tools that reinforce verbal explanations and reduce misunderstanding
- » Management tools that ensure activities of a similar type proceed under the same guidelines
- » Professional tools that enforce accountability, encouraging an examination of important issues and giving a more precise definition of expectations and practice

Elements of a policy should include:

1. *Identification of groups*—distinguishes the parties involved. It does not have to be specific, but can establish groups by the role they play: library, Friends, foundation, town council, sponsor, vendor, family, etc.
2. *Identification of relationships*—acknowledges the relationship as being one of oversight, supportive, community-oriented, pro-business, etc.
3. *Identification of settings*—use of physical or virtual space, presence of patrons.
4. *Identification of situations*—the nature of the revenue generation activity; sponsorship sales, crowdfunding campaign, vendor sales, passport assistance services, etc.
5. *Identification of behavior guidelines*—customer service expectations, adherence to contracts.
6. *Identification of penalty*—the rights to cancel or withhold funds based on improprieties, lack of service, moral turpitude, and harm to the library or its patrons.
7. *Identification of processes*—adherence to government oversight guidelines, internal budgetary processes, internal or external auditing procedures.
8. *Inference of outcomes*—acknowledgments of what can or cannot be done unless specified in contracts and approved by oversight authorities; an agreement's required revision if changes occur in laws, tax policy, etc.

Framing the relationship between your organization and the community is critical.

Almost every paragraph of the Akron-Summit Public Libraries Corporate sponsorship policy, which is a concise, page-and-a-half document, contains the words relationship, partner or partnerships. It's a positive, welcoming statement encouraging any potential sponsor to work with them toward uplifting the community, while reserving certain rights any good steward of public resources should have (Akron-Summit Public Library 2008).

Policy Comparison	EXERCISE

1 Many libraries post policies online. For this exercise, choose your favorite library and select three policies to analyze. If you don't have a favorite, go to http://pld.dpi.wi.gov/pld_policies, which links to the current library policies of the Wisconsin Public Libraries.

2 Googling "Corporate Sponsorship Policy" will return a number of good policies, including (at the time this book is being written) ones from YALSA and the city and county of Denver's Parks and Recreation Department. Both contain strong and clear language that spells out the value they see in accepting aid from commercial ventures while protecting the non-commercial nature of operations.

3 Analyze the policies using the eight aforementioned elements. Cut and paste the policy, indicate which characteristic you feel suits the particular paragraph best (more than one can be used, and might be used more than once) and briefly state the reason why.

Be aware of fiscal considerations. Fiscal officers, as well as your other top management and board members, should consult tax professionals as well as legal counselors to review what's allowable for fund-raising under your federal, state, and local laws. Libraries and NPs need to understand the legal and tax obligations relating to partnerships. You want to frame the arrangement so that neither party unnecessarily loses money to taxes but still gets good returns from the monetary exchange. Qualified sponsorship payments (also called "safe harbor"), and substantial return benefits are concepts that, while not deal-breakers in most cases, need to be clear to both the sponsor and your library (Martin 2004, 87.) You do not want to spoil a hard-earned relationship by having your sponsor believe they could write something off of their taxes, when they might only be allowed to deduct a partial amount. Likewise, you need to allow for being taxed on certain income you receive when planning your pricing.

For instance, under federal law, payments for advertising are taxable, but payments for which the payer receives an acknowledgment for underwriting are not. Sometimes to avoid a taxable situation in the past, advertisers could pay the costs of printing or materials as a gift, then get acknowledged. Again, check the current laws. Publication 598 currently reviews the Tax on Unrelated Business Income of Exempt Organizations (Internal Revenue Service 2012).

Know your lingo. What can make the difference between an underwriting acknowledgment and advertising? Review the Underwriting versus Advertising table in chapter 2. Avoid qualitative, comparative or inducement language. Keep it simple. A simple acknowledgment for providing support, and a brief (maybe even bland) description of the sponsor and their business is fine. Saying they're the best, or to call by Friday, or to show a library card for 10 percent off could turn a win-win into a lose-lose, even if fines for penalties are for minor amounts, if penalized. A few hours watching or listening to public media should give you an idea of the creative, positive ways you can acknowledge a sponsor without crossing the line into advertising.

Be aware of all municipal and other governmental guidelines. Libraries and other NPs must follow a number of rules that protect the public interest, just like broadcasting does. Below are some recent examples of a few clashes among city councils, the public, and libraries that have occurred, prompting libraries to change their naming strategies and event planning. You must consider the legal and political environment you're in before implementing significant change.

Understand the Signs of Taxable Revenue | TIP

Paying taxes on extra revenue is better than not having extra revenue. However, not paying taxes and getting penalized due to ignorance is something you want to avoid.

Unrelated Business Income Tax (UBIT) is something that any nonprofit, including libraries who are generating most of the revenue types discussed in this book should be aware of. Your fiscal officer should check regulations to determine whether or not they need to fill out a Form 990-T, the Exempt Organization Business Income Tax Return, and pay tax on income derived from the sale of advertising, library merchandise, vending machine candy, helping to issue passports, or other revenue-generating methods (Internal Revenue Service 2014).

In Santa Fe, a controversy over naming a branch after a deceased businessman caused his family to withdraw a donation offer of one million dollars (*American Libraries* 2007). Despite following the city's naming policy, when this person was the one picked from eight nominees, the city council delayed the approval, creating unwanted media attention and causing the family to withdraw its support.

In another million-dollar effort, the Hopkinton Public Library Foundation sought to supplement renovation and expansion funds through a naming rights campaign that ran into a little snag (Phelps 2014). Their town had no formal policy, and had regularly named properties during normal board meetings once or twice a year. The Foundation created thirty naming opportunities, from the building itself down to the bicycle racks. This prompted local authorities to ponder a policy giving them the authority for naming or renaming public assets. Whether you interpret this as micromanaging or good stewardship, it's nonetheless obvious you should be aware of policy vacuums around your organization.

In event planning, one library planned to assemble a fleet of food trucks at an outdoor event. However, local establishments protested and waivers needed to use public parking spaces nearby were denied (Berkowitz 2015). Problems like these can be a surprise if you don't consider all the consequences of planning anything beyond your own walls. Before looking outside for revenue, check with your government partners, from the IRS down to local selectmen, to make sure they're supportive stakeholders in your activities.

To use my earlier analogy, a policy is like a description of a meal. It has a general description, including basic ingredients, taste, presentation, number of servings provided, and nutritional value. Procedures and contracts are the actual recipe steps, which will be covered in the next chapter.

Never Promise Numbers!	TIP

You can use statistics to illustrate your environment or describe a past event, but don't promise a certain number of patrons will walk through a door, participate in an event, or guarantee anything else involving sponsorships. The Super Bowl traditionally has huge ad rates. But when there is a weak game and no one watches the end, the network offers "make-goods" to reach the Cume audience that advertisers were looking for. NPs can't really offer "make-goods." Current nonprofit law in this area says payments based on specific, promised returns would be taxed. When you use them in Stage 2, to cultivate a relationship with a potential sponsor, that's fine. Throwing them into a specific pitch, in Stage 3, changes the nature of the relationship, and is liable for UBIT tax. You are not just acknowledging their support, but delivering something. Payments contingent on measurements are not protected by safe harbor, so they would not be shielded from taxes and/or penalties for non-payment.

References

Akron-Summit Public Library 2008. "Sponsorship/Partnership Policy." http://akronlibrary.org/policy/sponsorship.pdf.

American Libraries. 2007. "Naming Flap Costs Santa Fe $1 Million." *American Libraries* 38 (7): 23–24.

Berkowitz, K. 2015. "City Nixes Food Trucks at Library's Event." *Chicago Tribune,* May 7. www.chicagotribune.com/suburbs/highland-park/news/ct-hpn-food-trucks-tl-0514–20150507-story.html.

Cervantes, N. 2013. "SM Library Benching Its Benches." *Santa Maria Times,* July 27. http://santamariatimes.com/news/local/sm-library-benching-its-benches/article_67d3c610- f677-11e2–874c-001a4bcf887a.html.

Internal Revenue Service. 2014. *Form 990-T, Exempt Organization Business Income Tax Returns.* www.irs.gov/uac/Form-990-T,-Exempt-Organization-Business-Income-Tax-Return.

———. 2012. *Publication 598, Tax on Unrelated Business Income of Exempt Organizations.* www.irs.gov/publications/p598/index.html.

Martin, P. 2004. *Made Possible By: Succeeding with Sponsorship.* San Francisco: Jossey-Bass.

Phelps, J. 2014. "Hopkinton Selectmen Consider Naming Policy." *Milford Daily News,* November 18. www.milforddailynews.com/article/20141118/News/141116751.

CHAPTER SIX

CONTRACTS AND PROCEDURES

IF POLICIES ARE DESCRIPTIONS OF A MEAL, CONTRACTS are the actual recipe steps! Contracts cover the logistics of a dish, ingredients, preparation time, timelines, etc. Contracts also form the parameters of how procedures should work. This chapter covers both.

The devil is in the details. In NYC, sixty-seven library branches were built between 1902 and 1929 for five million dollars (Maloney 2013). Many are landmarks, and almost all need costly updates and repairs. Something they didn't consider 100 years ago when Andrew Carnegie donated the money for construction but put the maintenance duties on the community. Part of a long-running naming rights contract should include an ongoing maintenance clause.

Writing contracts that include the phrase "in perpetuity" means something is forever. Many nonprofits, including not only libraries but also school districts, cities, and museums sell naming rights "in perpetuity," but smart business practices specify the length of the time period.

Here's a recent reason why. The Avery Fisher family gave ten million dollars in 1973 to rename Philharmonic Hall to "Avery Fisher Hall." Twelve years ago the family threatened legal action if the name was changed. In 2014 it was announced that the Fisher family will receive fifteen million dollars to allow the name to be changed. $500 million is needed for a major renovation and the center management want to be able to attract a large donor to rechristen the building. In 2015 entertainment mogul

David Geffen donated $100 million for the venue to be changed to David Geffen Hall. At the time of this writing no contract details were available (Pogrebin 2015).

KEY CONTRACT AND PROCEDURE POINTS

The contract is a formal aspect of the relationship between your organization and another. Despite the personal, friendly nature of a relationship you may have with a prospect, a professional contract proves you're interested in proper stewardship of the library, and respectful of their business. Do not be contract-phobic.

Procedures are multipurpose tools that support policies. They insure consistency, communicate specific action, and can be used for training as well as quality control. Procedures help everyone through a learning curve. Standard business operations include procedures that support the policies as well as accomplish the details required by your contracts.

The contract checklist below is what the library can control from a procedural viewpoint. You should standardize contracts as much as possible so that if your people change positions or you need to change partners, transition problems are minimal. Remember all contracts are subject to governmental oversight guidelines.

Each sales contract should contain these elements:

1. *Logistics Confirmation*—Who is producing what, and when will it be delivered?
2. *Copy Confirmation*—What exactly is being said? A screening process should be specified, checking not only for grammatical errors but content that may cross the line into advertising.
3. *Billing Process*—Document terms and deadlines for down payments, a payment schedule, auditing methods, and billing terms (net payment due in thirty days).
4. *Deposits Procedure*—This should be outlined, even though under some jurisdictions public entities like libraries may have no say in the process. However, the client should be made aware of what is or is not required of them.
5. *Implementation Process*—A timeline for all of the above, summarizing all the roles and due dates up until the final product is operational.

Standard Business Contract Organizational Sequence

1. *Identification of parties involved*—sometime involves condensing a legal name into a shorter term like "sponsor."
2. *The scope of agreement*—the description of the purchase. The start and end dates, rates, placement of name/brand, any extras involved.
3. *Financial arrangements*—payment and billing options, total costs, specific payment plans, advance payment discounts, credit card payments, security deposits, production, and/or maintenance fees.

4. *Cancellation policy*—right to refuse, costs of collection, substitution of placement, termination procedure, failure to comply, unacceptable material, use of non-inducement language, ability to reassign or transfer agreement to others.
5. *Liability issues*—no warranty, guarantees, adherence to truth in advertising.
6. *Governing*—state law under which this will be covered.
7. *Disposition of signed contract*—size of, and delivery schedule for graphics, other advertising material and payment; signature area for both parties.

For maximum efficiency, a library would use a standard form that included the dates of any subsequent revision. Check for any municipal guidelines, or polices of any entities that govern the library. Have someone in a legal oversight position proofread for you.

Be Flexible with Forms

The Denver Public Library and Foundation uses various forms based on the type of proposal, event sponsorship, event table purchase, naming rights, etc. To avoid too much bureaucracy, the proposal makes clear what's expected of each party. Their naming rights agreements are much more specific and need approval by the city's library commission and city attorney. When bond money has paid for a building, they need to be careful about what percentage is named and that the naming is specifically in appreciation of a gift to support the programming in the library, not as a purchase of any space in the library. They use common sense in decision-making when developing partnerships, about the use of logos, and involve the affected program/department managers before a proposal is sent to insure they don't over-promise anything and work with board and community members during the discovery process to find the best-suited local advertisers to approach (B. Ritenour, personal communication, July 13, 2015).

Other negotiating points to consider:

» Aim for general revenue fund contributions, rather than having a controlling partner saying the money has to go to X. They may be buying a sponsorship of the Medical Reference table, but that doesn't mean they pick what's shelved or added as part of the public collection.
» When accepting product or services in lieu of or in place of cash, be specific and avoid one-to-one dollar exchanges. For instance, if you've determined that a sponsorship of a summer reading program will cost $500, don't accept $500 of free ice cream from a grocery chain for an event. They will value it at retail costs rather than what they buy it for at wholesale. Strive for at least 1.5 times your cash target, and/or establish a limit for accepting in-lieu-of-cash product. Have a policy stating no more than a certain amount of non-cash product can go toward payments.
» Define the start-up and maintenance costs sponsor will pay. These are negotiating points outside of the fair-market value of the product being sold. Try to build in a maintenance endowment as part of the original endowment so you can refurbish, repaint, etc., as needed (Martin 2004, 80).

More contract considerations used by some public broadcasters include:

» Using ROS schedules, and not allowing proximity to programming in which the sponsor may have a vested interest.
» Offering a gift ladder of various scale announcements—for example, three units for $1,000 ($333 each), five for $1,500 ($300 each), ten for $2,700 ($270 each), etc.
» Specifying acceptable print, video, and digital signage techniques.

All these measures are relatively easy to put in place, and are made easier by having specific, standardized contracts with your sponsors and procedures for your staff to follow.

Be Flexible with Partnerships

Having various revenue streams requires good record keeping and flexibility. The clients may have unique procedures and schedules of their own that you'll have to accommodate in order to achieve proper payments. Librarians know the value of organization, but may be new to the nuances of partnerships with revenue stream clients. This brief section will review some basic business practices.

Types of clients include:

» *Businesses*—Usually concerned with event or area sponsorships. Simple billing and examples of final product usually suffice. Remember, payment based on numbers would move an acknowledgment into advertising, and certain tax consequences would come into play.
» *Foundations and Underwriters*—Often concerned with the above, plus issue-oriented strategic programs. They often require a before-and-after review of metrics to determine if the program was successful. Reporting that increasing the number of computers by 10 percent increased training attendance by 25 percent shows the scale of success for a program.
» *Third-Party Agencies, Vendors, or Internet Companies*—Billing associated with audits are common here. These are situations where the library is a go-between for passport assistance programs, vending machine sales, ebook sales through the library's website, etc.
» *Patrons*—Simple receipts for tax or other purposes are needed for the sale of printouts, ear-buds, faxes, notary services, etc.

In broadcasting and other media operations there is traditionally a traffic department that coordinates the sales and programming departments. Traffic department operations coordinate what could become chaos in a time-sensitive environment. Sales department staff needs to know what's for sale, and the programming staff (in radio, announcers) need to know what to say and when to say it. When a sales order comes in, traffic personnel check it against available spots to place the ad.

They then record that the time period is no longer for sale. They next do an audit to determine if the right commercial ran successfully, and arrange to have it invoiced. If for some reason it didn't, they note that, and if the contract allows create a "make-good" spot so the station won't lose the money. Depending on the revenue method you use, you'll need procedures like these traffic departments to manage inventory and content control, and auditing.

Always do a credit check for new clients before you invest too much of your inventory into the deal. You want to award a public resource only for someone with good credit, or cash in advance. You can reserve it for a new donor, but try to follow through on the credit check within a few days. Don't wait until you are two weeks out to find they can't produce a clean credit check, leaving you to find someone else to take over the inventory they claimed. Most broadcast operations have local salespeople bring in a filled-out and signed credit application form, then have the traffic or business department review it. For naming rights contracts, this is especially important.

The next step is getting an advertisement produced, reviewed, and okayed by both the client and management, and placing it in the appropriate time to air. The next day, a reconciliation is done to make sure the spot was aired, so it can be billed accordingly, or a "make good" spot is issued to run as a substitute for the missed placement. In broadcasting operations, the billing can be done at the end of a schedule, weekly, or monthly. In fact, there are two monthly cycles: a regular Gregorian calendar month and a standardized broadcast calendar month that goes from Monday to Sunday and has either four or five week months, depending on which day the first of the month falls. Some advertising agencies may want to be billed that way, something you may need to know when preparing your pitch. Just ask them during the cultivation stage.

A library developing a dynamic sponsorship program will want to develop the following reports:

An Inventory Report—what is available, and when. This is useful for making sure all available opportunities are being used, as well as when a contract needs to be renewed or resold to someone else. Many libraries use meeting room scheduling software, which works like systems that track inventory. You might be able to use that software for sponsorship inventory control as well.

A Revenue Projection Report—based on sales, and how much revenue will be coming in during a given month. This is especially critical if you do not collect an annual payment, which is the preferred method. This helps you track your revenue goals.

A Continuity Report—shows the status of the verbiage and graphics associated with an advertisement. The contract may be signed, and due to start next month. Do you need to create a special plaque? Have you received the verbiage from the advertiser? Has it been cleared by management before the plaque is created? Is it timely or seasonal in nature? These logistical questions about ad type, verbiage, graphics, rights clearance, production status, and expiration date can be tracked via a spreadsheet, written checklist, or any other method you prefer, but it's essential to keep organized, especially if you're rotating multiple sponsorships through various library branches and channels.

The Haverford Township Free Library has produced a sample tracking page that is an excellent tool in tracking the benefits a sponsor receives. It's in three parts:

1. Basic organization and contact information
2. Space for a contact log for comments
3. A three-column section that lists benefits in one column, date of benefit, and who completed it:

Benefits	Date of Benefit	Who Completed It
Thank-you letter sent		
Listing on website		
Sponsor badge for website provided		
Logo in promotional materials		
Spotlight on local business feature		
Special event tickets		

When juggling multiple sponsor duties within a team, this can be a great organizational tool (Haverford Township Free Library 2014).

Invoicing, Billing, and Collections—Invoices will need to show a description of the sponsored activity. It may be a brief sentence like "For acknowledgment slides at the front entrance of Main and branch libraries, $400," or more detailed, "Ten slides each day from March 1 through March 10 at both of the Circulation Desks of Main and Branch library. 10 slides x 10 days x 2 locations x $2 each slide = $400."

Based on your invoicing, reports on billing and accounts receivable will follow. Preferably, if paid in advance, your collection reports should show minimum amounts. As stated earlier, many libraries work under specific municipal or other governmental authorities that require specific tracking of revenue, billing, etc. Everyone does audits. Developing standard procedures, like libraries have had to do for various other complicated operations (e.g., interlibrary loans), will allow you to create valid reports auditors will respect. These reports will not only make your operations more efficient, but also should illustrate opportunities and help you plan better.

FIGURE 6.1
Standard Sequence of Broadcasting Business Activities

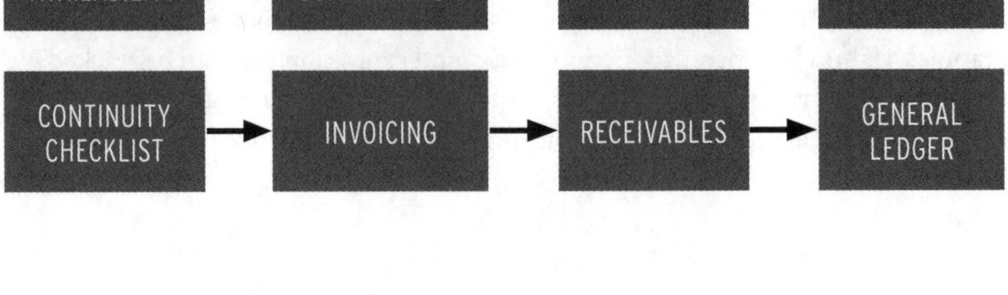

Standard Sequence of Procedures

Procedures are sequential descriptions of how things should be accomplished. They answer the "how" and "who" questions; the "whys" are covered in your policies. These are specific practices that may be self-contained or exist on their own. Yours wouldn't exactly mimic broadcasting operations, but conceptually follow the pattern above.

When creating them, you should:

» Use simple language (be reasonable)
» Be organized consistently

STRUCTURE OF INSTRUCTIONS

1. General introduction
   a. Why?
   b. When?
   c. Who?
   d. Is background information needed?

2. Step-by-step instructions
   a. Always number the instructions.
   b. Break down into reasonable parts.

3. Conclusion
   a. May not be necessary.
   b. Troubleshooting or "maintenance."

Checklist for Instructions
1. Does the introduction to the instructions
   a. State the purpose of the task?
   b. Describe background or safety measures necessary?
   c. List tools and materials?

2. Are the step-by-step instructions
   a. Numbered?
   b. Expressed in the imperative mood?
   c. Simple and direct?

3. Are appropriate graphics included?

4. Does the conclusion
   a. Supply any necessary follow-up advice?
   b. Include, if appropriate, a trouble-shooting guide?

» Be consistent in verbiage—for example, only use the word "warning" for possible human error situations, and "caution" for potential equipment or computer malfunctions
» Note how you can tell you are on the right track and indicate signs of effectiveness
» Point out if the practice is related to another procedure or policy

Try to have a triple perspective:

1. From above, as it fits into other activities
2. From the inside, as it is actually performed
3. From below, as its effects are felt by others

Always try to include an introduction, detailed instructions, and conclusion, rather than just listing bullet points. This will make comprehension and adaptation easier.

PROFESSIONAL NAMING RIGHTS CONTRACT TIPS

Myles Gallagher of the Superlative Group, who's arranged naming rights contracts for a number of schools, government entities, and hospitals, suggests a number of important points to consider (M. Gallagher, personal communication, September 2014). Some of his advice includes:

» For your sponsorships or naming rights, don't use request for proposals (RFPs) if you can avoid it (check your particular government oversight regulations). RFPs simply ask for bids, which isn't equivalent to the benefits you'll derive from the sales process—don't let bidders short-change you.
» When setting value in unusual places, like a local history archive, use an average of CPM values for print, outdoor, and electronic media in your area to determine the current market. Then raise or lower your own CPM accordingly. Remember the example formula from chapter 3?

Dollars / impressions (in thousands) = CPM $500 / 30 = 16 CPM

The local market CPM average for television, radio, billboard, and newspapers may be 20. You are undervaluing yourself! Raise your price to $600. If the market average is 12, drop your price to $360. If your financial goals are higher than that, this is where you need to produce a good sales presentation, which will be covered in chapter 7, on promotions.

OTHER POLICY QUESTIONS

Q: Will the sponsor be able to use your organization's logo on anything?
A: Why not? Don't quibble.

Q: Would you make your databases of Friends, etc., available to the sponsor?
A: Under what restrictions? Most places won't give out their Friends lists, and sponsors don't expect it; it's not a deal breaker, but mentioning having a policy takes it off the table quickly.

Q: Will you collaborate on program or event content?
A: It's work for the sponsor! Most will not, but it depends on the event.

A: Are any business categories off-limits (firearms, tobacco, or alcohol)?
Q: Check your local municipal marketing guidelines!

Some other practical wisdom:

» Always build in a moral turpitude clause, which allows a contract to be broken if a participant's actions undermine their public reputation.
» To prevent UBIT, watch rules on safe harbor; use very limited advertising messages, but acknowledge support.
» Have two money streams; one a 501(c)(3) gift, another either a UBIT or non-taxable revenue (acknowledgment) for advertising; the write-off will be an incentive. Check local regulations and current tax laws. But if you can do this, it definitely sweetens the pot for the prospect.
» Regarding naming rights, always try to build in a maintenance endowment as part of the original endowment so you can refurbish, repaint, etc., as needed.
» Strive for a twenty- to twenty-five-year commitment for naming rights. Use annual payments, with the current Consumer Price Index (CPI) increase of 2.9 percent per year.

Rookie mistakes Myles sees:

1. Over- or undervaluing. The nonprofit doesn't set the proper value, so their product is either never sold, or stolen.
2. Not doing due diligence, or neglecting to use credit applications. If dealing with one person or family for significant amounts, get a life insurance policy to protect against lost funding! For instance, if a husband wants to spend two million dollars over the course of twenty years to memorialize his wife, make sure a policy is taken out in case he dies and the surviving family members renege on payments. Likewise, do not let a business promise to sponsor an event or building area without first doing a credit application and having them furnish some other media references.

Focus Your Thinking

A standard practice in broadcasting operations is holding periodic full-day sales meetings with all concerned parties at the station. Full immersion in topics such as sales policies, rate cards, special event packages, program development, current client contacts, and cooperation should be included (Quaal and Brown 1976). Libraries and NPs also take time for "service days" that are devoted to building professional skills in a team environment. Whether it's with a full staff or special committee, a periodic review of your revenue-generating strategies and procedures is a critical factor for success in a dynamic business environment. You cannot afford to become stale.

After the initial wave of sponsored activity, you may be approached by more potential sponsors or third-party vendors. You may see within your organization areas or events that could be used to bring in revenue to enhance them. Now that you have strategic policies and procedures you will follow, and clear contractual arrangements ready, the next step is to choose what communication tactics you'll use to promote whatever revenue-generating methods you choose. Communicating well will improve your library's bottom line, keep branches open, offer outstanding materials, and keep people employed. That critical step, promotions, is in our next chapter.

References

Haverford Township Free Library. 2014. "Get the Business Bucks: Creating a Sponsorship Program on a Shoestring." Presented at PaLa Annual Conference, September 28.

Maloney, J. 2013. "Rethinking Andrew Carnegie's Library Gift to New York City." *Wall Street Journal*, July 7. www.wsj.com/articles/SB10001424127887324507404578 591901331381768.

Martin, P. 2004. *Made Possible By: Succeeding with Sponsorship*. San Francisco: Jossey-Bass.

Pogrebin, R. 2015. "David Geffen Captures Naming Rights to Avery Fisher Hall with Donation." *New York Times*, March 4. www.nytimes.com/2015/03/05/arts/ david-geffen-captures-naming-rights-to-avery-fisher-hall-with-donation .html?_r=0.

Quaal, W. L., and J. A. Brown. 1976. *Broadcast Management: Radio-Television*. New York: Hastings House Publishers, Inc.

CHAPTER SEVEN

PROMOTIONS
Getting the Word Out

NO MATTER HOW NOBLE THE CAUSE, YOU NEED EFFICIENT approaches for getting the word out to sponsors and getting them to work with you. This chapter will help you pitch your value, handle objections, and be able to reach media and advertising companies.

The *American Public Library Handbook* has a section devoted to explaining the field of public relations in both historical and current contexts (Marco 2012). "Advocacy" is now used as an umbrella term for various PR activities, and is geared toward activities used to gain funding for libraries, mostly through political means. These activities can be cross-pollinated into securing funding from the business sector as well.

You'll recall there are four stages to Moves Management sponsor development. This chapter is mostly concerned with Moves 2 and 3.

1. *Discovery*—Staff brainstorms a list of the top twenty-five businesses that could possibly be sponsors. Ask "does anyone here know someone working at ABC Widgets?" Arrange an introduction meeting, find out about their business, what they know about yours, and build rapport.
2. *Cultivation*—Make a second appointment. "Can we come back and talk about what it is you want to do? How we can help?" Show the promotional package.

3. *Solicitation*—Thanks for the conversation! You showed interest in doing X at Y cost. *We could do X at Y and throw in Z!* Here's the pitch/contract!"

4. *Stewardship*—Acknowledge their support; deliver on what you promised professionally. Invite them back to see their results. Keep connected.

Ideally, in Stage 2, cultivation, you'd discuss the monetization of the idea but not give the full pitch. Instead, emphasize the features, advantages, and benefits the library can offer to the sponsor or vendor. Because time is money, many organizations prepare materials that span both the areas of cultivation and solicitation.

THE DENVER PUBLIC LIBRARY PROPOSAL CHECKLIST

The Denver Public Library (DPL) works in a large media market with various levels of outside advertising agencies and marketing departments. Their successful approach to proposals combining Stage 2, cultivation, and Stage 3, solicitation, of Moves Management can be applied in any size market. It's composed of three elements:

1. An executive summary, introducing the library's mission statement and vision of its role in the community.
2. A more specific summary of the program with which they're approaching the sponsor, how it benefits the community, and subtly dropping in the sponsor's name to help them visualize participation.
3. Consideration statements that consist of what the library offers the sponsor, and finally, on the last page, what the library would like in return.

For example, considerations from the library might be inclusion of the sponsor in media releases, logos in event literature, storytimes done at the sponsor's location, tickets to special library fund-raising events, or even industry exclusivity. Considerations provided to DPL would be a specific dollar investment, logos in specific formats, and promotional materials for distribution at mutually agreed-upon locations (B. Ritenour, personal communication July 13, 2015).

The word "consideration" sounds nice and positive here. In connotes thoughtful, considerate, friendly action. It's a much better word for relationship-building than the word "payment"!

FEATURES, ADVANTAGES, AND BENEFITS

Using features and benefits is not a complicated process (Van Vechten nd); it's an age-old sales formula that can be used for any target audience: board, businesses, or patrons. The primary colors, red, green and blue, can combine to make any other attractive blend of colors. Likewise, features, advantages and benefits can be combined to create an attractive proposal for your prospects.

Features *(Characteristics)*	Advantages *(What they do)*	Benefits *(How they help)*
Example 1 Generating revenue	• No taxpayer burden • Convenience • Promotion and publicity • Underutilized space used	Providing more: • Materials • Programs • Services
Example 2 Supply vending machines	• Patron convenience • Promotion and publicity opportunities	• Support as needed • Enhancing library offerings to the public

The order can be reversed—for example, "Our patrons would appreciate being able to buy envelopes or other office and school supplies they forgot they needed before coming to the library. It'd be expensive to have the library stock, service, and charge them for items, but if we had a vending machine to direct them to, everyone wins!"

The Washington-Centerville Public Library Corporate Giving web page lays out the features of various relationship programs with businesses, including sponsorships, collaborations, and partnerships, as well as benefits and specific guidelines that must be followed for each type of relationship. It also covers shopping rebate programs and a unique welcoming activity geared toward rewarding new library card holders, entry into a drawing for a prize from a "Business of the Week." (Washington-Centerville Public Library nd).

Revenue Method Features and Benefits — EXERCISE

Go through the Money Matrix in Appendix A and apply this formula to five sample methods. Then check them against what's been suggested in the mini-chapters for those methods.

Example

REVENUE METHOD	PASSPORT SERVICES
FEATURES	Producing and processing photos and documents needed for passports.
ADVANTAGES	More convenient times than other government offices, trip preparation materials close by.
BENEFITS	Patron has fewer scheduling issues to get key documents. Conducted in a family-friendly location.

THE PROPOSAL BASICS

A proposal should include an introduction, facts, demographics, key selling points, a who-what-where-when-why section, and a summary. Think of it as the cover letter-resume combination that takes you into the interview, which is Stage 3, solicitation: the pitch.

The proposal will describe the features, advantages, and benefits you bring to the table. It should include the following:

Who	Your patron description	Feature (to win real pros, lead with your main value)
What	Activities the patrons are coming to the library's building/website/programming to do	Feature and advantage
Where	Would you position the sponsor	Advantage
When	How long a timeframe	Advantage
How	Signage, frequency	Advantage
Why	How the above matches the sponsors target audience	Benefit

In the book, *Made Possible By* (Martin 2004, 58), there's a list of sample selling points based on what your prospect will achieve from a sponsorship. These include:

» Generating leads and opening doors
» Building their brands and fostering loyalty
» Positioning against competition
» Gaining more advertising and media exposures
» Directly marketing to targeted audiences
» Getting reports and outcomes to gauge return on investment

Based on your policies, some of these may not be possible. It may not be permissible for a sponsor to obtain exclusive rights or do direct marketing on the premises. However, no one would argue that opportunities to build their brand and get more media exposure are honest and legal outcomes.

The Haverford Township Free Library gave an industry presentation in 2014 entitled "Get the Business Bucks: Creating a Sponsorship Program On a Shoestring." Among the ideas they shared was the concepts of "the ask." They emphasized that the ask be well-crafted, show clear benefits, include supporting materials, and be proofed by multiple people. Balance visibility opportunities and fun! When you are following up, make it a "soft sell," but keep in mind that you have to demonstrate that you truly believe in your cause (Haverford Township Free Library 2014).

PROFESSIONAL MEDIA KIT EXAMPLES

Monetize Pros (2015) uses seven examples of media kits, all of which share features that emphasize one goal: make it rain! "Make it rain" is business slang for generating a lot of money (or if not a lot, then enough to not have to cut back on service hours or personnel). All seven examples are great, and most share these common elements:

» A description of the audience
» Options and channels (opportunities) for reaching that audience
» Their reach into the target community
» Case studies of, and testimonials from, current partners

Many communities have several media companies under one corporate umbrella. In some markets, you can make a phone call about advertising for a Summer Reading Program to one radio station and rather quickly get great details from six different radio stations that are all part of the local jointly owned radio cluster. Information about each station's unique format and audience would be included, as well as a variety of options on rates, number of impressions via their combined websites, online streaming commercials, and 30- and 60-second daypart and ROS rate cards. Enhance your own proposals by becoming familiar with your local competitions.

MORE DETAILS ON THE PROPOSAL— HOW DO YOU WANT TO SAY IT?

This section deals with getting the word out, and not by using RFPs. The materials you present are part of the sales process, and are critical in working with agencies. Luckily, there are some free sources of help for this. Check into your local American Advertising Federation or American Marketing Association for pro-bono assistance. They might also be a great source of leads!

A great way to learn about marketing if you never had a chance to take a class in library school is through the Ohio Library Council's library marketing page. It includes a specific area for promotions that's geared toward the novice (Ohio Library Council 2008). It's a free web resource on promoting a library (or any business or nonprofit). The interactive tutorial discusses various tactical moves libraries can use to promote themselves in general and during their revenue-generating prospects during Stage 2, the cultivation stage; these include branding, press releases, advertising, and direct marketing publications (like library newsletters).

Agencies, as well as foundations, tend to want to see a clear analysis of the public you're serving. Graphics can quickly illustrate this in a compelling manner. Almost everyone learns better when visuals are involved.

The scatter diagram shown previously (figure 4.1), produced by Cengage's Analytics on Demand software (Cengage 2014), shows the library as the starred location, with heavy usage to the northwest quadrant above it, and some gaps to the east. It would be a great addition to your proposal.

Friends groups are equivalent to what broadcasters refer to as their core audience. People who've invested in and support activities, whether those activities are music concerts or book sales.

You can use analytics to spot Friends locations, which you can then use for strengthening your attraction with potential retail sponsors in the area. They might find themselves in the middle of an attractive audience and being one of your sponsors is a bridge to them. Using election data from past levies also gives you a good review of high support areas.

The use of infographics clearly illustrates NPR audience on their "Audience Profiles" page (National Public Media 2016). Bar graphs favorably compare the NPR audience to total US adults in the advertiser-oriented categories of income and education. They use creative pictures as well as statistics, and break out their audience descriptions using their own lifestyle categories, similar to the method Cengage's Analytics on Demand software uses as discussed in chapter 4. Their programming is also highlighted with the use of the logos of Morning Edition, Fresh Air with Terry Gross, and the TED Radio Hour. A technique other organizations could use in "branding" their most popular programming.

For example, Lakewood Public Library (OH) once used a cartoon family reflecting different demographics, such as a common sense mom, a sports-nut dad, an aging arts-oriented hippie grand-dad, etc. and used the individuals for visual cues in the library's program guide to focus on nutrition programs, art discussions, etc. After a few issues, people recognized the differences between the characters and their eyes were then drawn to that specific program.

THE PITCH

After the proposal, you're ready to move into the third stage of Moves Management:

> » *Solicitation*: Thanks for the conversation! You showed interest in doing X at Y cost. We could do X at Y and throw in Z!

Be prepared for the pitch—know what you have to offer, the fair value of your product, and the logistics involved. You should have a contract ready to keep the momentum going through commitment.

Proposals are essential parts of your overall strategy, but don't expect them to close a sale for you. The association with the library is sometimes all you will need for a successful pitch. One author says he doesn't use sales proposals for 30 percent of his sales! That's because he has a great relationship with his prospects (Gitomer 2006, 115). If you follow the rules of Moves Management, you have already discovered potential allies in Stage 1, discovery, and may already have built relationships with them. Depending on the business people you're approaching, you may or may not need to use a little proposal showmanship.

Proper Use of Promotional Packages

When working with advertising agencies, don't be too hasty on requests, that implies desperation, and you may get a low offer, if any. If you hurry and bend over backwards to get them a fair proposal for $500, they may sense your desperation and only offer $200. Insist on waiting to analyze the customer to insure there are no conflicts with existing sponsors or partners, and to better determine their needs. Don't buckle under their pressure to give them a custom proposal in forty-eight hours, or some other inappropriate timeframe.

Local Businesses

Packages for local businesses may not need to be quite as formal as those for agencies, but they still need to be professional. Use the same basic package elements formula for everyone, but look for ways to highlight data that will be of special interest to local businesses. Have a publicity angle ready, a sample news release showing how you'll positively project your partnership into the local media and public awareness.

The Public

Use your graphic art skills as well as social media to engage the public and encourage them to participate. People are bombarded by thousands of messages each day. Use a combination of communication channels to reach them. Unlike with businesses, one package won't do. There are a variety of email service companies that can help you get your message out inexpensively. Constant Contact is one well-known service, and there are others that specialize in our industry, like Ingram's Sendr program.

When and How Will You Say It?

Use your Friends organization for launching campaigns. Encourage them to spread the word. Social media like Facebook, Twitter, and the neighborhood-oriented platform nextdoor.com can help you launch a campaign, and be used for periodic follow-up.

Be aware that seasonal businesses (e.g., landscaping companies) plan their buys well in advance. Keep this in mind as you work through prospects in the discovery phase. For instance, for summer reading programs, start brainstorming sponsors in the fall! If you approach an amusement park in the spring, you're too late, their budget will be already committed.

Overcoming Objections

Use a features-benefits model to promote and justify your revenue generation techniques to your community. Features and benefits can be used in overcoming objections by anyone: board members, media, and public purists who insist all funds only come from government sources, no matter how bad conditions get. Simply put, to overcome objections to seeking money in the private versus government sector, this method:

1. Delineates the features—more money.
2. Shows advantages—less dependent on political cycles and opposition from non-library users.
3. Emphasizes benefits—better access, materials, and services!

REAL WORLD: THE ADOPTION FORM

The Bartow County Library System in Georgia has a creative "adoption program," where individuals or businesses can sponsor single books for $25 on up through an entire shelving section for $3,300.

This interactive form is accessed through a web page discussing the adopt-a-book-or-shelf program, serves both as a proposal and contract document. It offers an appealing rationale, very specific options for naming, and an easy procedure for communication and payments.

USING ANNUAL REPORTS FOR PROMOTION

Almost every library and NP produces an annual report for its stakeholders. You probably put some good work into it, but don't use it past the original distribution date. Brush yours off and use it for the next exercise.

Proposal packages are close cousins to annual reports. Both foster relationships between the library and the public. These are increasingly accessible through technology, like the interactive adoption form above, or the discussion of NPR's audience characteristics.

Speaking of technology, face-to-face communication seems to be less frequent these days, which dismays some, but helps others who are time-starved and reasonably technically competent. The next chapter discusses the opportunities technology opens up to develop new revenue resources.

Focused Annual Report Review	EXERCISE

- Take a look at your own library's publications to analyze the presentation of user profiles: is it using a well-balanced overview of outcomes and/or outputs? Or is it heavy on one or the other?

- Compare and contrast your annual report to at least three other nearby systems' annual reports.

- Some of the elements may not all be used, but look at each for proper comparisons.

- Which annual report is most likely to attract the dollars of an advertiser?

- How would you correct yours?

References

Auburn University. nd. "Simplifying Library Value for Non-Library Development Officers and Staff." https://aurora.auburn.edu/bitstream/handle/11200/48521/2016ALAPosterSimplifyingLibraryValue.pdf?sequence=1.

Bartow County Library System. "Adoption Form." www.bartowlibraryonline.org/assets/about/AdpotAbookForm.pdf.

Cengage Learning, Inc. 2014. *Analytics on Demand.* http://solutions.cengage.com/analytics/. from *Analytics on Demand* Patron Profile Report from Gale, a part on Cengage Learning. *Analytics on Demand* is a series of web-based apps that enable libraries to quickly blend data from their existing library systems with external demographic data, creating powerful insights.

Gitomer, J. 2006. *Jeffrey Gitomer's Little Red Book of Sales Answers: 99.5 Real World Answers That Make Sense, Make Sales, and Make Money.* Upper Saddle River, N.J.: Prentice Hall.

Haverford Township Free Library. 2014. "Get the Business Bucks: Creating a Sponsorship Program on a Shoestring." Presentation material from PaLa Annual Conference, September 28.

Marco, G. 2012. *The American Public Library Handbook.* Libraries Unlimited: Santa Barbara, CA.

Martin, P. 2004. *Made Possible By: Succeeding with Sponsorship.* San Francisco: Jossey-Bass.

Monetize Pros. 2015. "Seven Examples of Media Kits That Make It Rain." http://monetizepros.com/blog/2013/seven-examples-of-media-kits-that-make-it-rain/.

National Public Media. 2015. "NPR Profiles." http://nationalpublicmedia.com/npr/audience/.

Ohio Library Council. 2008. "Promoting the Library." www.olc.org/marketing/4intro.htm. Currently redesigning. If unavailable, use archive.org, March 24, 2014.

Van Vechten, L. nd. "Understanding Feature-Advantage-Benefit." www.sellingpower.com/content/article/?a=8554/understanding-feature-advantage-benefit.

Washington-Centerville Public Library nd. "Corporate Giving/Donations." www.wclibrary.info/donations/corporategiving.asp.

CHAPTER EIGHT

IMPACT OF TECHNOLOGY
Internet and Social Media

THE EARLY CHAPTERS DISCUSSED FOUNDATIONAL business frameworks for generating revenue. This chapter discusses both the strategic and tactical side of producing revenue through the use of the Internet, social media, and modern technology. As these are constantly changing and improving, this chapter will give a good grounding in both current activities and things to think about as new methods arise.

CROWDFUNDING

The most current and potentially best method for fund-raising is crowdfunding. Crowdfunding is the practice of funding a project or venture by raising monetary contributions from a large number of people via the Internet (Oxford 2015). Crowdfunding is done online, which makes it easy for supporters to share a cause or project with their social networks. Organizations, businesses, and individuals alike can use crowdfunding for any charitable cause, creative project, business startup, school, or personal expenses.

Crowdfunding is so easy, even elementary students can do it. In 2014, two second grade girls started a fund-raising campaign to re-open their school library. They started with a lemonade stand, then created an account on Indiegogo to reopen their closed school library in Sausalito, California (Barack 2014). It raised $23,000 from 178 people in two months for their "Dr. Seuss Wants You" campaign. Nice numbers! (Barack 2014).

The Foundation Center discusses this topic at length. Previously they concentrated on fund-raising through grants. Now it recognizes crowdfunding as a valuable new tool in any nonprofit's revenue-generating tool box. Our review is about what libraries and NPs will use, what is defined as donation-based funding.

Donation-based funding is where donors contribute toward a total amount for a new project. Often, the promised return is the product or service that will be developed with the revenue brought in by the crowdfunding campaign. For charitable projects whose ultimate beneficiary is not the donor, there may be some other perk or reward.

Know Your Terms: There's Crowdfunding and Crowdsourcing

Crowdfunding is just that, raising funds through a crowd. Crowdsourcing is where a group comes together to contribute volunteer work on a project. What's the definition of "crowdsourcing"? According to Jeff Howe, who coined the term in 2006, the short version is "the application of Open Source principles to fields outside of software," and the long version is "the act of taking a job traditionally performed by a designated agent (usually an employee) and outsourcing it to an undefined, generally large group of people in the form of an open call" (crowdsourcing.org 2015).

Crowdsourcing.org is an excellent portal into this field. It has a searchable database of projects that includes statistics about public library usage. A good example concerns New York City restaurant menus. The New York Public Library maintains a special collection of menus from the 1840's until the present, and even when scanned they were difficult to search. It developed a special software program that staff and volunteers could use for transcribing the fields into a database. In 2011 there had been 320,538 dishes transcribed from 6,143 menus, all through crowdsourcing!

We're more interested in raising money, and that's done through crowdfunding.

Real-World Examples

The United for Libraries documentary funding campaign is a good library-specific example. It was successful in raising funds for a ninety-minute documentary on public libraries entitled *Free for All: Inside the Public Library*. In fact, it exceeded the goal! Between September 17 and October 26, 2014, 980 backers pledged $79,000; the goal was $75,000 (*ALA News* 2014).

The Crowdfunding Bible: How to Raise Money for Any Startup, Video Game or Project is a recent book with solid advice (Steinberg 2014). There are six key crowdfunding characteristics the book emphasizes.

1. *Product*—Use of an established platform.
2. *Pitch*—The features, advantages and benefits of what you are raising money for.
3. *Video and graphics*—These inject a strong emotional element to the cause.
4. *Incentives*—Prizes awarded at certain levels of giving.
5. *Goal*—Within reach and justifiable.
6. *Campaign*—Specific short term timeframe, frequent updates, social media friendly.

Hudson Library Early Literacy Storytime Nook Campaign

The Hudson (NY) Public Library crowdfunding campaign focused on funding for a comfortable space to conduct an early literacy program. It used a specific time period, had a well-defined project, a specific monetary goal, and a brief video and incentives to help reward and recognize donors at higher levels. It raised 114 percent of their goal! $5,690 was raised between July 17–August 31, 2014 (Indiegogo 2014).

In looking at Hudson's successful campaign, we can see on the screen shot the six key areas the *Crowdfunding Bible* emphasizes.

1. *Product*—Use of an established platform; it used Indiegogo, a well-known, safe resource.
2. *Pitch*—Theirs was the "Importance of Early Literacy." They needed a comfort zone for storytime, which is both emotionally appealing and valuable to community.
3. *Video*—Great opening shot, impossible to miss.
4. *Incentives*—For $10 and $25 range contributions, plus others.

FIGURE 8.1
Screenshot of Hudson/Indiegogo Page

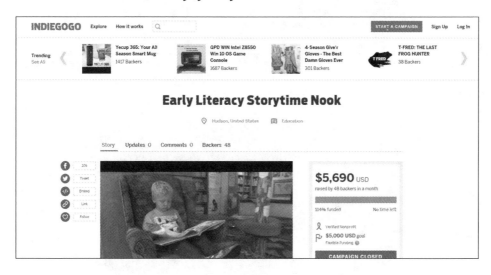

5. *Goal*—Not too far out of range for community.
6. *Campaign*—Specific short term timeframe, frequent updates, social media friendly, good timing with Summer Reading program.

Help Rebuild the Weed (CA) Library Campaign

The Weed (CA) Community Library was destroyed by a forest fire in 2014. A crowdfunding campaign from outside the community was launched and went beyond their goal.

FIGURE 8.2
Screenshot of Weed/Indiegogo Page

DISASTER RESPONSE AND CROWDFUNDING

The following interview with Erin Christmas, Branch Manager of the Old Town Newhall Library in California, explains how crowdfunding was used to assist the Weed Community Library. The following questions were asked:

AUTHOR. Does California have any special circumstances involved with libraries raising money via crowdfunding? Was your effort a library or grass-roots sponsored fundraiser? Were donors able to use their donations as tax write-offs? I see money goes to the Friends, but I also saw something about the Eureka 2014 Cohort?

CHRISTMAS. Here is the story: The director of the Siskiyou County Libraries is in the Eureka! 2014 Cohort (a leadership institute in California for librarians). The fire burned down the Weed library right before we all met up late last year for at our Encore Event. He asked if we as a group could help out. So this was done by five members of the cohort, I was the lead. I have never been to Weed, but we knew the best way to help would be through their Friends group. We asked them what they wanted their goal to be and we launched the campaign. Funds were tax write-offs as the Friends group is a 501(c)(3). This was a real grass roots effort.

AUTHOR. Regarding the platform Indiegogo, whom were you dealing with there? Was a rep assigned to you? Did you have much talk interaction or was everything done via email?

CHRISTMAS. A group of librarians figured it on our own. We did not reach out to anyone with Indiegogo. . . . [the process] is very intuitive.

AUTHOR. What types of questions did the community have about participating?

CHRISTMAS. How do we know it is a verified source? How do people get their tax receipts?

AUTHOR. What if someone wanted to contribute but didn't use computers? Did you recommend she find a friend, or did the library have a generic account that could be used?

CHRISTMAS. Our fundraiser was targeting computer users. I am not sure how the local Weed Community Library handled a situation like this. However, we did have an offsite fundraiser and the organizers contributed the money into the account.

AUTHOR. What was the time frame that you originally planned to achieve your goal? Did the platform stay up automatically after the goal was reached?

CHRISTMAS. We planned for the maximum it allowed which is 90 days. It stayed up after the goal was reached and once the goal was completed you were able to select to leave it up until you take it down.

AUTHOR. Did you use a video or many graphics other than what I see on the page today?

CHRISTMAS. No, it was very basic.

AUTHOR. Do you think using this unique form of fund-raising created more publicity from the media than a "normal" rebuilding fund-raiser would've gotten?

CHRISTMAS. We had no traditional media response.

Continued on next page.

DISASTER RESPONSE AND CROWDFUNDING (continued)

AUTHOR. I know you said you really didn't do incentives, but did you acknowledge donors in some way?

CHRISTMAS. On a California Library Association webinar, we did. Otherwise, no, we did not.

AUTHOR. The Crowdfunding Bible is a recent how-to book about crowdfunding. In looking at any successful campaign, there are six key areas the book emphasizes. The first is product, that is, the use of an established platform. You used Indiegogo, a well-known, safe resource. Any others a close second in choice?

CHRISTMAS. Kickstarter.

AUTHOR. What was your pitch?

CHRISTMAS. Rebuilding after a fire! It's emotionally appealing as well as valuable to community.

AUTHOR. Another key area concerns video and graphics. Did you use video?

CHRISTMAS. No. (Editor's note: Before-and-after photos were used to show the extent of damage)

AUTHOR. What about incentives for scalable dollar range contributions? Would you use one next time?

CHRISTMAS. Probably not for this type of fundraiser. It was specifically targeting the broader library community and most people understood the community could not afford incentives. Also, I have never been to Weed and I am not sure what an appropriate incentive would have been. I think our target was reachable without one.

AUTHOR. Was your *goal* within a good range for the community? You have exceeded that! How long has your "stretch goal" been up?

CHRISTMAS. We chose a number we thought would work based on a specific need. The stretch has been up a few months. I have not yet taken the site down, but I can at any time.

AUTHOR. *The Crowdfunding Bible's* final area is *campaign*. The book suggests a short-term time-frame. What was yours? Did you have frequent (weekly?) updates? Use social media much?

CHRISTMAS. For our campaign we used listservs and social media (Facebook, Twitter, etc.). We updated frequently. We also did it toward the end of the year so we were able to get a big boost with the end of the year giving.

(E. Christmas, personal communication, May 28, 2015)

Comparing Old and New Fund-Raising Campaigns

There are many conceptual similarities between a crowdfunding campaign and a traditional fund-raising campaign. In 2014, the Wright Memorial Public Library (WMPL) Foundation staged their annual fund drive, which incorporated the following elements:

1. *A Needs Assessment*—This contained a brief description of their service area and the theme it had chosen to highlight the campaign with. The library had just recently created a new logo, and wanted to achieve the following:
    a. Raise funds in support of the library's mission.
    b. Showcase the new logo.
    c. Increase WMPL's visibility in the community and refresh their image.
2. *Planning*—Contracting with the graphics expert who had created the logo and budgeting for planning incentive gifts at various levels.
3. *Implementation*—Using volunteers to create over 3,000 mail packets in order to promote the campaign. When the goal was achieved, a full-page local newspaper ad was placed to thank the community, and individual donors were thanked in a variety of other ways as well.
4. *Evaluation*—There was a net increase of 65 percent over the amount raised in 2013's campaign. The 2014 campaign did coincide with the seventy-fifth birthday of the library. The combination of the anniversary and the introduction of the new logo sparked extra publicity. (WMPL 2015).

All four of the above stages could—and should—be replicated in a crowdfunding effort. Perhaps the detail of sending old-school mail physically instead of electronically, could have had an impact on the rate of response. There's nothing wrong with creating a supplemental technology-driven effort with traditional campaign tactics, especially because the Millennial population and those even younger than them are tuned into using technology. This also leads to another potential revenue stream method—apps.

Software Development

Applications (apps) and widgets are computer programs usually designed to achieve efficiency in some type of information retrieval. In library settings, they can be used as access and advisory tools. Your source of revenue from this effort depends on what type of app you offer. If it's consumer-oriented it will appeal to the public—for example, a research app for genealogy, local trivia game, or something for building literacy skills. Businesses may purchase an app for localized research, or you might develop an innovative training or efficiency oriented app for other library systems. If you position it as a fund-raiser for the library, you might boost your revenue. Consumers and businesses generally want to download free or low-cost apps, unless there's an incentive like helping their favorite nonprofit (we'll review this method in part II in the Software Applications mini-chapter).

Social Media and Web Page Advertising

Most libraries have established themselves on the Internet. The nuances of acknowledgments and advertising were reviewed in chapter 2 but it would be remiss not
to discuss it here. The same concepts of delivering audience profiles and metrics
discussed in chapters 4 (on establishing value) and 7 (on promotions) still apply.

Due to the fact that these audiences still have yet to achieve a critical mass of
visitors at the local level, many broadcasters are adding online channels to enhance
their on-air sales packages. This value-added part of the sales proposal could also
be included as part of a library's proposal, or it can stand alone. Likewise, there are
a variety of third-party agencies that will handle online sales that just require you
to add a piece of code to your website, which will then automatically display ads.

Protect Your Integrity
You'll need to do your homework in dealing with these agencies, to insure they
respect your rules on certain product categories, images, or language.

More Revenue Options and Considerations

Self-publishing options for patrons are becoming more widespread. Libraries can
take advantage of the growth in e-publishing by providing publishing software to
prospective authors and organizations. There have been a number of books that
have been started as self-published digital books, such as *The Martian* by Andy Weir.
Local organizations that already partner with the library might be approached on
collaborative efforts, or if you simply let them know an option for self-publishing
exists they may want to create their own unique book through a trusted source—
their local library! IngramSpark (www. Ingramspark.com) is one option, and more
are being developed every day. More on these methods will be discussed in part II's
mini-chapter on publishing.

Online giving is not just for political campaigns anymore, although they were
some of the early innovators. Statistics show 75 percent of giving in this country
is from individuals, not institutions (Dowd 2014, 64). Tapping into the power of
Internet and mobile technology makes sense because that's what so many people
use to connect these days. A number of high-profile companies like Google and
Facebook are creating user-friendly platforms for nonprofit fund-raising.

Sometimes timing is everything. Don't underestimate the power of reminding
people about the tax advantages of end-of-year giving. The University of Massa-
chusetts Amherst libraries won a Gale-Cengage Learning Financial Development
award in 2013 for its "Second Ask" campaign (*ALA News* 2013). Essentially, donors
were contacted and asked to donate one more time to close the year out, and with
the focus on funds going to a sustainability campaign. They raised $160,000 from
almost 4,000 donors. Of course, the value of their sustainability programming was
critical to giving, but the audacity of an end-of-year appeal, a "second ask" provided a
great boost to the program and an extra write off for the donors, who may not have

---

Words Matter!

In another example of backlash against technology-based fund-raising, one school district board took offense with its teachers for an online appeal for school supplies. The board told the community that the classrooms had all that was required, and that their teachers were only asking for "classroom enhancements." Many schools do this, but the visibility that came from being online directed unwanted attention to district and board budget decisions. The teachers, trying to be diplomatic with the board while still reaching out to the public, changed their wording. They didn't ask for classroom supplies, but for what they called simply "projects." So far, ten "enhancement" projects have been funded by online appeals through Donorschoose.org (LaBorde 2015). Words do matter, as does representing the right, justifiable cause. Whether it's through a crowdfunding effort or other online method, even though they may seem to be based on common sense, make sure your efforts are defensible. And, as will be pointed out in part II, try to involve all stakeholders.

---

been contemplating such sizable donations when they first donated (perhaps due to cash flow concerns). In December, donors can step back, take a look at year-end circumstances, and make last-minute contributions (to those who ask).

Beware of losing relationships with donors! In *The Networked Nonprofit*, Kanter et al. advise that although all these tools are tempting to experiment with, remember that "people are partners, not ATM machines" (Kanter 2010, 141). Fund-raising is still all about relationships, and you're threatening them if you go to the fund-raising well too often.

For example, one college library recently created a $2,500 crowdfunding effort for additional power outlets in their academic library. Alumni were incensed that a major university that charged $40,000+ in tuition, and gathered millions from athletics, would bother their alumni base for such a small amount.

Raising funds online for partnerships creates great synergy. In the Moves Management stages of both discovery and stewardship, where you are meeting new businesses and solidifying your relationship with existing partners, you may get an opportunity to expand your fund-raising circle. You might be able to involve not only your organization's immediate donor base, but your partners as well. There should be very specific goals for doing this that will benefit all the partners' donors.

The Montclair Public Library in New Jersey teamed with two biking organizations, Bike and Walk Montclair and the Eat.Play.Live.Better Coalition, to raise funds to buy a bookbike, an eco-friendly alternative to a bookmobile. Equipped with a mobile hotspot device, the bookbike will visit parks, community events, senior centers, and other places people congregate to answer questions, request items for patrons, and enhance the visibility of the library and its partners (Copeland 2015). The fund-raising effort exceeded the goal of $6,000. It was earned by fifty-one funders in less than a month (Indigogo.com 2015b).

This chapter mapped new territory in fund-raising. In the next chapter we'll discuss applying some of these new fund-raising techniques to older revenue sources, like grants and partnerships.

References

ALA News. 2014. "United for Libraries Supports Award-Winning Filmmakers Raising Funds for Library Documentary." *ALA News*, September 16. www.ala .org/news/press-releases/2014/09/united-libraries-supports-award-winning -filmmakers-raising-funds-library.

———. "Gale Cengage Learning Financial Development Award Recipient Named." *ALA News*, March 14. www.ala.org/news/press-releases/2013/03/gale-cengage -learning-financial-development-award-recipient-named.

Barack, L. 2014. "Second Graders Aim to Restore School Library." *School Library Journal*, August 27. www.slj.com/2014/08/students/two-second-graders-pitch -to-restore-school-library-on-Indiegogo/#_.

Copeland, D. 2015. "Montclair Public Library Raising Funds for a Bookbike, a Greener Alternative to the Bookmobile." *NJ.com—True Jersey blog*, April 9. http://blog .nj.com/nj_off-road_biking/2015/04/montclair_public_library_raising_funds _for_a_bookbike_a_greener_alternative_to_the_bookmobile.html.

Crowdsourcing Consortium for Libraries and Archives. 2015. "Crowdsourcing 101." www.crowdsourcing.org/document/crowdsourcing-101/1406.

Dowd, S. (Ed.) 2014. *Beyond Book Sales: The Complete Guide to Raising Real Money for Your Library*. Neal-Schuman: Chicago.

Foundation Center. 2015. "What Is Crowdfunding?" www.grantspace.org/Tools/ Knowledge-Base/Funding-Resources/Individual-Donors/what-is-crowdfunding.

Indiegogo, Inc. 2015a. "Help Rebuild the Weed Library." www.Indiegogo.com/ projects/help-rebuild-the-weed-library—2#/story.

———. 2015b. "MPL Bookbike." www.Indiegogo.com/projects/mpl-bookbike#/story.

———. 2014. "Early Literacy Storytime Nook." www.Indiegogo.com/projects/ early-literacy-storytime-nook.

Kanter, B. 2010. *The Networked Nonprofit*. San Francisco: Jossey-Bass.

LaBorde, O. 2015. "Teachers Turn to Crowdfunding Websites for Classroom Extras." *KCENTV blog*, April 09. https://web.archive.org/web/20150412005713/ www.kcentv.com/story/28766112/teachers-turn-to-crowdfunding-websites-for -classroom-extras.

Mies, G. 2014. "Which Crowdfunding Platform Is Best for Your Organization?" *Tech Soup*, August 14. http://forums.techsoup.org/cs/community/b/tsblog/ archive/2013/09/03/which-crowdfunding-platform-is-best-for-your -organization.aspx?utm_source=newsletter&utm_medium=email&utm _term=blog&utm_content=sep1&utm_campaign=btc.

MLB Advanced Media, LP. 2015. "Scoreboard Messages." http://cleveland.indians .mlb.com/cle/fan_forum/scoreboard.jsp.

Oxford University Press. 2015. "Crowdfunding." *Oxford Dictionaries*. www.oxford dictionaries.com/us/definition/american_english/crowdfunding.

Steinberg, S. 2014. *The Crowdfunding Bible: How to Raise Money for Any Startup, Video Game or Project*. Raleigh, NC: Lulu Press, Inc.

Wright Memorial Public Library. 2015. Board of Trustees Special Meeting Minutes, March 5. www.wrightlibrary.org/files/WMPLBOTMinutes2015–03— FINALCOMPLETE.pdf.

CHAPTER NINE

GRANTS AND COMMUNITY PARTNERSHIPS

MOST LIBRARIES CURRENTLY FOCUS ON GRANTS WHEN they want to generate non-government revenue. This method works well when grants are available. Grants are obviously not under the control of the library in terms of timing or for what you want to accomplish.

Many of the tools and tips discussed in this book can be used to secure grants in any competitive field. This chapter discusses how to integrate techniques used to develop revenue sources to win grants and form productive partnerships.

One of the first things you need to do is establish a revenue baseline and determine how to grow from there. In your budget, determine where you are designating funds for specific programs. This is sometimes called "cost center budgeting." Some typical examples would be bookmobile or other outreach operations, literacy programs, or Smart Money Week activities.

Use the discovery process mentioned in earlier chapters to align both sponsor interest and grant possibilities. You have a variety of tools to do this, and this chapter will review possible methods for identifying and selecting the issues that could drive development of beneficial programs and services for your community, as well as techniques for uncovering the necessary funding for them, and approaches to using new revenue sources to strengthen grant proposal opportunities.

GRANTS AND ISSUES

Grants are tied to addressing specific issues, not just metrics (although the latter are still important). In 2015, the Aspen Institute produced a study entitled *Rising to the Challenge: Re-envisioning Public Libraries.* It identified issues libraries can use to build partnerships. They focus on four guiding opportunities (Aspen Institute nd, 33).

The first guiding opportunity is *aligning library services in support of community goals.* To be successful, libraries must "redefine the role of libraries as institutions that inspire learning, drive development, grow social capital and create opportunities." Libraries need to become more adaptable and flexible in both their vision and their relationships with the community. To bridge various special-interest silos maintain the core principle, "contributing knowledge to the community." An example is Nashville's "Limitless Libraries" model. This was a collaboration between the city's library and public-school program that extended library personnel and resources. The program affected tens of thousands of students and saved hundreds of thousands of dollars by using bulk purchasing and negotiated discounts.

The second guiding opportunity is *providing access to content in all formats.* "Ensuring access to e-books, other e-content and more-than-adequate high-speed broadband" is a major concern. The study cites two immediate challenges in the area: access to e-content and availability of sufficient broadband interconnectivity. Regarding the first, they recognize much is in flux due to the evolving copyright and other industry changes; despite the current growth spurt—or thanks to it— prices are still prohibitively high for a true library expansion into this field. Simply put, there's a lot of money to be made by the publishers if they play nice with the libraries, at this point in time. The study suggests libraries experiment with concepts like "buy it now," encouraging sales for hard-to-get e-books, and then encouraging the patron to donate the book back to the library for others. Although the study doesn't mention it, sponsored e-collections could also help achieve this goal. This issue will be addressed in a few mini-chapters in part II. Regarding the broadband issue, partnerships between public and private stakeholders as well as government and foundation backing will be needed to meet the constantly growing demand on current digital infrastructure. Imagine a civil engineer tasked with plotting a highway through a city, being told it needs four lanes for capacity now, five in two years, six in four years. Such is the digital challenge. An excellent case study uses the town of Chattanooga, Tennessee, and focuses on strong collaboration between the city and its public library system to convert underutilized library space into a technology showcase—part incubator, part classroom, part maker space. Like the Memphis Cloud901 concept, mentioned in part II's discussion on naming rights, this places the library in the center of that town's technological crossroads, and in the future no doubt will be prime for naming rights opportunities.

The third guiding opportunity is *ensuring long-term sustainability of public libraries.* "Perhaps the greatest challenge facing public libraries today is to transform their service model to meet the demands of the knowledge society while securing a sustainable funding base for the future." This is one of the core reasons that the book you're reading was written.

The fourth guiding opportunity is *cultivating leadership*; as the report suggests, "demonstrating the collective impact of partners working together" will be key in developing champions for the library's cause and valued place within the community. Generating revenue through local sponsorships will not only strengthen the library's bottom line, but will also help build these critical partnerships.

The Aspen Institute study could be a great compass to chart a course toward issues that will draw foundation funding. It emphasizes building a wide range of partnerships within the community.

Developing programs and services that are aligned with the preceding issues can be the basis of developing multiple revenue streams from the local public, businesses, and grant-giving organizations. Whether you're creating new revenue-stream relationships or developing existing ones, once you read the Aspen study's analysis of the particular nuances of the issues they raise, review the four stages. When revisiting the four stages of Moves Management, below, bear in mind that the process is similar to most other methods used for revenue-generator prospecting, but focused specifically on grants.

1. *Discovery*—Match issues with high-donor interest to the library mission. Staff should brainstorm a list of the top twenty-five foundations or organizations that could possibly award grants. After that, target whom within those organizations to approach, and determine if any staff already have a connection to these key people. Talk to them, share ideas, and find out what their objectives are. More importantly, what *issues* concern them? If you don't know anyone personally, most of these organizations make their requests for proposals quite clear as to when and how to submit grant proposals.

   The Foundation Center's Foundation Directory Online has long been a source that helps match grant seekers with grant funders. It may lack the personal touch, but it can efficiently present some ideas you may not have thought of in brainstorming (Foundation Center 2015). Their scalable packages can be a catalyst for a library wanting to foster partnerships with other NPs. At the Lakewood (OH) Public Library, the Friends organization funded the purchase of the database, and then the library held classes for other nonprofits in learning how to use it. As with the previous bike example, partnering with other NPs or private businesses can prove to be quite an asset in supplementing your own funding. (A grant often requires a portion of the total cost to be funded by the recipient or their partners. The grant may cover 75 percent of the total cost, requiring you to put up the other 25 percent. In other words, they want you to have skin in the game via some financial input).

2. *Cultivation*—Demonstrate need, metrics, and plans. In response to a foundation RFP, your appointment with them would be similar to a meeting with a business or crowdfunding partners. You will define your need, and be prepared to present metrics on how you're already addressing or will address it. Build your promotional package into your pitch, addressed below.

3. *Solicitation*—This is your response for the proposal, aka "the pitch." Combined with your promotional package, which you've tailored according to their requirements (e.g., focusing on a summer reading program for children and families), and with necessary procedural elements showing professionalism and thoughtfulness (how you will conduct the program), you ask for their funding. If you have already been able to raise money, demonstrate your ability to generate and use outside funds toward the proposal's goal as it is tied into the library's mission, in long term, sustainable ways (through annual events like art shows or athletic competitions).

   A significant difference between a grant from a foundation and an advertising or sponsorship contract will be in what you'll deliver. For most NPs, asking for dollars for advertising, sponsorships or naming rights based on measurable results will make them vulnerable to UBIT, which is sometimes a needless expense. However, when asking for foundation money, you need to state objectives (the more measurable and realistic the better), and present the evaluation methods that will be used to measure those outcomes. How did the project meet the needs as previously stated? How closely did the procedural process match reality? Were your objectives reached? This evaluation is addressed in the pitch, and followed through on in the last phase, stewardship.

4. *Stewardship*—Give an honest assessment and keep connected. This phase echoes Andrew Carnegie's belief that after he helped build a library, maintenance became the community's responsibility. You might say, "Help us get started and we will maintain the service," depending on the nature of the grant. If it's to jump-start a new service (e.g., a maker space area), they may only give a one-time infusion of funds. Acknowledge their support and deliver on what you promised. Invite them back to see the results. After 80 percent of the program length has passed, begin talking about renewal even if no formal RFP has been announced by the grantor. If you partnered with private businesses to help fund your portion of a grant, approach the business like you would a normal renewal. Perhaps justifying an increase based on if you have lost grant support due to the nature of a "jump-start"-type of grant. Or point out how well they are impacting the community.

   This phase is where you compile your outputs and outcomes. The outputs are the objective, measurable statistics and the outcomes are the subjective, emotionally driven testimonials about how this funded program had an impact on your patrons and community.

THE RELATIONSHIP BETWEEN GRANT AND PRIVATE MONEY

David Holmes, Cleveland Lead Foundation Center Midwest, was interviewed via email about changes in the world of grants.

AUTHOR. Grant-wise, is there an increase in grant-seeking and collaborative efforts such as crowdfunding?

HOLMES. Most RFPs would not get involved with crowdfunding, as most deal with non-profits that have a 501(c)(3) designation. They are less concerned with what type of fund-raising technique is going to happen, than the importance of an issue they are addressing.

AUTHOR. Are RFPs specifying what collaborative techniques are allowed?

HOLMES. Grants don't always need collaboration. Most RFPs don't require it.

AUTHOR. Do foundations allow direct contribution to the library fund accounts via fund-raising tools like Kickstarter, or would they prefer for a group to raise funds by whatever means, then make a direct cash deposit?

HOLMES. For effective use of a crowd funder, money should go to a 501(c)(3) organization. That way, the contribution for the public is tax-deductible. They would not structure money going directly into a foundation unless it was a gift.

AUTHOR. Do many libraries use Blackbaud or Fundraiser software to help their efforts? Who are their competitors? Are they also doing sponsorship sales assistance and analysis?

HOLMES. Yes, they're the biggest company in that field. They have modules for everything. A close competitor would be Donor Perfect.

AUTHOR. Do the grant providers have a deadline for submission? Is the grant offered at a particular time of year?? Does a collaborative history with a funding partner have to be two years? Does the collaborator have to give at least 25 percent of funding?

HOLMES. All RFPs tend to be unique in their requirements. They are not specific about your relationship with your collaborator. What they are concerned with is overlap of effort. If a library tries for a grant for something already existing in a community, what makes them a unique contributor?

(D. Holmes, personal communication, August 2014)

Real World: An Alternative View on Raising Extra Funds

Grant-giving organizations are more confident that their funds will be successfully invested in a cause if a request comes from an organization with proven community support mechanisms already in place. For example, if you and your partners raise 25 percent, they'll grant the other 75 percent, or use a similar formula.

Sometimes you may think you've hit the wall raising funds locally for grants or other purposes, but there's one more tactic you can use to raise more (see the tip below).

Part II will break down more than forty revenue-generating methods using capsule summaries of these foundational chapters, as well as introduce first steps toward implementation. Now that we've laid down a good business framework, let's move on to actually generating some revenue!

Pursue Co-Op Advertising   TIP

For years, media stations have been helping local retailers increase their advertising programs by having them use co-op (short for co-operative) advertising. This was mentioned in chapter 6 on contracts and procedure, for example, how a grocery chain might get money from one of its consumer packaged foods suppliers. The money can come in two ways (Entrepreneur Media Inc. 2015). The first would be when a local business, for instance, a computer services firm, uses manufacturers' money to help pay for an advertising campaign. Your library or NP might use a local logo for the computer store with another brand trademark (e.g., maybe for Dell, Google or Microsoft) next to it on a sponsorship acknowledgment page. Perhaps you want to promote your new streaming services beyond the tools the service provides you with. Finding a local technology-oriented company selling a national product to send streams to home televisions would be a prime example of the use of co-op money.

The second way is when advertisers within a local area, like a mall or several adjacent streets or that have a shared theme, partner on a project like the Montclair bikemobile project. In seeking revenue for a local cause, approaching major brands might be a waste of time, but finding a local community business with ties to the library might lead to a good, steady revenue stream.

National firms have the revenue for assisting local advertising budgets. A local hardware store may be so successful or face such minimal competition that they hardly advertise, and so the national funds available to them as exclusive dealers for a national brand, let's say ABC Lawnmowers, might go unused. You could enlist such a local business to aid in your cause and help them "move up the ladder" of sponsorship, from $100 to $200, using national ABC Lawnmower money.

Locally there is always more power in numbers, as the funding for the bikemobile demonstrates. Working individually, money for that effort would have been tight. More partners help ease the expense. It's up to you to target the right issues, find the right local businesses, and then help them seek national co-op money or non-competitive allies to back your cause and aid your community.

References

The Aspen Institute. nd. *Rising to the Challenge: Re-Envisioning Public Libraries.* http://csreports.aspeninstitute.org/Dialogue-on-Public-Libraries/2014/report.

Entrepreneur Media Inc. 2015. *Co-op Advertising—Small Business Encyclopedia.* www.entrepreneur.com/encyclopedia/co-op-advertising.

Foundation Center. 2015. *Foundation Directory Online.* https://fconline.foundation center.org.

PART TWO

REVENUE-GENERATING
METHODS MINI-CHAPTERS

WITHOUT SOME EXTRA CASH COMING IN TO VISIBLY improve library resources, traditional funding might be hard to come by in an economically hard-pressed community. Libraries need to reach out beyond taxes and levies to gather revenue to provide both the services the community expects and new services that the community will need in this fast-paced technology-oriented world. This part of the book uses brief "mini-chapters" to describe over forty revenue-generating methods that will help to achieve the necessary revenue. Each mini-chapter describes anticipated revenue, the amount of work and planning involved regarding contracts and promotions, as well as estimating the degree of board and government involvement you might have. These are summarized in the Money Matrix table found in Appendix A.

Perhaps the most important part of the mini-chapters is the "First Steps" section. Each method presents a plan and exercises to help you to begin implementation in an efficient manner. Whether you're running a solo operation or chairing a committee, these steps should guide your thinking as to how to use these methods quickly.

Perhaps the toughest part of working with the mini-chapters is their redundancy. If you are chairing or working with a committee, you might want to copy three to five mini-chapters to discuss at a strategy session. Due to many of the methods' similarities, I've had to repeat the same explanations wherever relevant in each mini-chapter. If you read through each one you'll see a number of similar statements, for example, about Board involvement. No matter which mini-chapter you select for discussion, rest assured it's as complete as possible, and includes information about its own unique challenges and opportunities.

Before you review the methods, here's an exercise that asks to have you set a "new revenue" goal and pick five of the methods to research.

Set a Revenue Goal

Previously we've used a $30,000 target. Determine which methods might achieve it using fair value and an honest assessment of start-up costs.

- Review all the revenue methods in the Money Matrix and select at least five to research.
- If the source will be businesses, determine fair value using the metrics discussed.
- If the source is public, do a market analysis to establish a competitive rate for services.
- Estimate start-up costs for your market.

Calculate the level of success you'll need to reach your goal. What number of sponsorships, meeting room rentals, vending machine sales, or passports issued would you need?

THE MONEY MATRIX

In the Money Matrix table, revenue methods are described according to nine characteristics.

1. **Source** is the first characteristic. Is it the public, a business, or a foundation? You might generate funding from many individual, smaller payments (public); several much larger payments (businesses); or a significant payment from one to three sources (foundations).

2. **Revenue amount** may vary according to the size of the budget of the organization or the population of its service area. For descriptive purposes, I'll use an organization with a three-million-dollar annual budget servicing an area with 30,000 people.
   For an annual amount of new revenue, the four categories below are used:
   - » Low—less than $1,000
   - » Moderate— $1,000–10,000
   - » High—$10,000–25,000
   - » Significant—greater than $25,000

3. **High start-up cost** is based on costs for design, construction, and initial operational costs such as extra personnel and training. It's a subjective attribute, but needs to be considered. It is also related to the risk factor involved in starting a revenue generator. For example, let's look at passport services. Certain amounts of hours and equipment will be needed to make it a working operation, but it has a defined revenue return. You know when and at what dollar amount your break-even point will be. Are the start-up costs still high after you know this?

4. **Public relations efforts** could be general, aimed at anyone in the community, or targeted toward specific business that might be interested in advertising or leasing your facilities.

5. **Board** involvement may also vary according to the situation. Action could include:
   » General involvement, or approval of policies that affect everyone, such as equipment rentals.
   » Specific involvement, or approval of an agreement with an individual or company, or a revenue stream that would have a significant impact on the library, such as naming rights.

6. **Policy requirement** may involve that special caveats be built into the policies depending on the type of contract required. Under a broad umbrella of a policy providing services to patrons, one section might involve vending machines, which would be different than providing meeting room space.

7. **Government involvement** is an alert to whether Unrelated Business Income Tax (UBIT) may be involved or not. This important concept is more fully explained in chapter 5's discussion of legal considerations.

8. **Contracts** are broken out by the length of the duration of the contract:
   » One-time—an author's visit, special anniversary, or recognition event
   » Continuing—as long as the partnership is working, renewal options might be placed into the original contract, with allowance for growth due to inflation
   » Seasonal—for a summer reading club sponsorship
   » Legacy—usually for a long-term memorial

9. The final characteristic is **resource** *category*:
   » Advertising (web page or newsletter ads)
   » Sponsorship (naming rights for branches or areas, special programs or resources)
   » Facility (meeting room rentals)
   » Product (books, equipment)

All of the above are situations that need to be specifically addressed. With some pre-planning, they can aid you in determining increases in your local revenue as well as building up your community partnerships.

INTRODUCTION TO THE MINI-CHAPTERS

In Appendix A, you'll find the Money Matrix in an efficient checklist format. This could be useful for brainstorming and group discussions.

The following mini-chapters will describe each method in narrative fashion using the matrix categories, review previously mentioned foundational concepts, and present details and exercises to help you get started. Below is the format of each mini-chapter:

1. **Description of method,** presented in narrative style, plus a synopsis of Money Matrix elements that address the source and amount of income to be achieved. Regarding revenue amount, this may vary according to the size of the budget of the organization or the population of its service area. For an annual amount of new revenue, the four categories below are used:
   - » Low—less than $1,000
   - » Moderate—$1,000–10,000
   - » High—$10,000–25,000
   - » Significant—greater than $25, 000

2. **Establishing value,** that is, the pertinent metrics and approaches involved. The revenue methods may use one or a combination of these.
   a. *CPM*: As introduced in chapter 3, on broadcasting, CPM is the method of objectively determining how many impressions of a message will be seen, and what every thousand impressions costs. It is useful for comparing costs in any audience-focused media. Because you're producing something measurable and tangible, the CPM method should work best as a starting point. From there, you can negotiate upwards based on the intangible benefits that being associated with your organization has to offer in terms of demographics and community goodwill.
      - Used in mini-chapters on all Advertising, Sponsorship, and Naming Rights methods, Bookplates, Charging Stations, Matching Challenges, Medical Services, Own-a-Day, Receipts, and Vendor Shows.

   b. *Public motivation*: The less objective but still real appeal the library has in the eyes of the public. A subjective value composed of emotional elements such as community pride, self-image, maintaining a "lifeline" for answers and assistance, etc.
      - Used in mini-chapters on Bookplates, Charging Stations, Crowdfunding, Own-a-Day, Publishing, Sponsored Materials and Rooms.

c. *Product value*: Estimate the cost of labor and materials. Then it's up to the organization to calculate the profit it would like to earn and set the price accordingly. Basically, the formula is: revenue (price) of each good minus costs equals your profit; multiplying that by the number of goods sold will give you your total value of the method over a period of time. Note: Breaking even does not help the cause, unless it's part of a package designed to sell a higher priced item, such as an entire collection area. In that case, it enhances, not dilutes, the overall sales package.

  – Used in mini-chapters on Art Shows, Author Sales, Community Book Sales, Third-Party Services, 50-50 Raffles, Gift Shops, Furniture Naming Rights and Sponsorships, as well as Sponsored Material.

d. *Market value*: What your local competition is charging (you don't have to match it). Usually based on three elements:

  – Visibility and prominence of the location (will determine how many impressions are delivered)
  – Size of the location (usually square footage, used in most real estate estimates)
  – The cost to outfit a particular location with furniture or equipment

Once your price is set the same objective profit calculation for product value above will apply.

  – Used in mini-chapters on Athletic Events, Cell Towers, Equipment, And Facility Rental, Gift Shops, Matching Competitions, Medical Services, Meeting Rooms, Naming and Sponsorship Rights for Rooms and Furniture, Own-a-Day, Publishing, Software Development, Third-Party Services, Tutoring, Vending Machines, and Vendor Shows.

3. **Board and policy considerations and other legal or government matters.** It's hard to give solid instructions outside of current federal laws because there are so many other state and local types of governance structures. This section does include advisories on possible UBIT charges. Other considerations could be general or specific.

  a. General considerations would not really involve any special discussion or votes. They're probably already incorporated into regular operations, such as Friends' revenue generation through book sales.
  b. Specific board considerations usually involve signing off on the terms of large contracts and long commitments such as naming rights.
  c. Specific policy considerations involve establishing the parameters of understanding as to how a method will be conducted—for example, what type of advertisement language will be allowed or whether only acknowledgment phrases can be used for certain methods.

Regarding tax matters, it's advisable to do proper research into what local, state, and federal laws regard as taxable income. See chapter 5, legal considerations, for more about this.

Below are two considerations for the federal level:
Taxable: The method is not substantially related to the furtherance of the organization's exemptions, and so it is probably subject to Unrelated Business Income Tax (UBIT). Factor that into your expenses, but double-check!
Non-Taxable: The method is related to the furtherance of the organization's exempt purpose, or

    i. Is an activity not regularly used
    ii. Is a convenience to the public or employees
    iii. Is rental income in a space that has no outstanding debt and no personal services are involved.

so that the revenue would probably not be subject to Unrelated Business Income Tax (UBIT). But double-check to avoid unanticipated expenses.

4. **Contracts and procedures**, a method-specific section that will help visualize how to put that method into action, broadly explained in chapter 6. Contracts are categorized by their renewability, reflecting the anticipated duration of the formal relationship: one-time, continuing, seasonal, or legacy. Some methods may use more than one type.
  a. *One time*: A simple exchange of a good for a price. No date span or renewability offered. This doesn't mean you can't partner again, but only standard contractual elements such as logistics confirmation and billing procedures would apply to this specific project.
    – Used in mini-chapters on Advertising on Calendars and Special Publications, Program Rebroadcasts, Art Shows, Author Sales, Crowdfunding, Equipment Rentals, Event Sponsorship, Facility Rentals, Matching Challenges, Meeting Services, Own-A-Day, Receipts, Software Applications, Sponsorship of Materials, and Tutoring Services.

  b. *Continuing*: All the standard contractual elements as previously discussed, but including a defined time period, and built-in renewability options. Something to insure the continuous message stream for the client as well as revenue stream for you. For example, a sponsorship contract for a computer lab for a year, with a defined renegotiation period three months before its end.
    – Used in mini-chapters on all Advertising methods, Bookplates, Third-Party Services, Cell Towers, Charging Stations, 50-50

Raffles, Gift Shops, Medical Services, Meeting Services, Passport Services, Publishing, Recycling, all Sponsorship methods, and Vending Machine Operator Contracts.

c. *Seasonal*: A modified version of a continuing contact, specifying an annual event and right of first refusal in case the business climate changes. Used when only a few high value slots on a gift ladder are available. For instance, "Gold" level sponsorship of a Summer Reading Program, which involves a variety of value-added enhancements such as the sponsor's name placed in a larger font than anyone else! The renewal period may be six months out to insure proper funding is in place for the program, as well as positively maintaining the relationship between you and the sponsor.
   – Used in mini-chapters on Art Shows, Athletic Events, Community Book Sales, Event Sponsorships and Vendor Shows.

d. *Legacy*: Used to establish a relationship that will last for a decade or more. It would have all the same contractual elements as a continuing contract but may have a special billing procedure and clauses for maintenance and cancellation under certain circumstances due to the longevity of the contract.
   – Used in mini-chapter on naming rights.

   Procedures reflect either standard business operations regarding sales, billing, and collections that support business details according to your contract details, or media-specific procedures and reports dealing with inventory and messages in copy. (See the earlier discussion of traffic department operations in chapter 6.)

5. **Promotions,** which guide the reader in using materials, communication techniques, and the feature and benefit approach for that method in a general or targeted approach. Some methods might use both, such as art shows that need general public awareness to build a crowd of potential buyers, and a targeted approach to convince quality artists to apply and sell their work.
   a. *General promotions*: Communication is aimed at the public, announcing new services, programs, or material availability. Use standard tools such as the library website, flyers, newsletters, etc.
      – Used in mini-chapters on selling Calendars and Other Special Publications, Medical Services, Meeting Services, Own-a-Day, Passports, Recycling, Third-Party Products and Services, Software Apps, Naming Rights and Sponsorships for Memorial Purposes, Tutoring, Vending Machines, and Vendor Shows.

    b. *Targeted promotions*: Communication is aimed at businesses or foundations, announcing new ways to improve their visibility in the community and/or opening up a new market for the sale of their products.
        – Used in mini-chapters on all types of advertising, Naming Rights and Sponsorships, Cell Towers, Facility Rentals, Matching Challenges, Medical Services, Meeting Services, Publishing, Receipts, Third Parties for Products and Services, Software Applications, and Vendor Shows.

The features and benefits tables list brief reviews of the characteristics, advantages, and benefits of that method. For instance, although your audience may be small, they may be exactly the profile your sponsor is looking for, a "smaller target but bigger bulls-eye." You could add more as you consider it for your particular circumstances.

6. **Moves Management contexts**, which are done on an individual method basis, these could also help give the reader a proper framework and idea of the entire customer relationship cycle for that specific method. Review non-governmental sources of revenue in chapter 2.

7. **First steps**, which are combinations of summaries of the above reinforcing their most important elements, plus vendor assessment suggestions. Considerations of what will either be low or high start-up costs are based on costs for design, construction, and initial operational costs such as extra personnel and/or training.

8. **Real world examples**, when applicable. Some methods are forecasts but have potential depending on the local conditions and will to pursue.

9. **Exercises**, because every method requires an organization that understands the costs and potential returns of the venture. Exercises in the following three areas will help establish this knowledge base and may affect your decision to use the method at this time:
    a. Determine value based on the CPM method (use the location audit exercise in chapter 4 as a model) and the techniques establishing product and market values discussed above.
    b. Analyze the competition, an environmental scan to determine if your uniqueness will allow entry into a marketplace that may be wide open, or oversaturated.
    c. Do stakeholder development: tap into your Friends groups, existing partners, patrons, and non-patrons for their input into the development and design of the methods used to achieve maximum exposure and usage. Using public opinion methods such as focus groups, surveys, etc. Successful entrepreneurs always involve others, although they recognize others may have agendas different than theirs. Knowledge of these can smooth roadblocks on the way to your organizations financial vitality.

ADVERTISING, ACKNOWLEDGMENTS, AND UNDERWRITING

General Concepts

THIS TOPIC IS THE CLOSEST TO THE BROADCASTING model we've discussed before. It's where the library becomes like a media outlet by packaging an audience that has value to certain businesses. And, as in public broadcasting, enacting proper rules and policies not only protects the independent, non-commercialized content of libraries, but also insures they use professional business practices.

Allowing either acknowledgments for underwriting or advertising through the library will generate moderate extra revenue, and might be liable for UBIT, depending on your approach. If you only allow acknowledgments of a business's support, without inducement language, promises of exclusivity and/or a specific number of patrons using a resource, you will probably not be liable for UBIT tax, and your patrons will not feel any intrusion when using your services.

However, if after checking your municipal guidelines, current policies, tax liabilities, and weighing those against opportunities for increased value for the sponsor and income for the library, you may well decide to allow advertising messages. From a contract or procedural side, many details will stay the same. You may have an audit for patron numbers at the end of a contract or a more dynamic copy flow, based on what the advertiser wishes to say, and when.

Go for acknowledgments as you begin this process. Over time, if the advertiser demand is there and/or if revenue from other sources goes down or expenses go up, you can take it to the next level. These procedural details are addressed in chapter 6 on contracts and procedures.

Acknowledgments or advertising can actually be used to develop new services, and generate more opportunities for revenue sources, as alluded to in the business revenue model in chapter 3. For instance, perhaps you're interested in creating Readers Advisory downloadable podcasts. By finding an initial sponsor for this new service, both the library and the sponsor gain from creating a service that can be publicized using both the library and the sponsor's brands. Even though the library (or nonprofit, using podcasts via their own website addressing recurring educational and/or encouragement themes) could face some high start-up costs at the beginning, as the service grows production will become more efficient, which should help the service break even, and then produce extra income. And as the service grows, it increases its value for the sponsor.

There are several channels of communication, many of which the library is already using, which are suited for acknowledgments or advertising a sponsor's name or brand. Among these are:

» Newsletters
» Website
» Podcasts and other Internet streaming technology
» Program rebroadcast and cable streaming
» Calendars and special publications
» Digital signage, like a carousel screen near a high-traffic area (e.g., an entrance) that plays a rotating presentation of ad messages

These six areas introduce the series of mini-chapters on revenue generation methods.

METHOD 1

Advertising in Newsletters

Newsletters are one of the most versatile methods of communications. They are prime real estate for anyone trying to reach a community. Newsletters can be either digital or print. Digital newsletters can be delivered by email or posted on the web. Print newsletters can be distributed at the library and at drop-off locations in the community. They can be entertaining and informative, and are an important way to connect with the public. Ads in a newsletter should generate a moderate amount of income.

Some organizations may offer professional services in exchange for ad placement. As mentioned earlier, be very careful about these exchanges. However, if it improves the quality of the newsletter, a one-for-one dollar exchange may be worth it, especially if the advertiser handles the production costs. An in-kind donation could also act as a catalyst. When the newsletter becomes profitable, the in-kind donation could be scaled back to a more cash-oriented contract.

Board Considerations, Policy Considerations, and Government Involvement
There are no special board considerations unless there are no advertising policies in place. There should be specific policies detailing the acceptable standards for acknowledgments or advertising. Depending on whether you use acknowledgments or advertising, taxes could be involved.

Establishing Value

Use CPM, the method of objectively determining how many impressions of a message will be seen, and what every thousand impressions costs.

Contracts and Procedures

» *Contract*: Continuing. One with a specific renewal process.
» *Procedures*: As a media operation, you would use both standard business operations procedures as well as traffic department operations procedures.

Promotions

» *Targeted*: Communication is aimed at businesses or foundations.

Revenue Method: Newsletter

Features	Advantages	Benefits
Specific advertiser contact information	Handy resource, offers promotion of products and services	Easier access to advertisers' services
Printed copies	Can be placed inside and outside library and/or passed around	Wider scope of distribution leads to more impressions

Moves Management Model

» *Discovery*: Use a media audit as well as personal contacts to find active local advertisers. Arrange an introduction.
» *Cultivation*: Come back and talk about what they want to do and how you can help them.
» *Solicitation*: Your proposal. Include a gift ladder that might involve value-added promotions.
» *Stewardship*: You can deliver copies of the newsletter. No matter what type of business they are, they could be a great drop-off point for hard copies. Run periodic status checks, especially if they use an advertisement that has inducement language such as "Bring this in for our 20 percent off Library Special." Also, follow through with attendance figures for the various programs mentioned in the newsletter—for example, "Last month, 300 children and 150 adults attended storytimes thanks in part to your help in advertising them." Make their day by having them feel they're part of the effort, which they are!

First Steps

Start-up costs will be high, mostly due to staff time. You'll need to review the newsletter design for placement areas, develop CPM and other metrics, create a proposal kit (possibly by integrating an existing annual report or you may need to start the kit from scratch), and develop media audit procedures to identify the most important logistical activities, as per the inventory and continuity reports in chapter 6.

Real-World Examples

Although your focus may be on libraries, investigate what other nonprofits produce. Take a look at local religious community bulletins. Many devote the entire last page to advertisements, encouraging their members to "support those who support us."

Exercises

» If you have a newsletter, determine how much space you'd like to devote to advertising. Determine if your space requirements will add to the publication expenses, and adjust your rates accordingly.

» If you don't produce a newsletter, have a brainstorming session and consider all these elements:

1. *Audience*—Everyone, or a certain group (e.g., teens or parents)?
2. *Purpose(s)*—Increase metrics (program attendance, circulation), share community resources, promote partnerships?
3. *Style*—Connected to your purpose: office style or playful?
4. *Elements*—Consistent features and columns?
5. *Structure*—Organization: heading size, fonts, brands?
6. *Regularity*—Monthly? Quarterly?
7. *Regular features*—Hot topics or circulation pieces, calendars?
8. *Seasonal features*—For example, summer reading activities?
9. *Special features*—Promotion of partnerships?
10. *Dissemination*—In-house, online and/or in the community? How many can be produced?

» Using advertising dollars as a catalyst, you will have a great opportunity to develop a new or greatly improved communications channel out into your community.

METHOD 2

Advertising on Websites

Almost every library and almost all nonprofits have some type of Internet platform. A web presence makes communication between the organization and public extremely efficient. Web advertisements can be placed in a variety of ways. Businesses could be page sponsors, or their message could be rotated through various pages. The source of revenue would be businesses, and should generate a moderate amount of income. If your organization is lacking in the technical skills required to program your web pages for ads, or uses a content manager that is not adaptable for advertising placement, rotation, and auditing, there are a number of firms that can handle this for you. They will even do the advertising sales, but your return on income will be lowered accordingly.

Establishing Value

Use CPM, the method of objectively determining how many impressions of a message will be seen, and what every thousand impressions costs. You could use Google analytics or other methods to determine how many page views you get.

Board and Policy Considerations or Government Involvement

There are no special board considerations unless there are no advertising policies in place. There should be specific policies detailing the acceptable standards of acknowledgments or advertising. Depending on whether you use acknowledgments or advertising, UBIT could be involved.

Contracts and Procedures

» *Contract*: Continuing. One with a specific renewal process.
» *Procedures*: As a media operation, you would use both standard business operations procedures and traffic department operations procedures.

Promotions

» *Targeted*: Communication is aimed at businesses or foundations.

Revenue Method: Website Advertising

Features	Advantages	Benefits
Visible	Convenience for promotion and publicity	Creates and fulfills impulse needs
Interactive	Links directly to advertiser' website or email	Customer control of message, offers

Moves Management Model

» *Discovery*: Use a media audit as well as personal contacts to find active local advertisers. Arrange an introduction.
» *Cultivation*: Come back and talk about what they want to do and how you can help them.
» *Solicitation*: Your proposal. Include a gift ladder that might involve value-added promotions.
» *Stewardship*: Have a publicity angle ready for them. Use their channels of communication whenever possible, no matter what type of business they are. Ask for reciprocal links from their website to yours. Run periodic status checks; this is especially important if they use an advertisement that has inducement language such as "Print this for our 20 percent off Library Special coupon." Also, follow through with attendance figures or other success stories. Make their day by having them feel they're part of the effort, which they are! Others would like their alliance. Strive to keep it.

First Steps

Start-up costs are relatively low, because chances are your website already exists. Placing ads would simply require asking for a graphic that meets your policies, inserting it on your page, and linking it to the advertiser directly, or to an intermediary page where you could further enhance the message and count how many initial clicks the ad received. You should also investigate your server's tracking capabilities, and use software for auditing purposes.

Get access to the statistics on your own page views, which will help in setting value for the ads.

Now that you have an estimate of page views, a method of verifying click-through activity, and have physically tested the web linkages, you can now go through the Moves Management process, starting with the discovery process. Have a demo page ready that you can show a potential sponsor. Let them see a copy of your home page, or wherever you're thinking of placing their ad with a mock-up already there!

Real-World Examples

Because we read English from left to right, in web design the left area of a webpage usually has navigational aids, the middle contains content, and advertisements are on the right. Take a look at ala.org to see how they use small block ads on the right of the page to advertise their programs and products.

Exercises

> » *Do a cost-benefit analysis.* Consider all the preceding steps and whether your current staff is capable of all the technical work before you begin. Check third-party Internet advertising companies that could handle all the web ad sales and placement. Based on your page view figures, see if their payment model might be worth using instead. You might also try contacting a local commercial media channel that seems to carry a lot of local and national web advertising to see whom they use and/or if they would be interested in acting as a partner with you.

METHOD 3

Advertising in Podcasts and Other Internet Streaming Technology

In many ways, traditional broadcasting is being supplanted by the Internet. Live streaming or delivery of programming in files accessible through a variety of devices run 24/7. This exciting area is growing thanks to the development of mobile technology. It's an especially significant change for a library to deliver programs outside its own walls, and a 24/7 delivery capability makes it more convenient for patrons to use the library for readers advisory discussions, genealogy lectures, storytime performances, or any other aural activities you offer. The source of revenue would be businesses, and should generate a low amount of money first and grow to a moderate amount over time. Start-up costs might be high depending on current access to needed equipment and software.

Establishing Value
Use CPM to determine objectively how many impressions of a message will be seen, and what every thousand impressions costs.

Board and Policy Considerations or Government Involvement
There are no special board considerations unless there are no advertising policies in place. There should be specific policies detailing the acceptable standards of acknowledgments or advertising. Depending on whether you use acknowledgments or advertising, UBIT could be involved.

Contracts and Procedures
» *Contract*: Continuing. One with a specific renewal process.
» *Procedures*: As a media operation, you would use both standard business operations procedures and traffic department operations procedures.

Please note that some organizations may offer professional services in exchange for placing their own advertising on your site. As mentioned earlier, be very careful about exchanges in this manner, known as in-kind donations, or simply "trade" in the broadcast industry. However, if it makes a difference that allows you to create a quality podcast, a one-for-one dollar exchange may be worth it, especially if an advertiser handles the production costs and logistics. An in-kind donation could act as a catalyst as well, and after the podcast is started and becomes a profitable operation, if need be the in-kind donation could be scaled back to a more cash-oriented contract. Be careful of cluttered advertising. If you have one advertiser doing an in-kind exchange for the production of the program, try not to be too greedy by using the innovative program to sell to five others, even if only for short acknowledgments. Limit it to maybe only two more, and if demand is high, raise rates. Start with annual contracts to give the service time to grow. After a year, the growth may have stabilized, or might continue to grow. Regardless, in the renewal stage you can either increase rates or use six-month contracts to give you time to adjust for an increasing audience.

Promotions
» *Targeted*: Communication is aimed at businesses or foundations.

Revenue Method: Podcast

Features	Advantages	Benefits
Aural delivery	Less distraction from message	Better focus on material, attention to client message
Digital delivery	Available on mobile devices	Consumer convenience

Moves Management Model

- » *Discovery*: Use a media audit as well as personal contacts to find active local advertisers. Arrange an introduction.
- » *Cultivation*: Come back and talk about what they want to do and how you can help them.
- » *Solicitation*: Your proposal. Include a gift ladder that might involve value-added promotions.
- » *Stewardship*: Run periodic status checks, especially if they use an advertisement that has inducement language such as "Ask for our 20 percent off Podcast Library Special." Also, follow through with attendance figures for the various programs performed live or downloaded. "Our storytimes had 300 downloads last month, thanks in part to your help in producing them." Make their day by having them feel they're part of the effort, which they are!

First Steps

Do a technical audit of what you have in-house in terms of microphones, recording software, and space needed for recording programs at various lengths.

Program development comes next. This is similar to the development of a newsletter.

1. *Audience*—Whom are you targeting? Moms? Mystery lovers?
2. *Purpose(s)*—Entertainment advisory or educational, an aural display table with specific subjects?
3. *Style*—One person's voice, or more? Conversational, or interviews?
4. *Elements*—How many themes would you do?
5. *Structure*—Do introduction and conclusion have standard scripts?
6. *Regularity*—Weekly, bi-weekly, monthly?
7. *Regular Features*—Author spotlight, current top circulating items, community news?
8. *Seasonal Features*—Easy to format, copy whatever you do inside your walls?
9. *Special Features*—Rise to the occasion—specialized focusing based on current events?
10. *Dissemination*—Can get complicated due to variety of delivery mechanisms. What are your in-house or a partnering advertiser capabilities?

Real-World Examples

The Seattle Public Library has been doing podcasts for almost a decade for various library programs and guest speakers. Their first forty seconds are a thank you to their sponsors (the Seattle Public Library Foundation) tastefully done with smooth background music and encouragement to visit the foundation's website to help support their efforts (Seattle Public Library 2015).

Exercises

» Do stakeholder development. Tap into your Friends groups, etc., for their input. Successful entrepreneurs always involve others. Get your Friends involved! Do a focus group listening party using whatever capabilities you have, and get feedback. Maybe do a few pilot episodes for focus groups before you roll out for real. If your Friends or volunteers are not a good cross-section of the community, recruit from the programs whose participants will be the target of your podcast. Some people may be reticent because they love coming into the library, but you might still get their feedback for "all those unable to come in" for one reason or another. Appeal to their desire to help the whole community take advantage of what the library can offer.

METHOD 4

Advertising in Program Rebroadcasts and Cable Streaming

Thanks to improved technology and better technical education in many school systems, there is an increased capability to capture on video and rebroadcast programming that can be both entertaining and educational for your community. It may be a historical actor giving a performance of Mark Twain, or a lecture on helping adults become part-time caregivers that uses photos of home improvement ideas for the elderly. If it's visual, you can capture it in a pretty cost- effective way. You can distribute it in cooperation with local broadcasters, and cable systems, or through your own server, YouTube Channel, or any other visual channels accessible to you and your community. The source of revenue would be businesses, and should generate a low amount of income first, growing to a moderate amount in time. Start-up costs might be high depending on current access to needed equipment and software.

Some organizations may offer professional services in exchange for placing their own advertising on your website. As mentioned earlier, be very careful about this kind of exchange. However, if it makes a difference between creating a good quality product or not, a one-for-one dollar exchange may be worth it, especially if an advertiser handles the production costs and logistics. An in-kind donation could act as a catalyst as well. After the rebroadcast service becomes a profitable operation, if need be the in-kind donation could be scaled back to a more cash-oriented contract.

Be careful of cluttered advertising. If you have one advertiser doing an in-kind exchange for the production of the program, try not to be too greedy by using the innovative program to sell to five others, even if only for short acknowledgments. Limit to maybe only two more, and if demand is high, raise rates. Start with annual contracts to give the service time to grow. After a year, the growth may have stabilized, or may continue to grow. Regardless, you can now either increase rates or use six-month contracts to give you time to adjust for an increased audience.

Establishing Value

Use CPM to determine objectively how many impressions of a message will be seen, and what every thousand impressions costs.

Board Considerations, Policy Considerations, or Government Involvement

There are no special board considerations unless there are no advertising policies in place. There should be specific policies detailing the acceptable standards of acknowledgments or advertising. Depending on whether you use acknowledgments or advertising, UBIT could be involved.

Contracts and Procedures

» *Contract*: Continuing. One with a specific renewal process.
» *Procedures*: As a media operation, you would use both standard business operations procedures and traffic department operations procedures.

Special broadcasts that may be offered live via Internet streaming should use a one-time contract. Traffic procedures would still apply.

Promotions

» *Targeted*: Communication is aimed at businesses or foundations.

Revenue Method: Program Rebroadcast and Cable Streaming

Features	Advantages	Benefits
Visual delivery	Better cognitive connection	Better message comprehension
On a schedule	Can time manage viewing/DVR	Audience convenience
Brand graphic	Builds brand recognition	Reinforces brand with connection to your organization

You should also employ whatever communications channels your organization uses (e.g., website, newsletter, flyers) to promote the program and build your audience.

Moves Management Model

» *Discovery*: Use a media audit as well as personal contacts to find active local advertisers. Arrange an introduction.
» *Cultivation*: Come back and talk about what they want to do and how you can help them.
» *Solicitation*: Your proposal. Include a gift ladder that might involve value-added promotions.
» *Stewardship*: Run periodic status checks, especially if they use an advertisement that has inducement language such as "Don't forget to ask for the 20 percent off Library Special." Also, follow through with attendance figures for the various programs when they were live, "Last month our Storytimes had 450 children and adults in attendance, and even more watching through cable, thanks in part to your help in producing them." Make their day by having them feel they're part of the effort, which they are!

First Steps

» Do a technical audit of what you have in-house in terms of cameras, microphones, recording software, and space needed for recording programs at various lengths.
» Determine what methods are available for use. You can distribute your program through:
    1. Cooperation with local broadcasters
    2. Cable systems
    3. Your own server
    4. A YouTube channel

Real-World Examples

The Lexington (KY) Public Library operates Library Cable Channel 20, which offers a variety of community and library programs. They also offer a YouTube channel that allows for rebroadcasts of author talks and spotlights on library services, with imbedded but non-intrusive links that take viewers immediately to a donation page. These could easily be swapped for an advertiser's link (Lexington Public Library 2015).

Exercises

» Do an environmental-scan of other library video programming. Utilize YouTube and scope out what other libraries produce. Although you want to tailor your programming to your own community, you can see how other productions use various elements such as settings, lighting, music, host dynamics, live audience shots, special effects, graphics, and captioning. For the ones you like best, investigate how they are produced. Ask questions about staffing, equipment, software brands, guest contracts, permissions from audience, and, yes, how they are funded.
» Do stakeholder development. Tap into your Friends groups, etc., for their input. Successful entrepreneurs always involve others.

METHOD 5

Advertising in Calendars and Special Publications

Is there a house or business that doesn't have a calendar visible somewhere? Not even smartphones have been able to dislodge these old-school time-management tools. Retail-wise, calendars, and geographic based publications (e.g., "The History of Old Town,") are ideal for advertising because they often include both entertainment and educational content. Some special publications, such as a tribute to local veterans, are more educational in nature and are better suited for acknowledgments. (Publishing is mentioned further down in this list as a standalone revenue generator with income mostly generated from the public.) In this type of revenue generator, the focus is on the advertising within, for example, a literary birthday calendar. The source of revenue would be businesses, and should generate a moderate amount of income. Start-up costs might be high depending on current access to needed software and staff time for research.

Establishing Value

Use CPM to determine objectively how many impressions of a message will be seen, and what every thousand impressions costs.

Board Considerations, Policy Considerations, or Government Involvement

There are no special board considerations unless there are no advertising policies in place. There should be specific policies detailing the acceptable standards of acknowledgments or advertising. Depending on whether you use acknowledgments or advertising, UBIT could be involved.

Contracts and Procedures

- » *Contract*: Continuing. One with a specific renewal process.
- » *Procedures*: As a media operation, you would use both standard business operations procedures and traffic department operations procedures.

With special publications such as for historical anniversaries, it will be a one-time contract. A copy approval process should still be in place, but only implemented once. No date span or renewability is offered, but you might build in a clause for more billing in a best-case scenario where you sell out your initial run of the publication and have to print more.

Promotions

- » *General*: The main goal is to get the public to buy.

Revenue Method: Calendar/Special Publication—General

Features	Advantages	Benefits
Time management tool	Organizing resource	Efficiency
Decorative	Enhance space aesthetics	More comfortable space
Library brand	Local and literacy-oriented	Shows you're supportive, classy!

> » *Targeted*: Communication is aimed at businesses or foundations. The goal is to get sponsors and advertisers.

Revenue Method: Calendar/Special Publication—Targeted

Features	Advantages	Benefits
Size/content of customer's ad or brand	Eye-catching, informative	Fosters image as supportive of community; more impressions over time

Moves Management Model

» *Discovery*: Use a media audit as well as personal contacts to find active local advertisers. Arrange an introduction.

» *Cultivation*: Come back and talk about what they want to do and how you can help them.

» *Solicitation*: Your proposal. Include a gift ladder that might involve value-added promotions.

» *Stewardship*: Deliver copies of the final product and possibly use the business as a retail location. In periodic status checks, mention the product's distribution success, production reorders, media mentions, and anything else positive with the effort. Again, it's another opportunity to thank them and show that their dollars were well invested.

First Steps

If you want to test the water with this concept, Workman Inc. publishes a 365-day book-lover's calendar at a great discount for schools and libraries (in 2015, the cost was $3.00 apiece, with a thirty-copy minimum order to retail for $13.99 [ALA-Workman 2015]). You could target the revenue goal you want, price competitively below retail, and develop enough revenue to afford to produce your own localized calendar for next year!

Assuming you'll raise enough cash to do your own calendar, other development steps would include:

» Conducting a technical audit to determine what types of production software you have in-house or would like to purchase to produce it yourselves

» Doing a vendor scan or request-for-proposal to find a company with the right skill set to produce your work (see the Publishing mini-chapter for options)

» Choosing a theme. Tap into Friends groups, existing partners, patrons, and non-patrons for their input into the development and design of the calendar or publication to achieve maximum exposure and usage. Look for correlations between the theme and the areas where you have the most circulation and public interest.

Real-World Examples

There are a wide variety of tools you can purchase to design and produce calendars. Googling "calendar software reviews" should find you plenty. You'll want to review them for such design options as whether or not they have a "wizard" for the technically challenged. How large is their range of templates: annual, monthly, weekly? How many images and fonts are available? Don't forget pricing and licensing details.

Exercises

» Determine value. Base this on the CPM method (use the location exercise in chapter 4 on establishing value as a model) and the techniques that establish product and market values described in the introduction to the mini-chapters.
» Analyze the competition for pricing and organizational tips. Don't needlessly reinvent the wheel.

METHOD 6

Advertising on Carousel Screens (Digital Signage)

This method uses a TV screen showing a revolving carousel of ad messages near a high-traffic location, such as an entrance or book pickup area. The source of revenue would be businesses, and should generate a moderate amount of income. Start-up costs may vary; if your organization is lacking in the technical skills required to set this up, there are a growing number of advertising firms that can handle this for you. They will even do the advertising sales, but your return on income will be lowered accordingly. You could also use screensavers for this, based on the way your computers were purchased; if they were purchased with grant funds, that may get complicated.

Establishing Value

Use CPM to determine objectively how many impressions of a message will be seen, and what every thousand impressions costs.

You will need to do a location audit to determine the CPM value. You'll obviously place them in a high-traffic area. For instance, if your screens are above the circulation desk, it'd be easier to get an average number of transactions that occur there and use that as a baseline. If they are located at a reference desk, measurements may not be as accurate, but should be sufficient as a starting point.

Board Considerations, Policy Considerations, and Government Involvement

There are no special board considerations unless there are no advertising policies in place. There should be specific policies detailing the acceptable standards of acknowledgments or advertising. Depending on whether you use acknowledgments or advertising, UBIT could be involved.

Contracts and Procedures

- » *Contract*: Continuing. One with a specific renewal process.
- » *Procedures*: As a media operation, you would use both standard business operations procedures and traffic department operations procedures described in chapter 6.

Promotions

- » *Targeted*: Communication is aimed at businesses or foundations.

Revenue Method: Advertising on Carousel Screens

Features	Advantages	Benefits
Visual delivery	Better cognitive connection	Better message comprehension
Prominent	Can't miss seeing message	More impressions
Brand graphic	Builds brand recognition	Reinforces brand with connection to your organization

Moves Management Model

- » *Discovery*: Use a media audit as well as personal contacts to find active local advertisers. Arrange an introduction. During this time, also search for other companies using this type of technology so you can develop a relationship with the people handling the logistics.
- » *Cultivation*: Come back and talk about what they want to do and how you can help them.
- » *Solicitation*: Your proposal. Include a gift ladder that might involve value-added promotions.
- » *Stewardship*: Because this is a location-based advertising vehicle, you might show a photo of their ad on display in a crowded environment. In your screen rotation, include one that says "Mention you saw our sponsors' ads at the library."

First Steps

» Consider the technology requirements. A simple PowerPoint slideshow or something more? What types of screens will you use? What type of visual range will they have? Please note there is a possibility that someone may try to hack into your digital signals and display something embarrassing. Make sure whatever technology you use is secure.

» Conduct a vendor assessment if you want to outsource this project. Who incurs what expenses? Will they act as an agency; if so, how will you be compensated?

» Consider the content of the screens. Will the verbiage be advertising or acknowledgments? Will it be seen from a distance? Remember things look different on a screen from 20 feet away, even on 50-inch large screens. Will it have static text or use special effects? Will a movie be inserted?

Real-World Examples

The Shaker Heights (OH) Public Library has contracted with an advertising company that handles all technical details and updates the carousel of messages remotely. The large screens are positioned over a circulation check-out area as well as near an exit door. If you're interested in more control over various locations, digital signage companies like Scala Signchannel (www.signchannel.com/) can be contracted to lease equipment and content such as weather information, and will let you place your own ads. Digitalsignagetoday.com is a leading portal into this industry.

Exercises

» Determine value by CPM, the method of objectively determining how many impressions of a message will be seen, and what every 1,000 impressions costs. Use the location audit exercise as a model.

» Try to gauge the optimum visual distance to read a message, and consider whether different locations and angles will maximize your audience.

METHOD 7

Art Show—Sales

Having a community art show is a great way to develop partnerships as well as gather a group of people that may or may not be library users. As the public becomes more accustomed to doing more and more online, it is a nice way to get them through your doors—in person. The source of revenue would be the public, artists, and gallery businesses, and should generate a moderate amount of income. The usual commission for the host, in this case library, is 10 percent. For the sake of discussion, I'll use that figure, but bear in mind the fee could be literally anything you can negotiate. This is a very popular program with the public, but it's somewhat labor intensive. You need staff or trusted volunteers to help find artists willing to participate, gather an inventory of what will be sold on your premises, and possibly compile a price list. This is the point where you'll see if the 10 percent commission makes it worthwhile (remember that profits will be susceptible to UBIT). If you can raise it to 20 percent to cover staff costs, loss of facility space, the UBIT tax, and still put some money toward increasing your general revenue, that's a winning situation for everyone.

After that fiscal determination, the library needs to prepare the presentation area, which could contribute to high start-up costs. The library will need to handle display area set-up and tear-down logistics, possibly photograph items, use their Internet and social media channels to promote the sale, and coordinate a schedule with the artist to have an "opening ceremony" and then have regular auditing procedures for the sales. Determine if it is going to be a one-night gala affair or an installation that runs for a specific time period when the public can come in, view, and/or vote. One makes money quickly, and the other is good for door counts and maybe other metrics. Do both if you can!

A sale involving a single artist is relatively easy. Multiple artists will be trickier to handle due to the increased scale, but can draw more patrons from each artist's core audience. A juried art show is the most complicated format. You need to find appropriate judges and set specific dates and locations for the art to be dropped off, juried, and returned to the artists. However, the quality of such a show may bring higher prices and, based on your host percentage, bring you higher commissions.

Whichever model you choose for art show sales, once the first one is done, the rest are much easier.

Establishing Value

Revenue comes in through commissions based on an agreed-upon figure. You can start off with the standard rate, then adjust based on the success of your event, which you should consider a product.

Use product value to estimate the cost of labor and materials. Then it's up to the organization to calculate the profit it would like to earn and set the price, or in this case commission, accordingly.

Board Considerations, Policy Considerations, or Government Involvement

There are no special board and policy considerations.

Revenue would probably not be subject to UBIT since this is an infrequent event. But double-check to avoid unanticipated expenses.

Contracts and Procedures

- » *Contract*: A onetime contract. The date span is the duration of the exhibit, but you may offer a renewability clause if you plan to partner with them online after the show. (See the mini-chapter on Gift Shops for more ideas.) For this method, standard contractual elements such as logistics confirmation (hanging from walls or using easels?) and billing procedures (payments directly to artist or to your organization?), would apply. You should also consider including a clause that gives permission from the artist to allow for discounting if your personnel handle sales, and you both want to move as much material as possible, perhaps on the last day or at other times. People do like to haggle! Determine from whose share the discount will be taken: the artist's, yours, or both?

» *Procedures*: Standard business operations procedures.

Promotions
» *General*: Use standard tools such as the library website, flyers, newsletters, etc., to draw a crowd that's ready to spend!

Revenue Method: General—Art Show

Features	Advantages	Benefits
Variety	Fits all decorative needs	Enhances space aesthetics
Local, In-person	Can discuss background of artist and topic, technique	Direct relationship with artists can enhances value of work, can reorder more

» *Targeted*. Communication is aimed at artists, to announce a new way to improve their visibility in the community, and/or open up a new market for the sale of their products.

Revenue Method: Targeted—Art Show

Features	Advantages	Benefits
In person	Can talk directly with customers	Builds relationships
Show best work	Shows the scope of your talent	Encourages gallery and website visits
Recognition possible from award	Publicity	Prestige and possibly money?

Moves Management Model
» *Discovery*: Use a media audit as well as personal contacts to find active local artists or galleries in the community that could take advantage of the cost-effectiveness and convenience of your facility.
» *Cultivation*: Come back and talk about what they want to do and how you can help them.

» *Solicitation*: Your proposal. Include a rate chart and/or incentives that might increase purchases.

» *Stewardship*: Have a publicity angle ready for them. Use their preferred channels of communication whenever possible, as well as your own. Run periodic status checks. Inspect inventory churn (what and how quickly items are moving). Insure both parties' contractual obligations are being met. Follow through with attendance figures or other success stories. Make their day by having them feel they're part of the effort, which they are! Others would like their alliance. Strive to keep it.

First Steps

» Check your event insurance coverage. Does it cover damage or theft of items?

» What venue can you use? If in-house, will you have to relocate other programs?

» What will be your costs in terms of staff time, special logistical purchases or rentals, or an opening night gala party? Considering these will help determine your break-even point.

» What are your objectives? What's your goal past the break-even point? Do you want to convert new library visitors into Friends or have them attend another program oriented toward the creative lifestyle? Do you want to build up a database of contacts? Offer a contest to gather contact information?

Real-World Examples

Rather than having fixed prices for art work you can also try the auction method. The Heermance Memorial Library (NY) recently received an unprecedented donation from their Friends group, thanks to both their annual appeal and a highly successful art auction. The Friends sold tickets for entry to the auction, which was held at a local restaurant, featured work by local artists (as well as some bottles of wine). They cleared over $6,000, allowing the Friends to present the library with a check triple the size of their original goal.

It probably helped that, thanks to earlier focus group work, the library knew extra community space was a major concern for their town. They promoted the fundraiser by stating funds raised would go toward that effort, which no doubt helped some people open up their wallets (Lekocevic 2014).

Exercises

» Determine product value. Determine your break-even point. Can you attract enough good artists to achieve your objectives?

» Analyze the competition for pricing and organizational tips. Don't needlessly reinvent the wheel.

» Do stakeholder development. Tap into your Friends groups, etc., for their input. Successful entrepreneurs always involve others.

METHOD 8

Athletic Competitions

Thanks to the increasing interest in health and fitness, more nonprofits are holding special athletic events as fundraisers. Determine which activity (e.g., biking, running, walking), establish various levels of achievement by distance and/or age, establish a route (get proper legal clearances), find sponsors to contribute prizes, and you're on your way! The source of revenue would be from the public and businesses, and should generate a moderate amount of income. Like Art and Vendor shows described in other mini-chapters, start-up costs, at least for the first one, may be high. Materials purchased might be used year after year afterward. Many such events have a registration fee to guarantee some type of revenue, and then ask participants to get sponsors to help support their efforts.

Establishing Value

Use

- » Public motivation, a subjective value composed of emotional elements.
- » Product value to estimate the cost of labor and materials. Then it's up to the organization to calculate the profit it would like to earn and set the price accordingly.
- » Market value, that is, what your local competition is charging.

Board Considerations, Policy Considerations, or Government Involvement

There are no special board and policy considerations.

Revenue would probably not be subject to UBIT, due to it being an infrequent event, but double-check to avoid unanticipated expenses.

Contracts and Procedures

- » *Contract*: One time. A simple exchange of a good for a price. No date span or renewability offered.
- » *Contract*: This method could also use seasonal contracts, a modified version of a continuing contact, specifying an annual event and right of first refusal in case the business climate changes.
- » *Procedures*: Standard business operations procedures.

Promotions

- » *General promotions*. Getting public attention and participation.

Revenue Method: General—Athletic Competitions

Features	Advantages	Benefits
Scalability	Family friendly	Bonding event with family and community
Activity	Variety of ages	Exercise
Challenge	Gives goal	Motivation

» *Targeted*: Communication is aimed at businesses or foundations.

Revenue Method: Targeted—Athletic Competitions

Features	Advantages	Benefits
Local event	Local promotion	More impressions
Cause-oriented	Inclusion in event publicity about cause	Brand connection with cause
		"Smaller target, bigger bullseye"

Moves Management Model

» *Discovery*: Use a media audit as well as personal contacts to find active local advertisers. Arrange an introduction. Target Friends groups, existing partners, patrons, and non-patrons (perhaps through flyers placed at locations outside of the library, for example, at coffee shops, grocery stores, etc.).

» *Cultivation*: Come back and talk about what they want to do and how you can help them.

» *Solicitation*: Your business proposal, including a gift ladder that might involve value-added promotions.

» *Stewardship*: Have a publicity angle ready for your business partners. Use their preferred channels of communication whenever possible, no matter what type of business they are. Follow through with attendance figures or other success stories. Make their day by having them feel they're part of the effort, which they are! Others would like their alliance. Strive to keep it.

First Steps

» Find experienced participants to help staff a committee.

» Determine who your participants will be—what demographic brackets will you establish?

» Determine the route and start researching the affected municipalities for permit requirements.

» Determine the date and time; use your archives to see the activities around town the last few years at that time. Some activities may be biannual, so check at least two years back.

» Determine your revenue-generation techniques. Individual registrations, and if so, how much will you charge? Vendor tables? Sponsorships? See the Event Sponsorship mini-chapter for more on this method.

Active.com has a free download on how to organize a race, covering tons of details (Eisler 2015). Their three main rules are:

1. Safety first.
2. Don't lose money.
3. Have fun!

Real-World Examples

The Brooklyn (NY) Public Library has been raising money for three years with their annual "Bike The Branches" one-day bike ride. They have various routes that feature Brooklyn history, breweries, music, even storytimes during extended rest stops for little ones. They finish with a two-hour awards celebration with activities for all ages. They use registration fees based on age, with discounts for families and groups, and entice people to ask for sponsors by awarding a limited-edition item for raising a certain amount of money (Bakija 2015).

Merrimack Public Library in New Hampshire has employed the efforts of a local karate school to help finance furnishings for their youth department through a well-publicized "Kickathon." Every year, around National Library Week, their Friends group helps find sponsors for the school's students to match a certain amount of money to each kick students can complete in a minute (or give a flat-rate contribution). The school also helps by offering two free weeks of classes for anyone making a $5 or greater donation to the library. The Kickathon drive lasts for two months prior to the event in early May, to capitalize on National Library Week publicity and cover a few book lending cycles to insure frequent exposures reaching their patrons (Merrimack 2015).

Exercises (All described in #9, page 92.)

» Determine value. Base this on the CPM method (use the location exercise as a model) and the techniques establishing product and market values.
» Analyze the competition. Bike MS has been conducting bicycling fund raisers for Multiple Sclerosis in many communities across the country for years. Their organization and sponsor development activities are good role models for any type of race.
» Work with relevant stakeholders for all three of these exercises.

METHOD 9

Author Sales

These are usually associated with book talks, which are very easy events to stage. Libraries are natural settings, but any nonprofit with a meeting space and cause could use this method. Sometimes the publisher will assist by providing publicity materials, or perhaps even arrange a media interview. These are much easier to do than art sales, because you're not concerned with presentation or protecting a long running art installation. The source of revenue would be from the public, and should generate a low amount of income. You can still generate commissions that will be a return on investment for your staff's time. You might designate an area for displaying and selling their work, independent of the circulating items in your collection. Some authors and publishers may bring their own copies to "sign and sell" and leave you with some on consignment. Details like this need to be worked out in your contracts and procedures for handling sales.

Technology can assist in this effort! There have been successful ALA presentations where the author Skyped in. Telephone conferences with authors are another option. In one case, a teleconference with an author who was a former resident of the community drew a large crowd, which included residents who wanted to catch up with an old neighbor. Depending on the author, this model might be used to spur book sales from a "name" author without the logistical issues of traveling to your library. With Gotomeeting.com and similar technologies that can support a web discussion for dozens, if not hundreds of people, a library or community organization that hosts such an event could also offer the author's books for sale.

Establishing Value

Revenue comes in through commissions based on an agreed-upon figure. You can start off with something standard, then adjust based on the success of the event, which you should consider a product.

- » *Product Value*: Estimate the cost of labor and materials. Then it's up to the organization to calculate the profit it would like to earn and set the commission, accordingly. Basically, the formula is revenue (price) of each good minus costs equal profit; multiplying that by the number of goods sold will give you the total value of the method over a period of time. You can then adjust your commission.

Board Considerations, Policy Considerations, or Government Involvement

There are no special board and policy considerations.

Revenue would probably not be subject to UBIT, as the sales are associated with your mission as a nonprofit, but double-check to avoid unanticipated expenses.

Contracts / Procedures

This method would use a onetime contract. The date span is obviously the duration of the author talk, but you may include a renewability clause if you later plan to partner with them online. See the mini-chapter on Gift Shops for ideas on this. For this specific method, standard contractual elements such as logistics confirmation (e.g., a podium or visual aids such as an LCD projector) and billing procedures (payments directly to author, their publisher's agent or your organization), would apply. You should also consider a clause that gives permission to discount if library personnel handle sales, and you want to move as much material as possible, especially during pre and post gift-giving seasons. Determine from whose money the discount will be taken—the author's, yours, or split between both?

» *Procedures*: Standard business operations procedures.

Promotions

» *General Promotions*: Use to encourage the public to go to the event.

Revenue Method: General—Author Sales

Features	Advantages	Benefits
Local	Can discuss background of author and topic writing technique	Direct relationship with author and/or signature can enhance value of work
In-person	Can meet new friends with similar interests	Can reorder more for gifts
Group setting	Can meet new friends with similar interests	Community/social bonding

Moves Management Model

» *Discovery*: Use a media audit as well as personal contacts to find active local writers in the community. Ask your Friends groups, existing partners, patrons, and non-patrons whom their favorite local authors are.
» *Cultivation*: Invite to your location and talk about what they want to do and how you can help them. Most want exposure and your setting will help seal the deal.
» *Solicitation*: Your pitch, include incentives that might increase purchases.
» *Stewardship*: Run periodic status checks, inspect inventory churn (what and how quickly items are moving or books circulating). Make their day by having them feel they're part of the effort, which they are!

First Steps

Considerations of what will either be low or high start-up costs are based on costs for logistics and operational costs such as extra personnel and/or training.

The Association for Library Service to Children (ALSC) has a great page on the steps to arrange an author visit. This page not only has a thorough timeline of steps to take but resources on locating authors (ALSC 2015).

Real-World Examples

Many publishers help their authors by acting as middlemen to arrange speaking engagements. If you have a local author, ask her about her publisher and see if they provide this type of service. You might be able to get an author via Skype, and arrange a sales and shipping agreement for certain titles, signed (perhaps dedicated in advance when ordering) or not. For example, Gray Publishing in Cleveland offers their authors through a Speakers Bureau page (www.grayco.com/speakers/index .shtml). It contains biographies and speaking topics, and can be extremely useful in the discovery process.

Exercises

- » Determine value. Examine the first step above to determine your break-even point. Can you get enough book sales to go beyond that?
- » Analyze the competition. Is this a hot author making rounds everywhere in your community? Would your turnout be lower if you don't host a program with them soon?
- » Do stakeholder development. Tap into your Friends groups, etc., for their input. Successful entrepreneurs always involve others.

BOOKS AND MATERIALS

General Concepts

VIDEOS, DVDs, CDs, BOOKS ON CD, AND EVEN PORTABLE personal devices such as Playaways can be part of this revenue stream mix. Also consider anything that can be downloaded. The first two methods below have been used in libraries for decades and are useful for memorialization as well as community involvement. The third is newer. Don't limit yourself as to using only books!

METHOD 10

Book and Resource Plates

These are labels applied to a book or other circulating material that acknowledge whomever helped purchase it. Make sure they don't cover up a key area of the cover! This is not necessarily a method limited to libraries, but also practical for religious nonprofits using hymnals, etc., community health centers or other organizations wishing to distribute printed or online material. The source of revenue would be from the public, businesses, and foundations. It should generate a moderate amount of income. Costs of the name template, labor, and book should be determined first; then set a price. If donations exceed that cost, the surplus goes to the general fund. If a beautiful plate costing $5 needs to be added to a $20 book and requires fifteen minutes of staff time at $12 an hour ($3), the total cost is $28. Making the price $35 will give you a 25 percent profit. You can do this individually or on a gift ladder that sets the costs to $33 for buying one to five books, $30 for six to ten, etc.

Establishing Value

Use

» CPM to determine objectively how many impressions of a message will be seen, and what every thousand impressions costs.
» Public motivation, a subjective value composed of emotional elements.

Board Considerations, Policy Considerations, or Government Involvement

There are no special board and policy considerations.

Revenue would probably not be subject to UBIT, but double-check to avoid unanticipated expenses.

Contracts and Procedures

This method would use both onetime and continuing contracts.

» *Procedures*: Standard business operations procedures. There should be a screening procedure if businesses are buying plates.

Promotions

» *General Promotions*: Communication is aimed at the public to get them to buy.

Revenue Method: Bookplate—General

Features	Advantages	Benefits
Prominent display	Helps promotion	Shows support of community/organization
Visual	Captures attention	Build pride, self-esteem
Long life	Once done, no need to renew	Long-lasting memorialization/support gesture

» *Targeted*: Communication is aimed at businesses or foundations.

Revenue Method: Bookplate—Targeted

Features	Advantages	Benefits
Prominent display	Helps promotion	Shows support of community/organization
Visual	Captures attention	Build brand awareness
Long life	Once done, no need to renew	Long-lasting memorialization/support gesture

Moves Management Model

» *Discovery*: Use a media audit as well as personal contacts to find active local advertisers. Arrange an introduction. Target Friends groups, existing partners, patrons, and non-patrons (perhaps through flyers placed at locations outside of the library, for example, at coffee shops, grocery stores, etc.).

» *Cultivation*: Come back and talk about what they want to do and how you can help them.

» *Solicitation*: Your business proposal, including an example plate or various available styles. Use the gift ladder approach mentioned below in first steps.

» *Stewardship*: Run periodic status checks, inspect inventory churn (what and how quickly things are moving), especially if you can target their books. Make their day by having them feel they're part of the effort, which they are!

First Steps

Costs on this will vary depending on the level of materials and detailed involved. Most organizations can build a successful program with low start-up costs and use the profit as a catalyst to enhance their offerings and earn more.

» Choose a design. One basic one or multiple templates? Will you engage an artist?

» Should you use a gift ladder approach? Have different rates for standard, genre-specific, or personalized with photograph or brand logo plates?

» Will the plate be only for books, or will you use non-print media such as DVDs, Books on CD, or online media? How will that affect costs?

Real-World Examples

Bookplates are ubiquitous in most libraries. There's a nonprofit organization, the American Society of Bookplate Collectors and Designers (www.bookplate.org) that acts as an online museum and resource guide for those interested in this area.

Exercise

» *Determine Value.* Base this on the CPM and the techniques that establish product values. (See part II's introduction to mini-chapters, #8.)

METHOD 11

Book Sales—Community

Any community organization, such as a family services-oriented nonprofit, could organize a book sale built along their particular services and demographic orientation, as well as general items. In libraries, these are usually coordinated with the Friends of the Library. The source of revenue would be from the public, and should generate a moderate to high amount of income. Depending on weather and publicity, it's best to schedule these sales on a regular basis so that if publicity goes awry, your core book buyers will remember that the library always has a sale the second week of months X and Y.

Establishing Value

Use product value to estimate the cost of labor and materials. Then it's up to the organization to calculate the profit it would like to earn and set prices accordingly.

Board Considerations, Policy Considerations, or Government Involvement

There are no special board and policy considerations.

Revenue would probably not be subject to UBIT, but double-check to avoid unanticipated expenses.

Contracts and Procedures

» *Contract*: Seasonal (a modified version of a continuing contact, specifying an annual event and right of first refusal in case the business climate changes). See the mini-chapter on Event Sponsorship for more on this.
» *Procedures*: Standard business operations procedures. You'll need to be especially clear on point-of-sale payment procedures, refund policy, deposits, and auditing procedures.

Promotions

» *General Promotions*: Communication is aimed at the public to get them to buy.

Revenue Method: Book Sales—Community

Features	Advantages	Benefits
Many choices	Good for all age levels and interests	Can hold books through the generations
Inexpensive	Cost-effective way to build personal libraries at home	Helping to support library cause

Moves Management Model

» *Discovery*: Target Friends groups, existing partners, patrons, and non-patrons (perhaps through flyers placed at locations outside of the library, for example, at coffee shops, grocery stores, etc.).

» *Cultivation*: Tap into Friends groups, existing partners, patrons, and non-patrons for their input into the development and design of the methods used to achieve maximum exposure and usage.

» *Solicitation*: Your proposal. Include incentives that might increase use and purchases.

» *Stewardship*: Run periodic status checks, inspect inventory churn (what and how quickly things are moving), follow through by publicizing attendance figures and dollars generated in real time on social media. Thank everyone at the exit doors. Make their day by having them feel they're part of the effort, which they are! Strive to keep them as future supporters for other efforts.

First Steps

Booksalemanager.com has an excellent guide for nonprofits setting up their first book sale. Sections include:

» How to obtain items
» Organizing the collection along lines of interest and media
» Pricing
» Advertising methods
» Sales day activities
» Cleaning up afterward
» Taking care of volunteers

Real World Example

Marketing your book sale can be a challenge in today's increasingly competitive environment. Booksalefinder.com will list the basics about your book sale, and for a relatively low rate will highlight a complete news-release type of announcement for you on their site.

Exercises

» Determine value. Base this on the CPM method (use the location exercise as a model) if going after an event sponsor and use the techniques that establish product and market values for item pricing.

» Analyze the competition for pricing and organizational tips. Don't needlessly reinvent the wheel.

» Do stakeholder development, tap into your Friends groups, etc., for their input. Successful entrepreneurs always involve others.

METHOD 12

Book Sales—Third Party

This method involves outsourcing book sales through Internet-based organizations. This is a tool of the twenty-first century, thanks to the Internet and advanced by downloadable technology. "Buy it now" deals that appeal with high-demand material might depress your circulation figures, but the hard dollars they produce will probably more than offset that. The source of revenue would be from the public or businesses and should generate a moderate amount of income after word spreads about the service in your community. There have been some success stories with these types of sales in terms of revenue. For a minor investment in setting up the contract, procedures, and method of sale, you should bring in some easy revenue. You might even grow your own "book fund-raisers" for popular authors. When a popular book comes out that has 1,000 holds for 100 copies, you might offer it for sale at a discount. (Add a message to your patrons: "Don't want to be on hold for material? Click below to buy your own copy and help support the library.") The proceeds could be reinvested in the library, and used for other books or services that enhance what the library has to offer the community. State what your earnings are going toward. Make money, not excuses! Some libraries purchase many copies of a best seller, only to see them languishing on the shelves a year later, which need to be weeded out of the collection, hopefully to go to book sales where they'll be sold for a few dollars. A library has to determine if buying a book for X price and having it circulate Y times is more valuable than selling a book in better condition due to less circulation and earning Z amount.

Establishing Value

Use market value, that is, what your local competition is charging.

Board Considerations, Policy Considerations, or Government Involvement

Specific board considerations usually involve signing off on the terms of large contracts and long commitments with third parties.

Specific policy considerations involve establishing the parameters of how procedures will be conducted—in this case, which administrative and financial policies have to be followed for a third-party commission-oriented relationship.

Revenue would probably not be subject to UBIT, but double-check to avoid unanticipated expenses.

Contracts and Procedures

- » *Contract*: Continuing. One with a specific renewal process.
- » *Procedures*: Standard business operations procedures.

Promotions

» *General Promotions*: Communication is aimed at the public to get them to buy.

Revenue Method: Book Sales—Third Party

Features	Advantages	Benefits
Worldwide	Wider sales area	More potential customers
24/7/365	Not restricted to library's hours	More access to inventory; more consistent cash flow, not just book sale week
Dynamic movement	Better monitoring of churn/ interests; track sales better	Can build up high moving inventory
Set higher price	Make more money	Better income

Moves Management Model

» *Discovery*: Target Friends groups, existing partners, patrons, and non-patrons (perhaps through flyers placed at locations outside of the library, for example, at coffee shops, grocery stores, etc.).

» *Cultivation*: Tap into your Friends groups, existing partners, patrons, and non-patrons for their input into the development and design of the methods used to achieve maximum exposure and usage.

» *Solicitation*: Your proposal. Include incentives that might increase use and purchases.

» *Stewardship*: Edit sales confirmation messages to make their day by having them feel they're part of the effort, which they are! Strive to keep them as future supporters for other efforts.

First Steps

This method should have low start-up costs, mostly for labor. You can use the following steps throughout the year, not just around book sale times.

» Separate the donated material from library material. The donated material usually has had one owner and is in much better condition, and may even be a first edition, so its value is much higher.

» Choose a platform to sell your books online through. This could be through an Amazon or Facebook store. There are various apps available to help you.

» If you chose Facebook, some decisions will have to be made about:
  – creating a theme and choosing one of their templates.
  – setting up the stores logistics: through their merchant application process you will be determining shipping procedures and costs, creating a PayPal account, return or other special contingency terms, sales categories and processes for tracking open, closed, and shipped orders.
  – how you'll promote your new "store"

Real-World: Memphis Friends of the Library Book Sales

Many libraries use their donated and weeded materials for annual book sales. Some also have "continuing" book sales with a smaller collection available all year in a high-visibility location. Memphis's library has added a third revenue stream for this material by using Amazon.com, where they offer a collection of over 7,000 titles. This online revenue stream contributed thousands of dollars over the last few years, thanks to the combined efforts of staff and Friends (Gill 2014). More of about this is discussed in the Gift Shop as well as the Recycling mini-chapters.

Exercises

Determine value via the following:

» Product Value. Estimate the cost of labor and materials. Then it's up to the organization to calculate the profit it would like to earn and set the price accordingly.
» Market Value. What your local competition is charging. Analyze the competition for pricing and organizational tips. Don't needlessly reinvent the wheel.
» Do stakeholder development. Tap into your Friends groups, etc., for their input. Successful entrepreneurs always involve others.

METHOD 13

Cell Tower Leasing

This could be a valuable revenue source for many NPs that own property in high elevation locations, or have high structures like church steeples (CEP 2012). Even twenty years ago, broadcasting towers were making nearly an extra five figure revenue stream from leasing their towers. Today the demand has jumped, and opportunities abound. For this revenue, what will hold you back is not competition, but complacency. The source of revenue would be from businesses, and should generate a high amount of income. Monthly rates can range in the mid-thousands, depending on market conditions. Leasing your space or allowing construction on your property can be a complicated affair. There are many consultants that can guide you through the process, as well as many Internet sites with FAQ's about the topic. Do your due diligence into these areas, and be prepared to specify conditions (e.g., the company picks up the extra insurance you'll need, and your right to a percentage of revenue they might charge others for using their tower).

Establishing Value

Use market value, that is, what your local competition is charging.

Board Considerations, Policy Considerations, or Government Involvement

Specific board considerations usually involve signing off on the terms of large contracts and long commitments.

- » No policy considerations should be involved.
- » Revenue would probably be subject to UBIT, but double-check to avoid unneeded expense calculations.

Contracts and Procedures
- » *Contract*: Continuing. One with a specific renewal process.
- » *Procedures*: Standard business operations procedures.

Promotions
- » *Targeted*: Communication is aimed at businesses or foundations.

Revenue Method: Cell Tower Revenue

Features	Advantages	Benefits
Under-utilized space used	Revenue generated without taxpayer burden	Extra income will provide more: • materials • programs • services

Moves Management Model
- » *Discovery*: Target communication companies that could take advantage of the cost-effectiveness and convenience of your facility.
- » *Cultivation*: Inquire about their cell tower policies; what they want to do and how you can help them.
- » *Solicitation*: Your specific offerings.
- » *Stewardship*: Run periodic status checks to insure both parties' contractual obligations are being met. Make sure they know doing business with you helps the wider community.

First Steps

There may be high start-up costs due to the expenses involved assessing your site for technical suitability. Assessment criteria can be covered by contacting cell tower acquisition companies that will act as your agents with the carrier companies, or you can contact the carriers directly. If you do hire an agent to represent you to those wishing to lease your space, you might negotiate with them to absorb the assessment costs and charge you after the sale. Basically, if you're a mile away from another site and have a high structure, and there are no nearby buildings that might impede the signal, you may be a good candidate (Airwave Management 2015).

Real-World Examples

Although this is a good source of income, depending on where you live you may experience some local homeowner push back due to health and aesthetic concerns (San Diego Union-Tribune 2014). AT&T withdrew from a cell tower deal with a California library after residents voiced opposition. If you suspect there may be some opposition but really need the extra revenue stream, prepare talking points about the benefits the cell tower will bring to the community.

Exercises

» Determine value. Base this on the techniques that establish market value.
» Analyze the competition for pricing and organizational tips. Don't needlessly reinvent the wheel.
» Do stakeholder development. Tap into your Friends groups, etc., for their input. Successful entrepreneurs always involve others.

METHOD 14

Charging Stations

Most libraries appreciate the need for their patrons to keep their personal devices charged. Usually it's an expense to the library, but now fulfilling that need can be a revenue stream. There are companies that host multiple chargers located off a screen that can show advertisements. The source of revenue would be from businesses and should generate a low amount of income.

Establishing Value

Use CPM to determine objectively how many impressions of a message will be seen, and what every thousand impressions costs. In this case, that includes anyone passing by the area, publicity you give the new service ("brought to you by"), as well as those charging their phones.

» *Public Motivation*: A subjective value composed of emotional elements. People will spread the word about this.

Board Considerations, Policy Considerations, or Government Involvement

Specific board considerations usually occur only when the board signs off on specific terms of contracts and commitments. Sometimes there is a monetary threshold that determines board involvement. This method may or may not reach that.

» There are no special policy considerations.
» Revenue would probably not be subject to UBIT, because it is a convenience to the public, but double-check to avoid unanticipated expenses.

Contracts and Procedures

» *Contract*: Continuing. One with a specific renewal process.
» *Procedures*: Standard business operations procedures.

Promotions

» *General Promotions*: Communication is aimed at the public, by making people aware of the new service.

Revenue Method: General: Charging Stations

Features	Advantages	Benefits
Safe area to charge phone (no leaving on floor)	Can multitask while charging	Free electricity, cost-effective

» *Targeted Promotions*: Communication is aimed at businesses or foundations.

Revenue Method: Targeted: Charging Stations

Features	Advantages	Benefits
Prominence	More impressions	Builds brand recognition and popularity
Providing multiple chargers	Popular activity, will be used often	"Pay it forward" gesture builds goodwill

Moves Management Model

» *Discovery*: Use a media audit as well as personal contacts through brainstorming to find active local advertisers. Arrange an introduction.
» *Cultivation*: Come back and talk about what they want to do and how you can help them.
» *Solicitation*: Your business proposal. Include a gift ladder that might involve a value-added promotion. or involvement in another sponsorship.
» *Stewardship*: Acknowledge their support and deliver on what you promised. Stay connected.

First Steps

There should be low start-up costs for this method, which will mostly involve research and negotiating. Many hard costs might be picked up by the vendor.

> » Choose a location for the station. Look at traffic, security, and how big a footprint (floor or desk space) you'll need. Is there special electrical or Internet connectivity needed?
> » Decide on a machine vendor, do a cost analysis of expense, possible furniture purchase, and increase in utility expenses. Can their station display multiple advertisers, like the digital signage carousel screen concept discussed earlier?
> » Search for advertisers.

Real-World Examples

One library has a charging station sponsored by a local insurance company that covers the leasing costs (P. Laurita, personal communication, July 7, 2015). The library has no expense, but they could, hypothetically, lease it themselves, and then make sure they cover the current $600 annual charge through sponsorships.

In a testimonial for one vendor, the library director had this to say:

> Both staff and patrons of the Hampton Bays Public Library are very pleased to have the public charging station through the partnership with EBSCO and Suffolk County National Bank. It is currently located in our adult reference department near the public computers. Many patrons come in on their lunch break or directly from work and are happy to be able to charge up their phones or tablets. The charging station is a great resource for our patrons and it is well utilized. The charging station also eliminates what was previously a tripping hazard when patrons would plug their device into a wall outlet with the cord snaking across the floor. (LaVista. nd)

Determine Value via the Following

> » CPM. Objectively determine how many impressions of a message will be seen, and what every thousand impressions costs. Use the location exercise as a model.
> » Product value. Estimate the cost of labor and materials. Then it's up to the organization to calculate the profit it would like to earn and set the price accordingly.
> » Market value. What your local competition is charging.

Do stakeholder development. Tap into your Friends groups, etc., for their input. Successful entrepreneurs always involve others.

METHOD 15

Crowdfunding

This is essentially a campaign technique for raising funds online, a tremendous new tool discussed in chapter 8. The source of revenue would be from the public, and should generate a moderate to high amount of income.

Most crowdfunding platforms handle the familiar Internet payment options, credit cards, Paypal, etc. It's truly a grassroots method of raising funds. Because of their targeted nature, most campaigns raise from $1,000 to $10,000. Also keep in mind that, according to the Foundation Center, fewer than half of all crowdfunding campaigns reach their goals, but the rate may be higher for libraries because of the more personal relationships libraries have with their communities, and the immediate payback of seeing what contributions can provide.

Establishing Value

Establishing the value of your crowdfunding project is easy. First, as part of your needs assessment, figure out the amount it will take to complete the project. Then add in any charges from the website for your campaign. Then, add any costs for giveaways or other awards you will be giving to your donors for contributing to your campaign. Consider rounding up for cost overruns or psychological effects. That total is your target!

Board and Policy Considerations

» *Board Involvement*: Specific. Due to the fact you're cooperating with an outside fund-raiser, the board would probably be charged with approving this effort. They may fully support it or may seek funding from other sources. You'll have to make a sales case by utilizing the features-advantages-benefits formula, and will need to do the same for the public.

» *Policy Requirements*: Specific. If there are no current guidelines to follow using the Internet as a fund-raising tool, there are probably some for fund-raising in general. Review these to see if they align with your contractual responsibilities from the platform you plan to use before committing to anything.

Government Involvement

This revenue would be directly related to library operations, so you should have no concerns about UBIT. You should check to see if the platform can generate a list of donors and contributions in case you're required to report donations over a certain size. Double-check to avoid unanticipated expenses for you or your donors! See chapter 5 on legal considerations for more about this.

In contrast to foundation funding, which almost exclusively flows to 501(c)(3) incorporated nonprofit organizations, many crowdfunding sites allow for a very broad range of projects in which the public can participate. Thus, crowdfunding may be a particularly relevant option for a startup organization, for unincorporated nonprofit projects, or those that have not received IRS recognition of a 501(c)(3) tax exemption (Foundation Center 2015).

Depending on your municipal guidelines, as a library and as a 501(c)(3) organization you should remain firmly in control of any crowdfunding effort for your library. Grassroots organizations may step up to support you, but be aware that if you stay in control, donors may be able to write off donations, which might not be the case for other basic, nonofficial organizations.

Contracts and Procedures

- » *Contract*: One time. The terms will depend on the platform you choose. Review information regarding contracts from chapter 6 and consult chapter 8 for more on crowdfunding.
- » *Procedures*: A crowdfunding campaign should be a dynamic outreach effort, like a media operation. You would use standard business operations procedures in dealing with your platform, as well as traffic department operations procedures to make sure you are keeping your campaign fresh on its web page and constantly updated in your social media efforts.

Promotions

- » *General Promotions*: Communication is aimed at the public.

Revenue Method: Crowdfunding

Features	Advantages	Benefits
Visual	Can graphically express need	Better emotional connection
Specific goal orientation	Know exactly what dollars contributed go toward	Gives sense of an efficient contribution
Incentives	Recognition for various levels of help	Feelings of prestige, inclusion

Moves Management Model

- » *Discovery*: Your needs assessment.
- » *Cultivation*: Craft your campaign's message, setting up your campaign's site, etc.
- » *Solicitation*: Announce your campaign and encourage others to share your message.
- » *Stewardship*: Follow up and thank your donors even if your campaign does not reach its goal. Send out the promotional-incentive giveaways when you reach your goal!

First Steps

Choose a platform for your project. Having a tough time deciding which one is right for your nonprofit? From Techsoup, Content Curator Ginny Mies advises:

> What platform you choose really depends on the size of your nonprofit and what sort of campaign you plan to run. If you're just doing a general fund-raising campaign, Razoo or CauseVox might be the way to go. If you are interested in offering merchandise, check out Teespring. If you're trying launch a project, like a community center or a film festival, KickStarter or Indiegogo might be the way to go. (Mies 2014)

Some of the best-known crowdfunding sites are Kickstarter, Indiegogo, Rockethub, and Gofundme, but many more exist. Most sites will:

1. Let you set up a page to describe, promote, and post updates about your project
2. Provide for donations in a wide variety of ways
3. Be easily and highly shareable on social networks
4. Specify the kinds of projects or campaigns that can be on the site (e.g., creative and artistic; entrepreneurial; personal needs)
4. Charge a percentage of funds raised plus a fee per transaction

Some sites have an "all-or-nothing" policy, meaning you have to reach your monetary goal to get any of the funds. Thus, if you use a crowdfunding site, read and understand its FAQs (frequently asked questions), guidelines, terms, and conditions before committing.

Take time to learn what makes crowdfunding campaigns for your type of project successful. With so many campaigns and platforms on the Internet, the biggest challenges are:

» To reach enough people
» To present a trustworthy, compelling story that will move them to give
» To compel them to share it with their friends

Real-World Examples

Review chapter 8 on technology for some case studies and an interview on crowdfunding.

Exercises

You might want to set up a grid like the one below to compare and contrast features of various crowdfunding platforms.

Platform	1. Customize	2. Donations	3. Social	4. Specific	5. Percentage to service?
Kickstarter					
Indigogo					
Rockethub					
Gofundme					

» Determine value using the steps described above.
» Analyze the competition. Do an environmental scan to determine if the market will provide a good opportunity, or is oversaturated with crowdfunding efforts.
» Work with relevant stakeholders. Tap into your Friends groups, existing partners, patrons, and non-patrons for their input into the development and design of the campaign to achieve maximum exposure and usage. Use public opinion methods such as focus groups, surveys, etc. Successful entrepreneurs always involve others.

METHOD 16

Equipment Rental

This method is especially suited for libraries that are branded as the community's resources experts. This goes beyond books, in that you are giving access to equipment that would be impractical for members of the community to purchase for limited use. Equipment aligned with the library's educational mission—for instance, presentation devices—might be practical in the beginning, and expand to anything from tools, sewing machines, or 3D printers. The source of revenue would be from the public and businesses, and should generate a low amount of income. The main cost to the library is the initial purchase of items like LCD projectors, kitchen equipment, etc., as well as personnel costs if they aid in set-up. To establish value, it would be best to scan your market and make your fee schedule reasonably competitive. As a public institution that wants to be a good steward of the public dollar, you can still justifiably use the fees as an investment and not give away material at under-market prices.

A standardized contract should be created that specifically states the various costs and obligations for both parties. Other factors could be necessary training before use, liability for damages, an in-out checklist of pieces, clean-up requirements, and/or deposit.

Establishing Value

Use market value, that is, what your local competition is charging, and/or the market value of the equipment.

Board Considerations, Policy Considerations, and Government Involvement

Specific board and policy considerations might involve the board signing off on the terms of contracts needed for the public to rent library property. Revenue would probably be subject to UBIT, but double-check to avoid unneeded expense calculations.

Contracts and Procedures

» *Contract*: This method would use a onetime contract. You may want to add a deposit clause.
» *Procedures*: Standard business operations procedures. You should have a tracking sheet for each item that shows the person or organization renting the equipment; date, duration of use, and a confirmation check that you have a signed contract before it leaves, and an inspection sheet to audit what's being returned for completeness and/or damage. You may not be able to do that at the time of return (e.g., five minutes before close), so if it's an item being rented with a deposit, a contract clause and process should be built in that the deposit will be returned in-person or by mail after a certain period, such as two business days. This shows good stewardship of the public's property.

Promotions

» *General Promotions*: Communication is aimed at the public.

Revenue Method: Equipment Rental

Features	Advantages	Benefits
Access to expensive equipment	Convenient; allows for infrequent use and no storage or paying for something rarely used	Saves money

Moves Management Model

» *Discovery*: Target other nonprofits or companies that could take advantage of the cost-effectiveness and convenience of your equipment.
» *Cultivation*: Standard meeting to discover prospects needs and goals.
» *Solicitation*: Your specific offerings, with a rate chart.
» *Stewardship*: Run periodic status checks to insure both parties' contractual obligations are being met. For example, call two weeks into a four-week loan for painting equipment as a friendly reminder on renewing, if possible.

First Steps

There will probably be high start-up costs due to equipment purchases.

- » Determine the need for, and where the equipment will be used—inside or outside the library, or both?
- » What types of equipment will be available? Office or academic oriented? House or yard tools?
- » Where would the initial funding come from, the general fund? Grants? Your Friends organization? Crowdfunding?

Real-World Examples

A good example of policy and procedures for leasing multimedia equipment in an academic setting from Case Western Reserve University in Cleveland clearly communicates the following policies (Kelvin Smith 2015):

- » Borrowing
- » Extended device loans
- » Fines
- » Damage and replacement fees

All would be covered in the contract.

Exercises

- » Determine value. Use the techniques that establish product and market values.
- » Analyze the competition for pricing and organizational tips. Don't needlessly reinvent the wheel.

METHOD 17

Event and Program Sponsorship

In addition to circulating material, special events and regularly scheduled programs are among the most visible and vital aspects of libraries. These include lectures, teaching computer skills, ice cream socials, and a myriad of other types of fun and/ or educational activities. Many other nonprofit service organizations use them for outreach and publicity as well. The source of revenue is from businesses and foundations, and this should generate a high to significant amount of income.

Membership perks are another type of community engagement program offered by many libraries, public broadcasters, and nonprofits. Membership perks are simply arrangements with vendors that may or may not be sponsoring other programs to give discounts to anyone identified as a member of a donation organization. This is a win-win situation, whereby a vendor (e.g., restaurant, hardware store) agrees to offer a discount for patrons who make a certain class of donation to a NP. The vendor and patron get a write-off, the patron saves money, and the NP gets a donation and, perhaps even more critical, provides proof of an active patron base interested in that vendor's product. This is a useful case to make when you are cultivating a relationship that may mean more revenue.

Establishing Value

Use CPM to determine objectively how many impressions of a message will be seen, and what every thousand impressions costs.

In terms of setting value, you need to use the CPM method to determine how many exposures, and how frequently, the sponsor's name or brand will appear in all prior promotional material and, of course, signage for day of the event. Program attendance and activity participation, such as in a summer reading program, can also be calculated for CPM. This then is compared to other media, and a fair cost can be set. You can also use a gift ladder approach, estimating factors such as extra exposure at entrances or performance stages to boost the CPM a bit more.

If your estimate of a CPM comes out low, you'll either have to increase the number of sponsorships, or partially abandon that model and emphasize less tangible, but still noteworthy value that a sponsorship will bring; being viewed as a community supporter, a champion of literacy, etc.

Board Considerations, Policy Considerations, and Government Involvement

Specific board considerations usually involve signing off on the terms of large contracts and long-term commitments such as event sponsorships.

Specific policy considerations involve establishing the parameters of understanding as to how a method will be conducted—for example, what type of advertisement language will be allowed or whether only acknowledgment phrases can be used for certain methods.

Revenue would probably not be subject to UBIT, but double-check to avoid unanticipated expenses.

Contracts and Procedures

This method would use a onetime contract. Also possibly seasonal, which is a modified version of a continuing contact, specifying an annual event and right of first refusal in case the business climate changes.

» *Procedures*: Standard business operations procedures. This normally has a specific wording or branding section as to how support will be acknowledged, but would not be rotating copy.

Promotions

» *Targeted*: Communication is aimed at businesses or foundations.

Revenue Method: Event and Program Sponsorship

Features	Advantages	Benefits
Local event	Local promotion	More impressions
Cause-oriented	Inclusion in event publicity about cause	Brand connection with cause
		"Smaller target, bigger bull's-eye"

Moves Management Model

» *Discovery*: Use a media audit as well as personal contacts through brainstorming to find active local advertisers. Arrange an introduction.
» *Cultivation*: Come back and talk about what they want to do and how you can help them.
» *Solicitation*: Your proposal. Include a gift ladder that might involve value-added promotions.
» *Stewardship*: Have a publicity angle ready for them. Follow through with attendance figures or other success stories. Make their day by having them feel they're part of the effort, which they are! Others would like their alliance. Strive to keep it.

First Steps

In terms of other practical considerations, if this is an ongoing program with a track record, chances are start-up costs will be minimal. If it's a brand new program, the personnel costs might be absorbed by the library, whereas other physical costs, tents, stage-building, etc., might be paid by the businesses or foundations as part of the sponsorship.

This is similar to the first steps in the mini-chapter on athletic competitions:

» Find experienced participants to help staff a committee.
» Determine who your participants will be and to which demographic brackets will you appeal.
» Determine the venue and start researching permit requirements.
» Determine the date and time; use your archives to check what the activities were around town at that time during the last few years. Some activities may be bi-annual so check at least two years back.
» Determine your revenue-generation techniques. Individual ticket sales, if so, how much? Vendor tables? Sponsorships?

When planning a project, you can often go through a list of basic research questions. In no specific order you should be able to answer the following in your first meeting:

» *Who* will be your audience or attendees?
» *What* type of event do you wish to stage: cultural, recreational, social?

> » *When* will it take place, how long will the event run, and have you picked a competitive time of year for this type of event?
> » *Where* will it take place, and will you need authorization if on a site outside the building, or any special preparation if it's inside?
> » *How* will the activities be chosen, for what purpose will they be used, what promotional techniques or sales methods will you employ?
> » *Why* have you chosen a particular theme—to achieve a strategic goal, or is it for the community's benefit (e.g., autism awareness, building literacy or STEM skills)?

Real-World Examples

Depending on the scale of your event, much of the work will focus on negotiating with all the relevant stakeholders. A successful example of this is the "Taste of Harrison" event sponsored by the Friends of the Harrison Public Library in New York (Harrison 2015). After three years working with the mayor and Chamber of Commerce, they've expanded the Taste so that all Harrison downtown businesses can be involved. By making a donation (which varies according to age) participants will get a special wristband they'll wear on a walking tour of downtown restaurants, while enjoying samples from each. The mayor even arranged for a Senior minivan to be available!

Exercises

Determine value via the following:

> » *CPM*: Objectively determine how many impressions of a message will be seen, and what every thousand impressions costs. Use the location exercise as a model.
> » *Product value*: Estimate the cost of labor and materials. Then it's up to the organization to calculate the profit it would like to earn and set the price accordingly.
> » *Market value*: What your local competition is charging. Analyze the competition for pricing and organizational tips. Don't needlessly reinvent the wheel.
> » *Do stakeholder development*: Tap into your Friends groups, etc., for their input. Successful entrepreneurs always involve others.

METHOD 18

Facility or Room Rental

Many libraries are renting under-utilized meeting space for social occasions or business functions. The source of revenue would be from the public and businesses. It should generate a moderate amount of income. Due to the wide scope of activities, very specific policies should be developed. Luckily, many are already online, so no one should ever have to totally reinvent the wheel.

Establishing Value

Use market value, that is, what your local competition is charging.

Board Considerations, Policy Considerations, and Government Involvement

» There are no special board considerations.
» Specific policy considerations involve establishing the parameters of contractual understanding as to how a method will be conducted.
» Revenue would probably be subject to UBIT, but double-check to avoid unneeded expense calculations.

Contracts and Procedures

» *Contract*: One time. A simple exchange of a good for a price. No date span or renewability offered.
» *Procedures*: Standard business operations procedures.

Promotions

» *General Promotions*: Communication is aimed at the public.

Revenue Method: General Facility Rental

Features	Advantages	Benefits
• Access to large group meeting areas	• Convenient; allows for infrequent use and/or paying for something rarely used	• Saves money • Great for family or community events

» *Targeted*: Communication is aimed at businesses or foundations.

Revenue Method: Targeted Facility Rental

Features	Advantages	Benefits
• Access to expensive equipment (if renting a computer lab) and large group meeting space	• Convenient; allows for infrequent use and no storage or paying for something rarely used	• Saves money • Enhances business training capability

Moves Management Model

» *Discovery*: Target other nonprofits or companies that could take advantage of the cost-effectiveness and convenience of your facility and arrange an introduction.
» *Cultivation*: Standard meeting to discover prospects needs and goals.
» *Solicitation*: Your specific offerings, with a rate chart.

» *Stewardship*: Run periodic status checks to insure both parties' contractual obligations are being met. Make sure they know doing business with you helps the wider community. Others would like their alliance. Strive to keep it.

First Steps

If you have an existing under-utilized facility, then the start-up costs should be low. The following elements would be good to have in a checklist format for staff trying to implement a new facility rentals program. It's advisable to check with the board and review your municipal guidelines (fire codes, etc.). Otherwise, these are generally the framework of decisions you'll need to make. You can then transform this into a combined checklist or contract for the person leasing the facility.

FACILITY RENTAL ELEMENTS CHECKLIST

Identification of facility: Location, capacity, pictures
Fee schedule:

- Separate fee tiers for business, social, or nonprofit use

- Discount for paying in advance

- Time period for due diligence on payment

- Late fee for late reservations

- Cleanup fee (provide examples of how charges will be assessed)

- Security service, if provided

- Deposit, if required

Reservation procedure: Many software packages are available, and some libraries are developing their own. Whether you allow the public to self-book or have staff handle it, procedures need to be in place to prevent over-booking.

Cancellation procedures: Proper notice or loss of deposit.

Publicity: Make sure the library is not viewed as a partner unless you approve; rules on signage and decorations should be specific to avoid excess custodial costs.

Appropriate conduct: Prohibit activities such as filming or photography within the library without prior permission; any sales unless a proportion of the proceeds go the library (which is a whole other revenue stream covered later); singing, alcohol, or other activities contrary to the library's code of conduct.

Parking and access issues: If a group eats up fifty parking spaces, do other patrons have access to the library?

Clean up and breakdown: Outline responsibilities and timeframes.

What the library can provide day of the event: Specify if it will handle seating set up or technical assistance.

Real-World Examples

As mentioned earlier, formulating good policies is critical to creating smooth procedures and operations. The Jacksonville Public Library has one of the better ones I've seen, covering all the contingencies above (Jacksonville Public Library 2015). They have fourteen specific sections:

1. Overview
2. Meeting and event space
3. General rental policies
4. Rental rates and service fees
5. Reservations and cancellations
6. Publicity
7. Filming and photography
8. Audiovisual services
9. Bag check
10. Logistics
11. Alcoholic beverages
12. Decorations
13. Parking
14. Clean-up and break-down

Exercises

» Determine value. Base this on the techniques that establish market values.
» Analyze the competition for pricing and organizational tips. Don't needlessly reinvent the wheel.

METHOD 19

50-50 Raffles

This is a simple and familiar way to generate cash from a lottery-oriented public. You sell raffle tickets, the winner takes half, and the organization keeps the other half. Obviously, you must check the legalities of offering these for a public institution, but then all you'll need is a roll of double-numbered tickets (labelled "need not be present to win"), a good promotional campaign, and you're all set! The source of revenue would be from the public, and should generate a moderate amount of income (Lamar Enterprises nd). As with the crowdfunding method, you might want to introduce this method to your community by having proceeds go to a specific cause within the library, to run for a specific time period or until a goal is reached. Perhaps a spring campaign to fund Summer Reading programs. Once that trial period is over you'll be able to determine whether to continue or not for some other organizational objective.

Establishing Value

Use public motivation, a subjective value composed of emotional elements. You could have an open-ended number of sales, or limit to a specific number to encourage sales before all the tickets are gone.

Board Considerations, Policy Considerations, and Government Involvement

» Specific board considerations usually involve the approval to use raffling as a fund-raiser.
» Specific policy considerations involve establishing the parameters of understanding as to how an activity will be conducted, based on all local, state, and federal law. Review IRS Publication 3079, Tax-Exempt Organizations and Gaming, which reviews what you'll need to know from the federal perspective.
» Revenue would probably be subject to UBIT, but double-check to avoid unneeded expense calculations.

Contracts and Procedures

» *Contract*: One time. A simple exchange of a good for a price. No date span or renewability offered.
» *Procedures*: Standard business operations procedures.

Promotions

» *General Promotions*: Communication is aimed at the public.

Revenue Method: 50-50 Raffles

Features	Advantages	Benefits
Simple	Can easily share with a group	Method to bond with library, friends, and family
Low cost	Can play often	High return potential, shows community support of library

Moves Management Model

» *Discovery*: Target Friends groups, existing partners, patrons, and non-patrons (perhaps through flyers placed at locations outside of the library, for example, at coffee shops, grocery stores, etc.).
» *Cultivation*: Tap into your Friends groups, existing partners, patrons, and non-patrons for their input into the development and design of the methods used to achieve maximum exposure and usage.

» *Solicitation*: Your proposal. Include incentives that might increase use and purchases (maybe non-monetary library promotional merchandise for second place).

» *Stewardship*: Run periodic status checks, inspect inventory churn (how quickly tickets are moving over time), if possible announce winners or jackpot sizes.

First Steps

There should be low start-up costs involved, mostly labor costs associated with setting up procedures, promotion, and buying the standard raffle tickets (perforated to tear into two pieces, one of which is used for contact information). After you develop the revenue stream you may want to spend some of the money on customized tickets with your brand on them.

» First check the statutory regulations governing your organization at every government level: local, state, and federal. If you receive funding from a school district, health board, or any other oversight organization, check with them as well. Laws may not apply to your type of organization, but there could be scenarios where a law applies to your funder. You wouldn't want to jeopardize that!

» Set up an easily auditable procedure for collecting and disbursing funds.

» Determine the timing of drawings. Once a week? Once a month? What would be sufficient to build and keep awareness, get people to participate, and still have a good size payout?

» What method will you use for both encouraging people to play and announcing winners? What are your legal obligations? Can you announce winners' or give them the option to remain private?

Real-World Examples

The Colchester East Hants Public Library Foundation (Nova Scotia, CN) began a one-million-dollar capital campaign that utilized many techniques, including naming rights, bookplates, and 50-50 raffles at two-week intervals (Tetanish 2015). This is a good timeframe to build up some nice winnings and keep interest alive—and it also extends through one checkout cycle for many libraries. Patrons can check out a best seller or DVD and play the contest every two weeks. Winners are announced on the library's website as well as through social media platforms.

When it comes to raising a million dollars, as with many other things in life, this old saying applies: "Yard by yard it's hard, inch by inch, it's a cinch!"

Exercises

» Determine market value. What is your local competition charging?

» Do stakeholder development. Tap into your Friends groups, etc., for their input. Successful entrepreneurs always involve others.

METHOD 20

Gift Shop Sales

These days you can establish a gift shop physically or online to promote your organization and profit from sales at the same time. Don't underestimate what a library brand offers to the self-esteem of your patrons. Using library-branded clothing, coffee mugs, or office accessories, or giving them as gifts, reinforces self-image, whether it's as an intellectual or geek. The source of revenue would be from the public, and should generate a moderate amount of income.

You might need a cash catalyst to start this type of operation. Definitely do the math on expenses, anticipated demand, and break-even points. Aim low at first, set a fair value for a small amount of product, then reinvest the profits accordingly. Clothing not doing as well as mugs? Then up the next mug order and hold off buying more clothing until stock is reduced. Anticipate seasonal demands. Use your Friends and volunteers to assist in brick-and-mortar stores and help spread the word about virtual efforts.

Establishing Value

Use

» Product value to estimate the cost of labor and materials. Then it's up to the organization to calculate the profit it would like to earn and set the price accordingly.
» Market value, that is, what your local competition is charging.

Board Considerations, Policy Considerations, and Government Involvement

» Specific board considerations usually involve signing off on the terms of large contracts and long commitments. Establishing a gift shop would qualify for this.
» Specific policy considerations involve establishing the parameters of understanding as to how gift shop sales on premises or online will be conducted.
» Revenue would probably be subject to UBIT, but double-check to avoid unneeded expense calculations.

Contracts and Procedures

» *Contract*: Continuing for vendors; one with a specific renewal process.
» *Procedures*: Standard business operations procedures.

Promotions

» *General Promotions*: Communication is aimed at the public.

Revenue Method: Gift Shop Sales

Features	Advantages	Benefits
On premises	See what you're getting, as opposed to online shopping	No surprises
Features brand	Shows support of organization	Personal identification with brand
Variety of items	Multiple choices for all ages and interests	Something of value for everyone, encourages library "habit"

Moves Management Model

» *Discovery*: Target Friends groups, existing partners, patrons, and non-patrons (perhaps through flyers placed at locations outside of the library, for example, at coffee shops, grocery stores, etc.) who would take advantage of the cost-effectiveness and convenience of a library gift shop.

» *Cultivation*: Tap into your Friends groups, existing partners, patrons, and non-patrons for their input into the development and design of the methods used to achieve maximum exposure and usage.

» *Solicitation*: Include a rate chart in the store and online to acquaint the public with your inventory and/or incentives that might increase use and purchases.

» *Stewardship*: Run periodic status checks, inspect inventory churn (what and how quickly items are moving). Thank everyone at the exit.

First Steps

High start-up costs would be based on costs for design, construction, and initial operational costs such as extra personnel and/or training. The website knowhow nonprofit.org details how to set up a "charity shop" includes some of the following in more detail, but this is the gist of what you'll need to consider:

» First check the statutory regulations governing your organization at every government level: local, state, and federal. If you receive funding from a school district, health board or any other oversight organization, check with them as well. Laws may not apply to your type of organization, but there could be scenarios where a law applies to your funder. You wouldn't want to jeopardize that!

» Where would the initial funding come from, the general fund? Grants? Your Friends organization? Crowdfunding?

» Do a location assessment. Do you need to construct a secure area, buy shelving and other display material?

» How will you acquire stock? Vendor relationships are discussed in the mini-chapters on Calendars, Publishing, and Third-Party Sales.

» How will it be staffed? Will there be an online presence?

» What types of signage will be used? What types of items will be sold?

» Set up an easily auditable procedure for handling funds and inventory control.

Real-World Examples

A recent article in *Library Journal* reviewed seven case studies of various successful library gift shops. One case study was of a shop in Ohio run by a Friends organization. It is a modest operation open only twenty hours a week, but viable enough to supplement Friends contributions to fund summer reading programs, ice cream socials, concerts, and even a customized delivery van. They're strictly on a one-on-one personal basis, nothing online. The volunteers like seeing the people to whom they're selling things (Peet 2015).

Exercises

» Determine market value. What is your local competition charging?
» Do stakeholder development. Tap into your Friends groups, etc., for their input.

METHOD 21

Matching Grants and Donation Challenges

The concept of corporate matching grants has been around for decades. They're essentially benefit programs whereby if an employee wishes to make a contribution to a nonprofit organization like your library, the corporation will match it (up to a defined limit). It requires a bit of front-end work for the nonprofit, but once that is done, the process takes minimal effort— periodic reminders to your patrons to bring in more donations. The source of revenue would be from the public, businesses, and foundations, and should generate a significant amount of income.

Regarding the campaign, you'll aim to achieve two goals: raising extra cash and demonstrating to the corporation that they might benefit from being a sponsor independent of the matching-grant program. The University of Kansas has published an excellent resource online about obtaining corporate funding that provides a number of tools and references as part of their Community Toolbox Initiative (2015).

Donation challenges could be used in conjunction with a crowdfunding project or other team events. Perhaps it's a "Ride for Literacy," where individuals or teams sign up for a bike ride and raise money through registration fees and/or individual sponsorships from family and friends. The team or individual raising the most wins an award. If the winning team is from a company offering matching donations, so much the better!

Establishing Value

Use

» CPM to objectively determine how many impressions of a message will be seen, and what every thousand impressions costs.
» Public motivation, a subjective value composed of emotional elements.
» Market value, that is, what your local competition is charging.

Board Considerations, Policy Considerations, and Government Involvement

» There are no special board or policy considerations.
» Revenue would probably not be subject to UBIT, but double-check to avoid unanticipated expenses.

Contracts and Procedures

» *Contract*: One time. A simple exchange of a good for a price. No date span or renewability offered.
» *Procedures*: Standard business operations procedures.

Promotions

» *General Promotions*: Communication is aimed at the public.

Revenue Method: General—Matching Grants and Donations Challenges

Features	Advantages	Benefits
Matching money from employer or	Uses under-utilized employment benefits	Multiplies donation
Cause advocate	Provides motivation to participate	Positive feelings of community pride, self-image

» *Targeted*: Communication is aimed at businesses or foundations.

Revenue Method: Targeted—Matching Grants and Donations Challenges

Features	Advantages	Benefits
Morale	Bonding with employees	Builds pride in workplace
Cause/community advocacy	Shared publicity and promotion of event or cause	Aids community image

Moves Management Model

» *Discovery*: The work involved can be integrated into any of the sponsor searches for the other methods.
  – Identify the area's largest employers.
  – Determine if there's a matching grant program through employees you know, or by calling the benefits department.
  – Provide them with the proper paperwork.
  – Prepare a campaign in which they can participate.

» *The Great Nonprofits Blog* (2015) reports that almost ten billion dollars in matching money goes unused annually. They provide a search engine you can use to research companies both nationally and locally that have matching programs.
» *Cultivation*: Contact the company and talk about what it is they can do in accordance with their policies. How can you help them implement those policies?
» *Solicitation*: Your proposal. Include a gift ladder that might involve value-added promotions, a rate chart, and/or incentives that might increase use and purchases.
» *Stewardship*: Have a publicity angle ready for them. Use their preferred channels of communication whenever possible to reach their employees, vendors, etc.

First Steps

Start-up costs may be low if you're simply establishing a matching donation program—just the costs of research, administrative paperwork, and publicity. Costs will be high if you stage a full event, and have teams competing against each other both in fund-raising and during the event itself. See the real world example below.

When planning a project, you can sometimes use a list of basic research questions. In no specific order, you should be able to answer the following in your first meeting:

» *Who* will be your audience or attendees? Who will be matching the money raised?
» *What* type of event do you wish to stage: cultural, recreational, social?
» *When* will it take place, how long will the event run, and have you picked a competitive time of year for this type of event, when it will conflict with other fundraisers? Plan several months that begins before the event by creating a timeline with preparatory activities, and which runs a few months after the event for pledge follow ups, thank-you messages, and publicizing the next fund-raiser.
» *How* will the activities be chosen? Will they be team or individually oriented? What promotional techniques or sales methods will be used?
» *Why* have you chosen a particular theme—to achieve a strategic goal, or is it for the community's benefit (e.g., autism awareness, building literacy or STEM skills)?

Real World Example: A Corporate Knowledge Bowl

The Memphis Library Foundation has been offering a Corporate Knowledge Bowl for eighteen years. It's a trivia contest with teams from various local businesses competing for bragging rights as being "The Smartest Company in Memphis" (Memphis Library Foundation 2015). The library asks for a good-sized contribution, which is a write-off for the company, and encourages spectators to watch four-person teams go through sixty questions in twenty minutes.

Involving sponsors' employees adds an intangible value for the employer; you're giving them an opportunity to demonstrate corporate support of an indispensable community asset—the local library!

Exercises

» Analyze the competition for pricing and organizational tips. Don't needlessly reinvent the wheel.
» Do stakeholder development. Tap into your Friends groups, etc., for their input. Successful entrepreneurs always involve others.

METHOD 22

Medical Services Partnerships

Using your meeting room space for various health screenings, eye exams, massages, and other services geared toward boomers or children could be the catalyst for an ongoing relationship between your organization and a healthcare provider. It's good for the bottom line, as well as library circulation and programming figures. The source of revenue would usually be from businesses, but possibly from the public, depending how you structure as the event (as explained below), and should generate a moderate amount of income.

This requires space and electrical capacity, but it could serve as a good platform for the vendor, free or low-cost services for the patron, and it's a way for the library to attract people who might not otherwise visit.

Based on your municipal and other governing guidelines, you could structure your revenue streams in various ways:

1. Have the vendor provide the library with a tax-deductible donation that pays for the space and the library's promotional costs. This shifts more work to the library but, on the upside, you can promote the event as a library program.
2. Have the vendor pay a standard charge for an event or meeting space and let them handle the publicity on their own.
3. Having participating patrons make a partial tax-deductible donation to the library in exchange for the service. Perhaps even offer the service at a discount as a "one-day perk" for Friends of the Library, which should attract new members.
4. Take a commission on paid services rendered, much like an art, book, or plant sale.

What an efficient way to combine generating revenue while building up your base of supporters! Timing the event can also be key. Imagine a program offering massages after a big community bike race. What about hearing tests to prepare for the "sounds of summer" outdoor music and theater performances? You'll be helping provide a tangible service, become more involved in the community, and generate some income for both the library and the wellness service involved. Do not agree to a request for free space from a commercial entity or well-funded nonprofit hospital because the event is for the "community good." As responsible stewards, you should strive to shore up your finances as well as participate in the well-being of your community.

Establishing Value

Use

> » CPM, the method of objectively determining how many impressions of a message will be seen, and what every thousand impressions costs.
> » Market value, that is, what your local competition is charging.

Board Considerations, Policy Considerations, and Government Involvement

> » Specific board considerations usually involve signing off on the terms of large contracts or outside party involvements on library property.
> » There are no special policy considerations.
> » Revenue would probably not be subject to UBIT, but double-check to avoid unanticipated expenses.

Contracts and Procedures

> » *Contract*: One time. A simple exchange of a good for a price. No date span or renewability offered.
> » *Procedures*: Standard business operations procedures.

Promotions

> » *General Promotions*: Communication is aimed at the public to increase attendance.

Revenue Method: General—Medical Services Partnerships

Features	Advantages	Benefits
Practical health care	Convenience	Efficient; can use library with family or your own purposes besides medical
Access to more knowledge	Can get reference suggestions on subject material	Quick follow-up on subject matter; preparation for future steps

> » *Targeted Promotions*: Communication is aimed at businesses or foundations.

Revenue Method: Targeted—Medical Services Partnerships

Features	Advantages	Benefits
Local event	Local promotion	More impressions; build client base
Cause-oriented	Inclusion in event publicity about cause	Brand connection with cause "Smaller target, bigger bull's-eye"

Moves Management Model

» *Discovery:* Target other nonprofits or medical companies that could take advantage of the cost-effectiveness and convenience of your facility.
» *Cultivation:* Standard meeting to discover prospects needs and goals.
» *Solicitation:* Your specific offerings, with a rate chart.
» *Stewardship:* Run periodic status checks to insure both parties' contractual obligations are being met. Make sure they know doing business with you is a win for you, them, and the community.

First Steps

Start-up costs could be low if you're simply using your existing facility.

When planning a project, you'll want to use some basic research questions. You should be able to answer the following in your first internal meeting:

» *Who* will be your audience or attendees?
» *What* type of medical event you wish to stage: informational, screening, both?
» *When* will it take place, how long will the event run, and have you picked a time of year for this type of event concerning competing with other activities in the area?
» *Where* will it take place, and will you need authorization if on a site outside the building, or any special preparation if it's inside?
» *How* will the activities be chosen, and what promotional techniques or sales methods will you employ?
» *Why* have you chosen a particular service? Can you develop this relationship into a regular sponsorship?

Real-World Examples

Both the discovery move above, and one of the exercises below, involve an environmental scan for services that could work for this method. Googling "medical screening services" will produce a number of national companies you can contact for specific logistical information. Next, you could look at local chains and hospital groups, and finally individual practices. Also talk to local drug stores and medical equipment suppliers for their input.

Exercises

» Determine value with CPM, Use CPM to determine objectively how many impressions of a message will be seen, and what every thousand impressions costs.
» Analyze the competition for pricing and organizational tips. Don't needlessly reinvent the wheel.
» Do stakeholder development. Tap into your Friends groups, etc., for their input. Successful entrepreneurs always involve others.

METHOD 23

Meeting Services

Business incubators, entrepreneurial zones, maker spaces, and various other names are being used to describe collections of individual services under one roof that, combined, would be too expensive for new or smaller businesses. For a library that can win grants more easily than a new business can get funding, developing a list of services and equipment could be very helpful to the community. The source of revenue would be from the public and businesses, and although it would probably generate a low amount of income, it makes you a more attractive prospect for grant money. Renting facilities like training labs for competitive market prices takes advantage of under-utilized resources and shows good stewardship of library resources. Real estate, insurance, and tax regulation training are just three areas that experience dynamic and reoccurring changes. If you target companies like this in your area, perhaps in cooperation with professional membership organizations, it could be beneficial not only for this revenue stream, but for discovering other sponsors.

A partial list of what kind of business services that could be offered follows.

REVENUE-GENERATING EQUIPMENT AND SERVICES

Possible Equipment

- LCD projector
- Laptop with current presentation software
- Sound system
- Video cameras
- Color printers and laminating equipment
- SMART Boards

Services

Meeting space for various capacities and lengths of time

You could "lease" space. The Shaker Heights Public Library hosts a Community Entrepreneurial Office (CEO) that offers spaces at varying costs. The highest charge is for a dedicated office cubicle that you can outfit with signage, and where you can leave items. A less-expensive option is for a flexible arrangement for guaranteed space, or "walk-in" office, where you can use one of several cubicles, but can't leave anything behind. (Shaker Heights Public Library 2015).

Many libraries now have semi-private training labs that are used for classes and general public use. With more and more companies holding virtual meetings, and more government programs requiring access via computer, these areas can be rented, thereby alleviating the costs of setting up a training facility for a business that rarely needs one.

Establishing Value

» Use market value, that is, what your local competition is charging.

Board Considerations, Policy Considerations, and Government Involvement

» There are no special board and policy considerations.
» Specific policy considerations involve establishing the parameters of contractual understanding as to how a method will be conducted.
» Revenue would probably not be subject to UBIT, but double-check to avoid unanticipated expenses.

Contracts and Procedures

» *Contract*: Continuing; one with a specific renewal process. For labs and spaces.
» *Contract*: One time; A simple exchange of a good for a price. No date span or renewability offered. For equipment leasing.
» *Procedures*: Standard business operations procedures.

Promotions

» *General Promotions*: Communication is aimed at the public.

Revenue Method: General—Meeting Services

Features	Advantages	Benefits
Access to expensive equipment	Convenient; allows for infrequent use and no storage or paying for something rarely used	Saves money

» *Targeted Promotions*: Communication is aimed at businesses or foundations.

Revenue Method: Targeted—Meeting Services

Features	Advantages	Benefits
Access to expensive equipment	Convenient; allows for infrequent use and no storage or paying for something rarely used	Saves money

Moves Management Model

» *Discovery*: Target other nonprofits or companies that could take advantage of the cost-effectiveness and convenience of your facility.
» *Cultivation*: Standard meeting to discover prospects needs and goals.
» *Solicitation*: Your specific offerings, with a rate chart.
» *Stewardship*: Run periodic status checks to insure both parties' contractual obligations are being met.

First Steps

There will probably be high start-up costs due to equipment purchases. These steps are similar to the Equipment and Facility Rental mini-chapters:

» Determine the need for the equipment to be used.
» What types of equipment will be available? Office- or academic-oriented?
» Develop a rate chart.
» Determine the policies and procedures for handling reservations, cancellations, damages, appropriate conduct, etc.
» Have contingency plans for parking.
» Where would the initial funding come from? The general fund? Grants? Your Friends organization? Crowdfunding?

Real-World Examples

Services like these are on a tiered scale at the Shaker Heights Public Library. You can have a permanent, flexible, or walk-in office at different rates. They also have a well-equipped computer lab with a SMART Board, twelve work stations, and an instructor's station available for specific technology training. This service is used by private and nonprofit organizations alike (Shaker Heights Public Library 2015).

Exercises

» Determine value. Base this on the techniques that establish product and market values.
» Analyze the competition for pricing and organizational tips. Don't needlessly reinvent the wheel.
» Do stakeholder development. Tap into your Friends groups, etc., for their input. Successful entrepreneurs always involve others.

NAMING RIGHTS

General Concepts

EVERYONE READING THIS PROBABLY IS FAMILIAR WITH community examples of naming rights, which are most visible on public sports venues. However, schools, libraries, and other institutions also supplement their tax and bond monies with naming rights. One library with a seven-million-dollar bond campaign supplemented that over 10 percent—$724,000—in naming rights money (O'Connor 2013). This is a traditional approach to naming rights, which can and should evolve to a more proactive and renewable fund-raising method. To use broadcast model verbiage, they can also be sponsorships. The source of revenue could be from the public, businesses, or foundations, and should generate a significant amount of income.

Naming rights opportunities abound in libraries. To gauge the use of various revenue-generating methods, as mentioned in the introduction, a survey of libraries was conducted in December of 2013, the results of which are examined below.

The top three naming rights designations in the survey were 28 percent for areas (e.g., children's department), 28 percent for collection items (e.g., bookplates) and 18 percent for special collections (e.g., business databases). Only 13 percent were for buildings. Creative opportunities exist no matter how small or large the library. You do not need to wait for a construction project to raise funds via this method.

The Library Foundation of Cincinnati and Hamilton county uses a web page as one tool to attract attention to their naming rights program. They focus on the value being more personal than corporate-oriented. They emphasize that this is a very special way to memorialize someone in a way that touches lives every day. "Donors may name endowments for programs, technology enhancement, collection development, and physical spaces at the Main Library and branch libraries" (Public Library of Cincinnati nd).

The book *Naming Rights* lists three different source types for naming rights revenue: legacy gifts, event sponsorship, and corporate partners (Burton 2008, 57).

This third category is the opportunity to establish recurring revenue streams by using time-based, fairly valued contracts.

About 22 percent of the survey respondents that didn't use naming rights cited concerns over interference with traditional funding. The professional cadre in the early years of public broadcasting shared those concerns, as well as worries about commercialism interfering with the non-commercial quality of their content. Over time, this has faded. Even commercial broadcasters have been concerned about over-commercialization. It can cause a temporary spike in revenue, but it can also reduce effectiveness of advertising over time due to over-saturation, loss of audience, and even cause a backlash in causing more government regulation (Quaal and Brown 1976, 276).

Based on the survey, this is a familiar technique that many libraries large and small have used over the years. Many libraries use undervalued legacy contracts for memorialization purposes. Corporate naming rights have not been as visible as they are in the sports field, but the potential is there.

Four Factors in Choosing Naming Rights Locations and Value

In another example, as part of a $500,000 capital rights campaign, over twenty-three locations within the renovated Thomas Memorial Library have been selected for naming rights opportunities. There were four factors involved in choosing the locations (Collins 2014):

1. Visibility and prominence of the location (will determine how many impressions are delivered)
2. Size of the location (usually square footage, as used in most real estate estimates)
3. Cost to outfit a particular location with furniture or equipment
4. Importance of the location to the donor

Although it might be hard to do an "apples-to-apples" comparison with other NPs naming rights using the fourth element, which would be subjective based on the prospective donor's marketing goals, the first three elements are objective numbers that real pros could appreciate and factor into their decision-making formula.

Promotions

» *General Promotions*: Communication is aimed at the public.

Revenue Method: General—Naming Rights

Features	Advantages	Benefits
Prominence	Simple	Efficient memorialization

» *Targeted Promotions*: Communication is aimed at businesses or foundations.

Revenue Method: Targeted—Naming Rights

Features	Advantages	Benefits
Prominence	Simple	Shows support of community
Used in multiple organization announcements	High number of impressions	Builds brand recognition

Contractual Considerations

» *Contract*: Legacy. Used to establish a relationship that will last for a decade or more. As discussed in earlier chapters, it is important to design
  - A specific, long term contract
  - A payment schedule taking in the cost of inflation, or specific annual or bi-annual payments
  - Well-defined maintenance and escape clauses
  - Value closely tied to both objective metrics and subjective community prestige

» *Procedures*: Standard business operations procedures.

There are five main areas that naming rights can be applied to which will be discussed in detail next. Four are also potential sponsorship opportunities, but the first, for buildings, is unique to naming rights.

METHOD 24

Naming Rights—Buildings

Naming rights for buildings are granted usually for a large portion, at least 25 percent, of construction costs. In granting a long-term contract, you are building and associating the library with a name for a long period of time. Emotions need to be put aside when developing a contract. From a value perspective, look at it this way. One million dollars divided by 25 = $40,000 a year. If you have an open-ended contract, in thirty years, that's about $33,000 a year, forty years = $25,000, fifty years, $20,000. The shorter the timeframe, the more value those rights give to the library. Although corporations understand this, families may not. Libraries can shift the emphasis of naming rights for memorialization to lower-value, but still visible and important, channels, such as the next four options. The source of revenue would be from the public, businesses, or foundations, and should generate a significant amount of income.

Establishing Value

Use

» CPM to determine objectively how many impressions of a message will be seen, and what every thousand impressions costs.

» Market value, that is, what your local competition is charging.

Board Considerations, Policy Considerations, and Government Involvement

» Specific board considerations usually involve signing off on the terms of large contracts and long commitments such as naming rights.

» Specific policy considerations involve establishing the parameters of understanding as to how a method will be conducted—for example, what type of advertisement language will be allowed or whether only acknowledgment phrases can be used for certain methods.

» Revenue would probably not be subject to UBIT, but double-check to avoid unanticipated expenses.

Contracts and Procedures

» *Contract*: Legacy. Used to establish a relationship that will last for a decade or more.

» *Procedures*: Standard business operations procedures.

Promotions

» *Targeted Promotions*: Communication is aimed at businesses or foundations.

Revenue Method: Targeted—Naming Rights—Buildings

Features	Advantages	Benefits
Prominence	Simple	Shows support of community
Used in multiple organization announcements	High number of impressions	Builds brand recognition

» *General Promotions*: Communication is aimed at the public.

Revenue Method: General—Naming Rights—Buildings

Features	Advantages	Benefits
Prominence	Simple	Efficient memorialization

Moves Management Model

» *Discovery*: Use a media audit as well as personal contacts to find active local advertisers. Arrange an introduction.

» *Cultivation*: Come back and talk about what they want to do and how you can help them.

» *Solicitation*: Your proposal. Include a gift ladder that might involve value-added promotions.
» *Stewardship*: Acknowledge their support and deliver on what you promised. Stay connected.

First Steps

Obviously, high start-up costs are involved if you consider the expense of constructing a building to be part of the naming-rights expenses. Others include:

» Investigating the statutory restrictions on all government and oversight levels.
» Clarifying your organization's policies for awarding rights. If it's a contribution toward construction costs or past meritorious service, to avoid controversy it should be clear which method will take prominence.
» Developing a price based on what you estimate will be the construction costs, as well as the value of current and future CPM estimates, and your market value estimates (as indicated above in the Value section). If the building already exists, the construction costs can be taken out of the equation.
» Putting together a proposal outlining the costs + value + intangibles (such as the sponsor's image as one who supports the community) that you can use to start shopping the rights around. A recent TV show, *Billions*, had an episode entitled "Naming Rights." To paraphrase one of the lines of dialogue, naming rights not only *signify* a company but *dignify* it as well. This is an intangible for which some companies will pay a great deal.

Real-World Examples

Well-designed policies on naming rights for buildings can offset a number of issues down the road. The Madison Public Library (2015) has a very succinct page on policies that gives them a wide range of options and protects the value of the property. The board allows the option of awarding naming rights for buildings on factors other than donations. However, in the case of donations, they specify that there must be at least a 51-percent contribution to the costs of the building, and the agreement must last twenty-five years.

Exercises

Determine value via the following:

» *CPM*: The method of objectively determining how many impressions of a message will be seen, and what every thousand impressions costs. Use the location exercise as a model. Is there a commercial billboard nearby that catches approximately the same number of traffic views? Keep that statistic in mind. Yours will be much greater due to its use in forms, publicity, etc.
» *Product value*: Estimate the cost of labor and materials. Then it's up to your organization to calculate the profit it would like to earn and set the price accordingly.

» *Market value*: What your local competition is charging.
» *Stakeholder development*: Tap into your Friends groups, etc., for their input. Successful entrepreneurs always involve others.

METHOD 25

Naming Rights—Collection Areas

This method is specifically geared toward libraries that separate books and materials in a hierarchical fashion. At the top of the categories are fiction and non-fiction. Underneath these are other ranked categories. This is a great way to organize collections, and to help market them to both the public and potential donors. To families seeking a memorial, the power to share a favorite subject or genre with others is an intangible of its own. The process for awarding these rights should insure a fair, well-vetted end result. The source of revenue would be from the public, businesses, and foundations, and should generate a significant amount of income.

Establishing Value
Use
» CPM to determine objectively how many impressions of a message will be seen, and what every thousand impressions costs.
» Public motivation, a subjective value composed of emotional elements.

Board Considerations, Policy Considerations, and Government Involvement
» Specific board considerations usually involve signing off on the terms of large contracts and long commitments such as naming rights.
» Specific policy considerations involve establishing the parameters of understanding as to how a method will be conducted—for example, what type of advertisement language will be allowed or whether only acknowledgment phrases can be used for certain methods.
» Revenue would probably not be subject to UBIT, but double-check to avoid unanticipated expenses.

Contracts and Procedures
» *Contract*: Legacy. Used to establish a relationship that will last for a decade or more.
» *Procedures*: Standard business operations procedures.

Promotions
» *General Promotions*: Communication is aimed at the public.

Revenue Method: General—Naming Rights—Collection Areas

Features	Advantages	Benefits
Prominence	Simple	Efficient memorialization

» *Targeted Promotions*: Communication is aimed at businesses or foundations.

Revenue Method: Targeted—Naming Rights—Collection Areas

Features	Advantages	Benefits
Prominence	Simple	Shows support of community
Used in multiple organization announcements	High number of impressions	Builds brand recognition

Moves Management Model

» *Discovery*: Use a media audit as well as personal contacts to find active local advertisers. Arrange an introduction.
» *Cultivation*: Come back and talk about what they want to do and how you can help them.
» *Solicitation*: Your proposal. Include a gift ladder that might involve value-added promotions.
» *Stewardship*: Acknowledge their support and deliver on what you promised. Stay connected. Perhaps share information about best-sellers in their area.

First Steps

Obviously, high start-up costs are involved if you consider constructing a special collection area, but they should be low if you're keeping the current collection in its present location. Then it's a matter of the labor involved developing and pitching the rights, and the physical signage involved.

Others Steps Include

» Investigate the statutory restrictions on all government and oversight levels.
» Your organization's policies for awarding rights should be crystal clear to avoid controversy.
» You should develop a price based on what you estimate will be the construction costs, as well as the value of current and future CPM estimates, and your market value estimates, as indicated above in the Value section. If the collection area already exists, the construction costs can obviously be taken out of the equation.
» Put together a proposal outlining the costs + value + intangibles (such as the sponsor's image) that you can use to start shopping the rights around.

Real-World Examples: Denver's Rules on Bond Funding

As mentioned in chapter 6's discussion on contracts and procedures, designating certain areas for naming rights or sponsorships could be complicated by certain legal restrictions that can be smoothed through proper contractual elements. Denver must submit agreements needing approval by the city's library commission and city attorney. When bond money has paid for a building, they need to be careful about what percentage can be named and that the naming is specifically in appreciation of a gift to support the programming in the library, and is not a purchase of any physical space in the library (B. Ritenour, personal communication, July 13, 2015).

Exercises

- » Determine value. Base this on the CPM method; use the location exercise as a model. Also use the techniques that establish product and market values.
- » Analyze the competition for pricing and organizational tips. Don't needlessly reinvent the wheel.
- » Do stakeholder development. Tap into your Friends groups, etc., for their input. Successful entrepreneurs always involve others.

METHOD 26

Naming Rights—Furniture

Naming rights for furniture like desks, benches, or even chairs should include maintenance and weathering agreements. The source of revenue would be from the public, businesses, and foundations, and should generate a high amount of income.

Establishing Value

Use

- » CPM to determine objectively how many impressions of a message will be seen, and what every thousand impressions costs.
- » Public motivation, a subjective value composed of emotional elements.
- » Product value to estimate the cost of labor and materials. Then it's up to the organization to calculate the profit it would like to earn and set the price accordingly.

Board Considerations, Policy Considerations, and Government Involvement

- » Specific board considerations usually involve signing off on the terms of large contracts and long commitments such as naming rights.

» Specific policy considerations involve establishing the parameters of understanding as to how a method will be conducted—for example, what type of advertisement language will be allowed or whether only acknowledgment phrases can be used for certain methods.
» Revenue would probably not be subject to UBIT, but double-check to avoid unanticipated expenses.

Contracts and Procedures
» *Contract*: Legacy. Used to establish a relationship that will last for a decade or more.
» *Procedures*: Standard business operations procedures.

Promotions
» *General Promotions*: Communication is aimed at the public.

Revenue Method: General—Naming Rights—Furniture

Features	Advantages	Benefits
Prominence	Simple	Efficient memorialization

» *Targeted Promotions*: Communication is aimed at businesses or foundations.

Revenue Method: Targeted—Naming Rights—Furniture

Features	Advantages	Benefits
Prominence	Simple	Shows support of community
Used in multiple organization announcements	High number of impressions	Builds brand recognition

Moves Management Model
» *Discovery*: Use a media audit as well as personal contacts to find active local advertisers. Arrange an introduction.
» *Cultivation*: Come back and talk about what they want to do and how you can help them.
» *Solicitation*: Your proposal. Include a gift ladder that might involve value-added promotions.
» *Stewardship*: Acknowledge their support and deliver on what you promised. Stay connected.

First Steps

High start-up costs might be involved if you plan to buy new furniture immediately, but should be low if you're keeping the current furniture (e.g., a legal reference work table) in place or waiting until you have funding for purchases. Then it's a matter of the labor involved developing and pitching the rights, and the physical signage involved.

Other Steps Include

» Investigate the statutory restrictions on all government and oversight levels.
» Your organization's policies for awarding rights should be crystal clear to avoid controversy.
» Develop a price based on what you estimate the construction will be, the value of current and future CPM estimates, and your market value estimates, as indicated above in the Value section. If the furniture already exists, that expenditure can obviously be taken out of the equation.
» Put together a proposal outlining the costs + value + intangibles (such as the sponsor's image) that you can use to start shopping the rights around.

Try not to accept in-kind one-for-one dollar exchanges, because the vendor often charges full retail although the value diminishes over time. Unless you seriously need to replace furniture and no other donor can be found, you should avoid this.

Real-World Examples

The Fort Worth library system knows the value of specific definitions when it comes to naming rights. Their page on this subject breaks down naming opportunities into these five categories, noting for each the minimum and maximum contribution levels and time span the rights will last for: building, section of a building, outdoor feature, collection and furnishings, and equipment. Contribution levels are $5,000 for individuals and $10,000 for corporations; for donations exceeding these levels a special mention is made in a prominent place in the library. If contributions are under the thresholds, a plaque or book plate is created. Rights last for the life of the purchased item (City of Fort Worth 2015).

Exercises

» Determine value. Base this on the CPM method; use the location exercise as a model. Also use the techniques that establish product and market values.
» Analyze the competition for pricing and organizational tips. Don't needlessly reinvent the wheel.
» Do stakeholder development. Tap into your Friends groups, etc., for their input. Successful entrepreneurs always involve others.

METHOD 27

Naming Rights—Materials

This is one of the more widespread revenue-producing tools libraries use—buying best sellers; specialty books; or items like DVDs, Playaways, or laptops and including an acknowledgment of the person or business that purchases it. The source of revenue would be from the public, businesses, and foundations, and should generate a moderate amount of income.

Establishing Value

Use

» CPM to determine objectively how many impressions of a message will be seen, and what every thousand impressions costs.

» Public motivation, a subjective value composed of emotional elements.

» Product value to estimate the cost of labor and materials. Then it's up to the organization to calculate the profit it would like to earn and set the price accordingly.

Board Considerations, Policy Considerations, or Government Involvement

Specific board considerations usually involve signing off on the terms of large contracts and long commitments such as naming rights.

Specific policy considerations involve establishing the parameters of understanding as to how a method will be conducted—for example, what type of advertisement language will be allowed or whether only acknowledgment phrases can be used for certain methods. Paying money does not give the right to decide content.

Revenue would probably not be subject to UBIT, but double-check to avoid unanticipated expenses.

Contracts and Procedures

» *Contract*: Legacy. Used to establish a relationship that will last for a decade or more.

» *Procedures*. Standard business operations procedures.

Promotions

» *General Promotions*: Communication is aimed at the public.

Revenue Method: General—Naming Rights—Materials

Features	Advantages	Benefits
Prominence	Simple	Efficient memorialization

» *Targeted Promotions*: Communication is aimed at businesses or foundations.

Revenue Method: Targeted—Naming Rights—Materials

Features	Advantages	Benefits
Prominence	Simple	Shows support of community
Used with specific materials	Aimed at a targeted audience	Brand development

Moves Management Model

- » *Discovery*: Use a media audit as well as personal contacts to find active local advertisers. Arrange an introduction.
- » *Cultivation*: Come back and talk about what they want to do and how you can help them.
- » *Solicitation*: Your proposal. Include a gift ladder that might involve value-added promotions.
- » *Stewardship*: Acknowledge their support and deliver on what you promised. Stay connected.

First Steps

High start-up costs might be involved if you consider buying materials and then look for funding, but they should be low if you wait until you have the funding for purchases. Then it's a matter of the labor involved developing and pitching the rights and the physical signage involved.

Others Steps

- » Investigate the statutory restrictions on all government and oversight levels.
- » Clarify your organization's policies for awarding to avoid controversy.
- » Develop a price based on what you estimate will be the material purchases cost, as well as the value of current and future CPM estimates, and your product value estimates, as indicated above in the Value section. If the material already exists that cost can obviously be taken out of the equation.
- » Put together a proposal outlining the costs + value + intangibles (such as the sponsor's image) that you can use to start shopping the rights around.

Try not to accept in-kind one-for-one dollar exchanges, because the vendor often charges full retail although the value diminishes over time. Unless you are seriously in need of material replacement and no other donor can be found, I would avoid this.

Real-World Examples

The city of Fort Worth and its library system know the value of specific definitions when it comes to naming rights. Their city page on this subject breaks down naming opportunities into these five categories, noting with each with the minimum and maximum contribution levels and time span the rights will last for a building, section of a building, outdoor feature, collection, and furnishings and equipment. Contribution levels are $5,000 for individuals and $10,000 for corporations. For donations exceeding the levels a special mention is made in a prominent place in the library. If contributions are under the threshold, a plaque or book plate is created. Rights last for the life of the purchased item (City of Fort Worth 2015).

Exercises
» Determine value. Base this on the CPM method; use the location exercise as a model. Also use the techniques that establish product and market values.
» Analyze the competition for pricing and organizational tips. Don't needlessly reinvent the wheel.
» Do stakeholder development. Tap into your Friends groups, etc., for their input. Successful entrepreneurs always involve others.

METHOD 28
Naming Rights—Rooms

Instead of referring to a space as "Meeting Room 1," it can be named for a person, company, or foundation. After building rights, this method has the potential to be the highest-value naming rights award. That's because the name can be included in any publicity about activities in the meeting room. If it's a well-used room, that makes the name highly visible—not only in your publicity efforts, but in publicity done by the organizations that use the room, for example, "Tonight, the local auxiliary club will be meeting in the Ed Rossman room at Anytown Public Library." The source of revenue would be from the public, businesses, and foundations, and should generate a high amount of income.

Establishing Value
» Use CPM, the method of objectively determining how many impressions of a message will be seen, and what every thousand impressions costs.
» Public motivation, a subjective value composed of emotional elements.
» Product value, to estimate the cost of labor and materials. Then it's up to the organization to calculate the profit it would like to earn and set the price accordingly.

Board Considerations, Policy Considerations, and Government Involvement
Specific board considerations usually involve signing off on the terms of large contracts and long commitments such as naming rights.

Specific policy considerations involve establishing the parameters of understanding as to how a method will be conducted—for example, what type of advertisement language will be allowed or whether only acknowledgment phrases can be used for certain methods.

Revenue would probably not be subject to UBIT, but double-check to avoid unanticipated expenses.

Contracts and Procedures

» *Contract*: Legacy. Used to establish a relationship that will last for a decade or more.
» *Procedures*: Standard business operations procedures.

Promotions

» *General Promotions*: Communication is aimed at the public.

Revenue Method: General—Naming Rights—Rooms

Features	Advantages	Benefits
Prominence	Simple	Efficient memorialization

» *Targeted Promotions*: Communication is aimed at businesses or foundations.

Revenue Method: Targeted—Naming Rights—Rooms

Features	Advantages	Benefits
Prominence	Simple	Shows support of community
Used with Organization program promotion and publicity	More impressions	Brand development

Moves Management Model

» *Discovery*: Use a media audit as well as personal contacts to find active local advertisers. Arrange an introduction.
» *Cultivation*: Come back and talk about what they want to do and how you can help them.
» *Solicitation*: Your proposal. Include a gift ladder that might involve value-added promotions.
» *Stewardship*: Acknowledge their support and deliver on what you promised. Stay connected.

First Steps

Obviously, high start-up costs are involved if you consider constructing new rooms as part of the naming-rights expenses. If not, then it's a matter of the labor involved developing and pitching the rights and the physical signage involved.

Other steps:

» Investigate the statutory restrictions on all government and oversight levels.
» Clarify your organization's policies for awarding rights. If it's a contribution toward costs or past meritorious service, to avoid controversy it should be clear which method will take prominence.

» Develop a price based on what you estimate will be the construction costs, as well as the value of current and future CPM estimates, and your market value estimates, as indicated above in the Value section. If the building already exists, the construction costs can obviously be taken out of the equation.

» Put together a proposal outlining the costs + value + intangibles such as community support that you can use to start shopping the rights around.

"Cloud901" stands for both the Memphis area code and a cutting-edge technology, cloud computing. In an effort to raise funds for a teen center that will allow teens to use high technology as well as other maker skills, the Memphis Library Foundation is working on a number of sources and techniques, including naming rights for a variety of labs and spaces within the area. When finished, it will be a

Teen Learning Lab (Cloud901) Naming Opportunities

SPONSOR	SPACE	DESCRIPTION	PRICE
	Audio Production Lab	Music studio, recording, editing	$100,000
	Video Production Lab	Video, film, editing, green screen	$100,000
	Maker Space	3D printers, laser cutters, tools	$75,000
Friends/Lichterman Lowenberg Foundation	Gallery	Display area for art, digital projects	$75,000
	Performance Stage	Stage for performances, presentations	$50,000
The Memphis Grizzlies	Gaming Zone	Gaming, design, and creation	$50,000
The Children's Foundation	Art Studio	Painting, printing, design, sculpture	$50,000
The Belz Family	Lounge	Open space for formal or informal use	$50,000
	Hi Tech Tree House	Graphic design, illustration, animation	$25,000
Memphis GP Cellulose	Collaboration Zone	Small group space, writable walls	$25,000
The Canale Foundation	Homework Central	Study area, tutors available	$25,000
AutoZone	Brainstorming Zone	Free space, seating, books, materials	$25,000
Orion Federal Credit Union	Dreamcatcher Space	Inspiration and relaxation	$25,000
Honey Scheidt & Lawson Arney	Dream Store	Genius Bar, printing station	$20,000
Ron and and Jan Coleman	Info Desk / Tool Check-Out	Check-in, equipment access, workshop sign-up	$17,500
Doug Ferris and Dot Neale	Play Cafe	Food and drink area, free space	$15,000
Society for Information Management (SIM)	Gadget Garage	Equipment storage, charging station	$10,000

(as of July 10, 2015)

state-of-the-art social, creative, production, research, and performance lab that will use technology to engage teens. This need was established via strategic planning groups—another example of using local stakeholders to confirm the direction an expensive endeavor should go. See page 171 for current sponsors, the space's designation (very creative in some cases), their description, and prices. You can see the wide range of opportunities.

The discovery process used for these donors consisted of the aforementioned discovery brainstorming techniques, including perusing the development director's Rolodex (D. Jalfon, personal communication, July 29, 2015).

Exercises
» Determine value. Base this on the CPM method; use the location exercise as a model. Also use the techniques that establish product and market values.
» Analyze the competition for pricing and organizational tips. Don't needlessly reinvent the wheel.
» Do stakeholder development. Tap into your Friends groups, etc., for their input. Successful entrepreneurs always involve others.

METHOD 29

Naming Rights—Own a Day

In this method, someone's name is placed on available spaces on an organization's promotional channels, like the website, a calendar of events, and on all the receipts slips for a particular day. They are also featured on other electronic media like the library's emailed newsletters, the Facebook page, and Twitter account. The source of revenue would be from the public and businesses, and should generate a moderate amount of income. A commercial example is the Cleveland Indians Scoreboard Announcement program, which has a limit of fifteen names per game at $50 a name; these can be used to commemorate someone's birthday, retirement, or almost anything (MLB 2015).

Establishing Value
Use
» Public motivation, a subjective value composed of emotional elements.
» CPM to determine objectively how many impressions of a message will be seen, and what every thousand impressions costs.
» Market value, that is, what your local competition is charging.

Board Considerations, Policy Considerations, and Government Involvement

Specific board considerations usually involve approval of special commitments, such as spotlighting any private name on public material.

Specific policy considerations involve establishing the parameters of understanding as to how a method will be conducted; for example, what type of advertisement language will be allowed or whether only acknowledgment phrases can be used for certain methods.

Revenue would probably not be subject to UBIT, but double-check to avoid unanticipated expenses.

Contracts and Procedures

- » *Contract*: One time. A simple exchange of a good for a price. No date span or renewability offered.
- » *Procedures*: As a media operation, you would use both standard business operations procedures and well as traffic department operations procedures. Executing this method requires better-than-average precision in scheduling. It's embarrassing to miss a birthday announcement!

Promotions

- » *General Promotions*: Communication is aimed at the public.

Revenue Method: General—Own a Day

Features	Advantages	Benefits
Prominence	Simple	Efficient recognition or memorialization

- » *Targeted Promotions*: Communication is aimed at businesses or foundations.

Revenue Method: Targeted—Own a Day

Features	Advantages	Benefits
Prominence	Simple	Efficient recognition or memorialization method
Used in multiple organization announcements	High number of impressions	Shows support of community and builds brand recognition

Moves Management Model

- » *Discovery*: Use a media audit as well as personal contacts to find active local advertisers. Arrange an introduction. Let the rest of the community know about the program through your promotional efforts.

» *Cultivation*: Talk about what they want to do, how, and when they want to "own a day." Discuss how you can help them achieve their business or personal goals.

» *Solicitation*: Your proposal. Include a gift ladder that might involve value-added promotions for companies, or other memorialization methods for the public.

» *Stewardship*: Acknowledge their support and deliver on what you promised. Stay connected.

First Steps

This method should have a low start-up cost. The following questions should be answered before putting this method into place:

» *Who* will participate? Should you have separate rates for the public and businesses? Will there be certain categories of businesses not allowed to participate?

» *What* will be the parameters on name or brand prominence? Text only, or can images also be used?

» *When* will you need to set deadlines? Because a specific date is being used, you will need a good calendar system to handle reservations as well as cancellations. You'll need a due date for deposits or payments, as well as pictures or images if those will be used. If you do use patron pictures, have a backup image to superimpose their name over in case they are shy or can't get the image to you in time.

» *Where* will the sponsor's name be displayed? This decision helps set the value in terms of CPM. Determine every location where the name is displayed, then the average impressions it will receive.

» *How* will you handle the mechanics? Determine your procedures for copy. How far out does your copy/name need to be submitted to be placed on your website, lobby sign, newsletter calendar, due date receipts, or any other place?

» *Why* will you allow advertising messages, or simple acknowledgment language for businesses? Will you have suggested copy or word limits so you don't have to reinvent the wheel for memorials, recognitions, celebrations or branding?

Real World Example

The James V. Brown Library in Williamsport, Pennsylvania, won the Gale Cengage Learning Financial Development Award for 2015 by successfully implementing the "Own-a-Day" concept. The award citation praised how the

> James V. Brown Library developed an annual fundraising campaign that allowed patrons to Own a Day at the library to honor or memorialize someone, or to celebrate a birthday or anniversary. The honoree's name is placed on the library's website, the calendar of events and on all the receipts for that day. They are also featured on other electronic media like the emailed newsletter, the library Facebook page and Twitter account. In 2013 they hoped to sell 120 days to raise $12,000. They were able to meet this goal and increase the amount of participation each year. As of 2015, they are on track to keep up or

expand the program with 120 dates already spoken for. Word of mouth has been a vital part of making this program successful. The program clearly works as a supplemental revenue stream to maintain services while it strengthens ties to the community. The James V. Brown Library notes with pride that patrons make a point of coming to the Library on their special day to take pictures of the digital displays reinforcing a sense of ownership and pride in the Library (American Library Association 2015).

Exercises

Determine value via the following:

- » *CPM*: The method of objectively determining how many impressions of a message will be seen, and what every thousand impressions costs. Use the location exercise as a model.
- » *Product value*: Estimate the cost of labor and materials. Then it's up to the organization to calculate the profit it would like to earn and set the price accordingly.
- » *Market value*: What your local competition is charging. Analyze the competition for pricing and organizational tips. Don't needlessly reinvent the wheel.
- » *Stakeholder development*: Tap into your Friends groups, etc., for their input. Successful entrepreneurs always involve others.

METHOD 30

Passports

Being a Passport Acceptance Facility that helps people get passports is a public service with the huge advantage of extended hours versus most government office schedules. There is also a plethora of travel materials and online assistance libraries can offer (Rua 2011). The source of revenue would be from the public, and it should generate a high amount of income. The current execution fee the library earns for each passport (adult or child) is $25.

It's a relatively easy process that involves some paperwork in the beginning, a dedicated working space, self-paced online training from the government that takes five to eight hours and requires annual recertification, and initial start-up costs for the purchase of photographic equipment. You will have annual inspections by the State Department.

Due to funding cutbacks in 2009, the Cuyahoga County (Ohio) Library System had shut down all but seven branches on Sundays. After they introduced their passport services, the extra income helped restore Sunday hours to all of their twenty-eight branches. (Cuyahoga County Public Library 2013).

They made money, not excuses—something most libraries can do. If there's one thing you can do to pay for the cost of this book—this is it!

Establishing Value

A fixed execution fee by the State Department determines what you will receive in revenue. You can set your own price for taking photos based on local market value.

Board Considerations, Policy Considerations, and Government Involvement

» There are no special board and policy considerations.
» Revenue would probably not be subject to UBIT, since this is a convenience to the public, but double-check to avoid unanticipated expenses.

Contracts and Procedures

» *Contract*: The library would use a onetime contract for public services like photography. Only standard contractual elements would apply. The State Department would create and manage the continuing contract required for the program, which you may need to keep on file to renew your status as an Acceptance Facility.

Promotions

» *General Promotions*: Communication is aimed at the public.

Revenue Method: Passport Services

Features	Advantages	Benefits
Producing and processing photos and documents needed for passports	More convenient times and locations than other government offices; other trip preparation materials like books and DVDs close by	Efficiency in trip preparation and planning • Customer has fewer scheduling issues to get key documents • Conducted in a family friendly location

Moves Management Model

» *Discovery*: Target other internationally-oriented nonprofits or companies that could take advantage of the cost-effectiveness and convenience of your facility. Inform the public of your availability via promotions.
» *Cultivation*: Standard meeting with companies to discover prospects needs and goals.
» *Solicitation*: Your specific offerings, with current rates chart.
» *Stewardship*: Run periodic status checks to insure both parties' contractual obligations are being met. The government is pretty thorough on this issue, so be prepared internally.

First Steps

You must begin by sending a letter of intent to the State Department, then follow whatever current schedule of forms they require before becoming a Passport Acceptance Facility.

Assuming you clear the paperwork, your start-up costs may be high, depending on whether you need to construct a special location, buy equipment, and labor costs for staff training requirements. The San Mateo experience described below will give you a good example of what is required.

Real World Example: San Mateo Public Library's Passport Service

Jan Busa of San Mateo, California, gave a presentation at 2015 ALA Annual Conference in San Francisco on this topic. The San Mateo Public Library started their passport services in 2014. FY 2014 statistics were:

- » 1,956 applications
- » 894 photos
- » Gross revenue = $62,215
- » Net revenue = $36,574
- » 60 percent profit margin!

Requirements include designating a Site Program Manager, who oversees staffing, training, and document security and shares communications from the State Department.

Start-Up Costs Included

- » Passport camera with printer and cutter—$500
- » Film—$1.25/print
- » Office supplies—$250
- » PC and copier/printer paper
- » Incidental marketing supplies

You will also need some dedicated space for operations and photography processing.

The passport fees are determined by the State Department. In 2016, passports were $110 for adults and $80 for children.

There is a $25 Execution Fee that goes to the Acceptance Facility (you), which is used to cover Passport Acceptance Agent wages, priority traceable mail postage, and supplies.

Want to increase profit? Jan says to offer a passport photo service (you can set your own fee) and also maximize the number of applications accepted during your service hours. This proved to be a challenge in the beginning of the San Mateo service. Their original first-come, first-served service led to chaos. They discovered that fifteen-minute appointments were optimal, and that communication with appointment seekers was a key element to efficiency. They turned to technology to streamline their operation. They now use a prerecorded phone message line with key information, then use Microsoft Outlook calendaring to schedule appointments and to send important information and appointment reminders.

They offer customer-friendly hours—Monday and Tuesday evenings and all day Saturdays—and as of June 2015 they were booked seven weeks in advance! This is their average wait time no matter what the season.

The main staffer is a part-time library assistant, with four other trained acceptance agents for backup. Having a backup system when you have a booking backlog like this is *very* important.

To sign up, contact your Regional Passport Agency (RPA) through www.travel .state.gov and submit a Letter of Intent. The RPA will look at the number of existing acceptance facilities in your area to determine need. If one exists, you'll need to submit a Request for Designation form. (J. Busa, personal communication, June 29, 2015).

Exercises

» Determine what is charged for photographic services in your community. Base this on a local environmental scan for photographic services.

METHOD 31

Publishing

Self-publishing has been around for a while, but is growing in popularity thanks to social networks and easier-to-use publishing software. Libraries are uniquely gifted with skilled, creative researchers and writers who are equipped to take advantage of this growing trend. It's also an important tool to show how libraries can unite and transform communities through creative partnerships and locally focused themes.

Long-time library vendor Ingram has created a new publication program (www .ingramspark.com). For a relatively low cost (less than $50 for a set-up fee), libraries can publish books and e-books on a wide variety of local topics. The source of revenue would be from the public, and should generate a moderate amount of income.

Establishing Value

Prior to dedicating resources, use the publishing calculator on ingramspark.com to determine how much revenue will be generated. This could be used as a baseline when discussing costs with other publishers.

Three methods should also be utilized:

» Public motivation, a subjective value composed of emotional elements.
» Product value: to estimate the cost of labor and materials. Then it's up to the organization to calculate the profit it would like to earn and set the price accordingly.
» Market value, that is, what your local competition is charging.

Board Considerations, Policy Considerations, and Government Involvement

» Specific board considerations usually involve approval before entering the world of publishing.
» Specific policy considerations involve establishing the parameters of understanding as to how a method will be conducted—if others created the work, have a disclaimer on ownership and/or liability.
» Revenue would probably not be subject to UBIT, but double-check to avoid unanticipated expenses.

Contracts and Procedures

» *Contract*: Continuing. One with a specific renewal process between all parties involved. Possible payment changes based on success or reprints required.
» *Procedures*: Standard business operations procedures.

Promotions

» *Targeted Promotions*: Communication is aimed at businesses, schools, or foundations to help produce the book.

Revenue Method: Publishing—Targeted for Schools and Other Partners

Features	Advantages	Benefits
Access to publishing software	Convenient; allows for infrequent use and/or paying for it to be used only once	Saves money
Work with research experts	Supplements skills	Faster, efficient production

Moves Management Model

» *Discovery*: Target Friends groups, existing partners, patrons, and non-patrons (perhaps through flyers placed at locations outside of the library, for example, at coffee shops, grocery stores, etc.).
» *Cultivation*: Tap into your Friends groups, existing partners, patrons, and non-patrons for their input into the development and design of the themes used to achieve maximum exposure and usage.
» *Solicitation*: Your proposal. Include incentives that might increase use and purchases.

» *Stewardship*: Run periodic status checks, inspect inventory churn (what and how quickly things are moving), follow through with information about sales generated, thanks in part to the help of your sponsors and partners. Make their day by having them feel they're part of the effort, which they are! Strive to keep them as future supporters for other efforts.

First Steps

Depending on what software you use, start-up costs should be low. Labor costs are another story. Perhaps this will be a volunteer effort, or you'll be able to devote staff time to it. Regardless, the following questions should be answered:

» *Who* is the target audience for this publication?
» *What's* your topic or theme? Local architecture? Recipes?
» *When* do you plan to publish? Are you timing a release for an anniversary? Seasonal sales? Will it be an annual publication, perhaps a juried anthology with an award?
» *Where* do you plan to distribute the publication? Distribution channels could include local shops, online platforms, in-house, or schools.
» *How* will the books be designed? Publication logistics would include decisions on trim size, the use of color and graphics, binding, and page count.
» *Why* have you chosen a topic? Are you spotlighting community history? Are your goals educational or focused on building the community?

Real-World Examples

Tennessee's Williamson County Public Library published a book on a local Civil War battle that was adopted into the curriculum of middle schools throughout the state. *Bullets and Bayonets: A Battle of Franklin Primer*, commemorated the sesquicentennial of the Battle of Franklin, nicknamed the "Gettysburg of the West." The project was a collaboration by library staff and a local writer and historian (Williamson Public Library 2014).

Exercises

Determine value via the following:

» *CPM*: The method of objectively determining how many impressions of a message will be seen, and what every thousand impressions costs.
» *Product value*: Estimate the cost of labor and materials. Then it's up to the organization to calculate the profit it would like to earn and set the price accordingly.
» *Market value*: What your local competition is charging. Analyze the competition for pricing and organizational tips. Don't needlessly reinvent the wheel.
» *Do stakeholder development*: Tap into your Friends groups, etc., for their input. Successful entrepreneurs always involve others.

METHOD 32

Receipts

Libraries hand out slips of paper for almost every circulation transaction that shows the date the item needs to be returned. This is a potential space for outside advertising. This is something Toronto Public Library and other commercial retailers have independently tried in many cities. The library should negotiate the initial start-up costs into the package so that the receipt business absorbs the initial paper and equipment costs. If nothing else, have them absorb your current expense on receipt paper! (L. Hazzan, personal communication, May 18, 2015).

Libraries already track circulation, and can estimate how many receipts are printed on an annual basis—you probably already have a figure. Some libraries also use the same printer to give patrons a listing of items on which they are being fined on (not that these patrons are necessarily the best target demographic, but regardless, it gets the advertiser's name out there). Some local grocery chains use a targeted system that highlights local establishments within a mile, even competitors like pizza parlors. Those grocery receipts drive customers to the parlors, and they renew year after year. Many cities have companies that offer this cost-cutting type of advertising service. There was a slow evolution of this idea in Toronto (Receipt Media 2013). The company claims receipt advertising is one of the least expensive advertising channels there is, less than half a cent per impression, thereby making it accessible to many businesses. The source of revenue would be from businesses and foundations, and should generate a moderate amount of income or cost-savings.

Establishing Value

Use CPM, the method of objectively determining how many impressions of a message will be seen, and what every thousand impressions costs.

Board Considerations, Policy Considerations, and Government Involvement

» Specific board considerations usually involve approval of the terms of large contracts and long commitments such as this advertising method.
» Specific policy considerations involve establishing the parameters of understanding as to how a method will be conducted—for example, what type of advertisement language will be allowed or whether only underwriting types of acknowledgment phrases can be used. Revenue would probably be subject to UBIT, but double-check to avoid unneeded expense calculations.

Contracts and Procedures

» *Contract*: Continuing. One with a specific renewal process.
» *Procedures*: If you handle the advertising as a media operation you would use both standard business operations procedures and traffic department operations procedures. If not, then only standard procedures would apply.

Promotions

» *Targeted Promotions*: Communication is aimed at businesses or foundations.

Revenue Method: Receipts

Features	Advantages	Benefits
Prominence	More impressions	Brand recognition
Coupon capability	Complements media plan	Cost efficiency; able to monitor return on investment

Moves Management Model

» *Discovery*: Use a media audit as well as personal contacts to find active local advertisers. Arrange an introduction.
» *Cultivation*: Come back and talk about what they want to do and how you can help them.
» *Solicitation*: Your proposal. Include a gift ladder that might involve value-added promotions.
» *Stewardship*: Acknowledge their support and deliver on what you promised. Stay connected.

First Steps

Start-up costs will probably be low because the vendor you choose should provide the proper printing supplies and handle advertising logistics.

» To pursue this method, you should scan your community for existing use. This method involves the agency handling it to print direct requests for clients. Our local grocery chain uses this method and after every three to four ads there's a "be part of this" ad with the advertising agencies' contact information.
» If not, Google "receipt advertising" and you should come up with a wide variety of national suppliers that could match you up to a local agency.
» Prior to contact, have statistics ready on how many due date receipts you issue daily, weekly, monthly, and annually, as well as how many current rolls of paper you use. These are important tools to establish CPM, as well as the frequency of the impressions, based on how many ads the vendor usually includes per foot of receipt paper.

Real-World Examples

The Toronto Public Library did not make that much money on the actual program, but did save thousands due to the fact the receipt company supplied paper (L. Hazzan, personal communication, May 18, 2015). Because this was a potential point of controversy, Toronto's Chief Librarian acknowledged, "The goal here is to raise revenue in a context that is sensitive to the library environment," which includes providing a broad range of information in a neutral environment. They of course reserved the right to decline anything they would deem inappropriate (*American Libraries* 2013).

Exercises

» Determine value. Base this on the CPM method. Try to determine how many due date receipts (or rolls of receipt paper) you're currently issuing on a weekly, monthly, and/or seasonal basis.

» Analyze the competition for pricing and organizational tips. Don't needlessly reinvent the wheel.

METHOD 33

Recycling

Many libraries use local options to recycle the enormous amount of discarded and donated books they receive each year. Usually these are bulk transactions, meaning they are paid by the sheer weight of the books, not their true potential value. The source of revenue would be from the public and businesses, and should generate a low amount of income, but is a great "green" public relations gesture.

Prior to discarding them, the books may have been offered at a library book sale, often conducted by Friends organizations that diligently screen books to insure quality of covers, pages, etc. However, most books are sold at a flat rate, no matter who the authors are; at the end of the sale, they might be heavily discounted just to move them. There are wonderful benefits from having periodic book sales as a community effort, but there are ways to produce a year-round revenue stream using technology.

There are a few private companies that use the Internet and offer shipping options to help libraries try to achieve a better return on these items. Some vendors even offer the ability to become an affiliate sales channel for their entire inventory, not just what that particular library has contributed. One vender says they've helped thousands of libraries of all types in the last ten years with this concept. This would not be the case if there was no profit to be made.

These companies are ideal for small and rural libraries to take advantage of what would otherwise be a labor- and technology-intensive effort. As a bonus, many of the companies work with literacy programs around the country to donate unsold books in a way that's beneficial to society. If they don't find a home for these books, they recycle them.

Recycling programs for regular paper, including making your library a collection point for public donations of newspapers, phone books, etc., is also a good option. It's another magnet to draw people to your organization. Goodwill stores are a good example. Some people go to donate clothing, then stay to shop for more!

Establishing Value

Regular recycling revenue is usually determined by weight. Most recycling companies don't ask you to provide anything other than the materials.

Board Considerations, Policy Considerations, and Government Involvement

Specific board considerations usually involve approval of the terms of contracts and long-term commitments such as a recycling agreement.

Specific policy considerations involve establishing the parameters of understanding as to how a method will be conducted. There may also be other local rules regarding government-purchased material that you'll have to consider.

Revenue would probably not be subject to UBIT, but double-check to avoid unanticipated expenses.

Contracts and Procedures

» *Contracts*: Each company will have some type of continuing contract service agreement and establish standards as to what they will accept. These usually deal with the packing of items, shipping options and timing, and tracking and paying out revenue.

» *Procedures*: Many companies now have real-time sales dashboards that you can review at any time to see how well you're doing. They might distribute checks to you only after a certain plateau is reached, or on a regular basis. Chances are you might not be liable for UBIT, but you need to have a good reporting mechanism in place whenever you dispose of government-purchased material. Some library software vendors may have parts of their packages you could use to regularly target books to resell based on age, circulation, and recent activity. You might need to create reports with different parameters than you would for normal weeding. For instance, if you normally generate a report showing no activity for one year after purchase, you might want to change that to fewer than one transaction in six months for books bought within one year. If you have multiple copies, if you keep some and sell some while the title is still relatively fresh, you'll get a higher value online than a flat rate in an annual book sale would give you. This is good stewardship of the investment you've made in books.

Promotions

Your community needs to be informed that you want them to donate items. It can be done in a general way, emphasizing the benefits of a year-round revenue stream that helps your organization, and helps the environment. Many people visit you anyway, so you can position this method as a way to kill two birds with one stone—recycle newspapers while picking up books.

» *General Promotions*: Communication is aimed at the public.

Promotions are not usually relevant because this method requires a vendor relationship. However, as a library promotion that will eventually yield metrics you can boast about, it does offer an opportunity to engage the community, and to make the library a leader in the local "Green" efforts. For example, you might use the following statement in annual reports or other PR material:

> Anytown Public Library, through its recycling partners, ABC Company, raised $10,000 dollars last year through used book sales, distributed 2,000 old but usable books to literacy programs, and recycled 100,000 pounds of books, keeping them out of landfills.

This also gives you an opportunity to partner with local media and other community partners concerned with the environment. Who knows how much you can increase donations by this exposure?

Revenue Method: Recycling

Features	Advantages	Benefits
Location	Convenient	Can develop a time-management routine
Specific material accepted	Lets patrons know about recyclables and how to collect them	Efficiency in improving environment

Moves Management Model
- » *Discovery:* Target other nonprofits or companies that could take advantage of the cost-effectiveness and convenience of your facility. Do an environmental scan for competing recycling services.
- » *Cultivation:* Standard meeting to discover vendors needs and charges.
- » *Solicitation:* Your specific offer. Make sure they know doing business with you helps the wider community. They also share being associated with a community asset.
- » *Stewardship:* Run periodic status checks to insure both parties' contractual obligations are being met.

First Steps
1. Do an audit of companies that provide this service to determine if your location will be an issue. Some vendors may charge for shipping based on location, volume, and shipping frequency.
2. Meet with current book-sale personnel and discuss this option with them. You may have volunteers who are sensitive to losing their connection to the library, or having their efforts changed in some new way. Be prepared with a list of features and benefits to introduce the concept to them.

3. Check with municipal guidelines to see if collection resales or material recycling require specific standards or reporting mechanisms. For materials recycling, determine if standards for safe traffic flow or other issues have to be followed. If a collection bin is used, can you sacrifice a certain amount of parking spaces and would that conflict with any ordinances?

4. A designated staff person should be the liaison between your organization and the chosen vendor.

5. Review your policies with your board to determine if a new policy regarding the issue of reselling or recycling library material needs to be addressed. Some may already have policies on donations. Should wording be added to emphasize that once donated, the library will use the books or material to the library's best advantage? This would avoid patrons insisting their donations be put into circulation or stay in the community due to local sales.

Real-World Examples

Friends of the Memphis Public Library receives 175,000 books a year, many in unusable shape. They partnered with a nonprofit recycler, Better World Books, and have built up a revenue stream recycling their books that costs only some volunteer hours (Urban Libraries Council nd).

Exercise

» Do a cost-benefit analysis. Determine the costs currently involved for doing periodic book sales, weeding the collection, and handling discards and donations.

» Work with vendors and come up with estimated revenue from their services.

» Contact other libraries that use them and ask about unexpected costs, public reaction, and net revenue from the effort.

» Check with your current inventory-control vendor and to learn from their experiences what you might change in your current system of reports and procedures.

» After completing the previous steps, determine if the extra revenue will offset costs, and how soon. Consider "what-if" scenarios that will help you achieve results faster. For instance, can you achieve faster weeding using technology, produce weekly promotional announcements, and develop special community events and challenge contests?

METHOD 34

Software Application Development

Some libraries, most notably the New York Public Library System, have developed special computer programs and apps that they then try to sell to other library systems (Library Hotline 2014). At the very least, developing your own software solutions saves you money in licensing fees. That's the reason why many libraries are moving to open-source software to outfit their computer labs. Software development is out of the reach of most libraries, but for those that own mobile application software, and have staff who can program, there's potential. Your app might be something fun to encourage reading, or a practical tool to do remote registrations. The programming technology is accessible—all that's needed is a creative application and an entrepreneurial spirit. Working with creative partnerships is also a benefit of this type of project for any nonprofit, as the real world example below will show. The source of revenue would be from the public and businesses, and should generate a low amount of income.

Establishing Value

Use market value, that is, what your local competition is charging.

Board Considerations, Policy Considerations, and Government Involvement

» There are no special board and policy considerations, unless a high amount of money was to be spent on development.
» Revenue would probably not be subject to UBIT, but double-check to avoid unanticipated expenses.

Contracts and Procedures

» This method would use a onetime contract.
» *Procedures*: Standard business operations procedures.

Promotions

» *General Promotions*: Communication is aimed at the public.

Revenue Method: General—Software Development

Features	Advantages	Benefits
Mobility	Always handy	Handles impulse request
Various services offered	Addresses most in-demand needs	Efficient bonding to products and services

» *Targeted Promotions*: Communication is aimed at businesses or foundations.

Revenue Method: Targeted—Software Development

Features	Advantages	Benefits
Prominence	Simple	Shows support of community and helps brand development
Various services offered	Addresses most in-demand needs	Efficient bonding to products and services

Moves Management Model

» *Discovery*: Target other nonprofits or companies that could take advantage of the cost-effectiveness and convenience of your product.

» *Cultivation*: Standard meeting to discover prospects needs and goals.

» *Solicitation*: Your specific offering.

» *Stewardship*: Run periodic status checks to insure both parties' contractual obligations are being met regarding updates or other logistical issues, if applicable.

First Steps

This has the potential for high start-up costs due to the specialized labor development time it can take. Unless it's a volunteer effort—see the section on crowdsourcing in chapter 8.

The first step is to do a need assessment. Is this a project that could be commercialized for a revenue stream, or produced for the community benefit with financial support from the public, businesses, or foundations?

Because it is so labor intensive, if you determine that there is a need, you should do a staff, Friends, and/or community talent audit to see if you have access to someone with the skill set you need to do the proper programming.

Real-World Examples

Once the creative theme of the app is selected, it's then a matter of clarifying your marketing targets (institutions or public?), your marketing channel (iTunes store?), estimating costs associated with developing and selling, then setting the appropriate price. Set a price to get past the break-even point.

Exercises

» Establish product value. Estimate the cost of labor and materials. Then it's up to the organization to calculate the profit it would like to earn and set the price accordingly.

» Analyze the competition for pricing and organizational tips. Don't needlessly reinvent the wheel.

INTERVIEW WITH A DIGITAL CURATOR

Erin Bell has helped manage a software development effort for Cleveland State University that focuses on the history of local neighborhoods. The university uses apps to provide walking tour and other information about historical districts, which are gaining popularity as younger workers choose to live in cities rather than the suburbs. Bell shares these insights. The Cleveland Historical app/website (clevelandhistorical.org) is one instance of a larger international project called Curatescape (curatescape.org) that we operate from the Center. It began as a grant-funded NEH project (via the Digital Humanities Startup and Implementation programs), but has grown over the past few years and is now a significant source of revenue for the Center. We also provide contractual services, which you can read about at http://csudigitalhumanities.org/services/.

Additionally, we build some of our public history projects around financial support from partner organizations and family foundations.

As far as using software development to generate revenue, it is an uphill battle, especially when dealing with mobile apps, whose characteristics and underlying technology change rapidly and are, thus, expensive to maintain. For a while we were working with a third-party software developer, which allowed us to focus on the operational, promotional, educational, and research aspects of the Curatescape project, but that eventually became untenable for a variety of reasons, so we're now moving the project 100 percent in-house.

One of the biggest challenges—besides funding continuing development—is project management. Software development is a complex process, usually involving many dependent phases and more people than you might expect. There's also not much money in selling apps to consumers in most cases, so the work usually needs to be subsidized in some other way. In our case, clients pay for app store management and deployment (which itself borders on impossible for individuals and public institutions to do themselves, especially in academia), web and graphic design, training, long-term support, etc. All of this goes toward paying for continued development, which is (more or less) enough to cover a single full-time employee (myself). In other words, it's not a money-maker in itself. Thankfully, we have motives other than profit and this happens to fit well into our organizational mission and opens up other opportunities, including additional funding and research projects.

As far as sponsorships, we treat each of our Curatescape projects as their own entity. They have their own funders who generally help pay for the project and get to place their own logos in the app and on the website. We haven't pursued a more comprehensive form of sponsorship (that would say, place an American Airlines logo on every Curatescape app) but we would be open to that if someone offered!

Worth noting, though, some of the content on Cleveland Historical is actually "sponsored" by local organizations (e.g., Metroparks, family foundations, civic organizations, etc.–nobody with what you might call a profit motive). That funding basically helps us pay for student employment and for our small part-time research team.

(E. Bell, personal communication, October 29. 2015).

SPONSORSHIPS

General Concepts

SPONSORSHIPS HAVE THE SAME BENEFITS AND CHALLENGES as naming rights, but can be more efficient due to the scalability of the contract. In essence, they can be more dynamic, with various other value added options that can have a more flexible, higher impact on an audience in a shorter period of time.

Sponsorships can use the "ladder" approach whereby various physical areas and other means of exposures can be arranged based on the size of the contract. For example, a $5,000 annual sponsorship covers a Dewey range, a display table two times a year, and a newsletter article about the collection area they're sponsoring. $7,500 could include these plus two special programs. The extra funds could be used for guest honorariums, refreshments, or talent fees that will help insure a great draw!

A ladder approach to the benefits of being a business sponsor for the Haverford Township Free library (note the use of impressions) is shown in Appendix B.

These are generic sponsorships. They also have separate plans and benefits for individual event sponsorships (Haverford Township Free Library 2014).

The following four areas are the same as those used in naming rights, minus the one about building names. The contractual terms, setting of value, and use in publicity when apropos are pretty much the same. The major differences are generally the lengths of the agreements and special concerns about dealing with businesses seeking a form of advertising as opposed to families wishing to memorialize. Review the table on acknowledgment or advertising in chapter 2 to reacquaint yourself with the specific topics involved.

That being said, the major difference between naming rights (NR) and sponsorship (SP) is a matter of semantics. NR will be how something is known. SP is how something is provided. In reviewing the broadcast model, the difference between these would be like having an advertiser's name imbedded in the title, like "Mutual of Omaha's Wild Kingdom," as opposed to "the following presentation is brought to you in part by Mutual of Omaha."

Sample SP acknowledgement phrases:

» *For collection areas:* "Enjoy this new fiction, partially sponsored by . . ."
» *For furniture:* "Enjoy this bench, chair, or work desk, compliments of . . ."
» *For materials:* "This book/DVD/Playaway is available thanks to a generous contribution by . . ."
» *For rooms:* "The library thanks . . . for helping us maintain this space for your meetings."

METHOD 35

Sponsorship—Collection Areas

This method is specifically geared toward libraries that separate books and materials using a hierarchical organization method. At the top of the categories are fiction and non-fiction. Underneath these are more ranked categories. It's a great way to organize collections, and help market them to both the public and potential donors. The source of revenue would be from the public, businesses, and foundations, and should generate a high amount of income.

Establishing Value

Use
» CPM to determine objectively how many impressions of a message will be seen, and what every thousand impressions costs.
» Product value to estimate the cost of labor and materials. Then it's up to the organization to calculate the profit it would like to earn and set the price accordingly.
» Market value, that is, what your local competition is charging.

Board Considerations, Policy Considerations, and Government Involvement

» Specific board considerations usually involve signing off on the terms of large contracts and long commitments such as sponsorships.
» Specific policy considerations involve establishing the parameters of understanding as to how a method will be conducted—for example, what type of advertisement language will be allowed or whether only acknowledgment phrases can be used for certain methods.
» Revenue would probably not be subject to UBIT, but double-check to avoid unanticipated expenses.

Contracts and Procedures

» *Contract*: Continuing. One with a specific renewal process.
» *Procedures*: As a media operation, you would use both standard business operations procedures and traffic department operations procedures.

Promotions

» *General Promotions*: Communication is aimed at the public.

Revenue Method: General—Sponsorship: Collection Areas

Features	Advantages	Benefits
Prominence	Simple	Efficient memorialization

» *Targeted Promotions*: Communication is aimed at businesses or foundations.

Revenue Method: Targeted—Sponsorship: Collection Areas

Features	Advantages	Benefits
Prominence	Simple	Shows support of community
Used in multiple organization announcements	High number of impressions	Builds brand recognition

Moves Management Model

» *Discovery*: Use a media audit as well as personal contacts to find active local advertisers. Arrange an introduction.
» *Cultivation*: Come back and talk about what they want to do and how you can help them.
» *Solicitation*: Your proposal. Include a gift ladder that might involve value-added promotions.
» *Stewardship*: Have a publicity angle ready for them. Acknowledge their support and deliver on what you promised. Stay connected.

First Steps

Obviously, high start-up costs are involved if you consider constructing a special collection area, but they should be low if you're keeping the current collection in place. Then it's a matter of the labor involved developing and pitching the rights and the physical signage involved.

Other steps:

» Investigate the statutory restrictions on all government and oversight levels.
» Insure your organization's policies for awarding rights are crystal clear to avoid controversy.

» Develop a price based on your estimate of the construction costs, as well as the value of current and future CPM estimates, and your market value estimates, as indicated above in the Value section. If the collection area already exists, the construction costs can obviously be taken out of the equation.

» Put together a proposal outlining the costs + value + intangibles (such as the sponsor's image) that you can use to start shopping the rights around.

Real-World Examples: Denver Rules on Bond Funding

As mentioned in chapter 6's discussion on contracts and procedures, designating certain areas for naming rights or sponsorships might be complicated by certain legal restrictions that can be smoothed through proper contractual elements. Denver's agreements need approval from the city's library commission and city attorney. When bond money has paid for a building, it's important to be careful about what percentage of a facility is named and that the naming right has been granted in appreciation of a gift to support the programming in the library, not as a purchase of any space in the library (B. Ritenour, personal communication, July 13, 2015).

Exercises

Determine value using the following methods:

» *CPM:* The method of objectively determining how many impressions of a message will be seen, and what every thousand impressions costs (use the location exercise as a model).

» *Product value:* Estimate the cost of labor and materials. Then it's up to the organization to calculate the profit it would like to earn and set the price accordingly.

» *Market value:* What your local competition is charging.

» *Work with relevant stakeholders:* Successful entrepreneurs always involve others.

METHOD 36

Sponsorship—Furniture

Sponsorship for furniture like desks, benches, or even chairs should include maintenance and even weathering agreements, depending on the length of the contract. The source of revenue would be from the public, businesses, and foundations, and should generate a high amount of income.

Establishing Value

Use

- » CPM to determine objectively how many impressions of a message will be seen, and what every thousand impressions costs.
- » Product value to estimate the cost of labor and materials. Then it's up to the organization to calculate the profit it would like to earn and set the price accordingly.

Board Considerations, Policy Considerations, and Government Involvement

- » Specific board considerations usually involve signing off on the terms of large contracts and long commitments such as sponsorships.
- » Specific policy considerations involve establishing the parameters of understanding as to how a method will be conducted—for example, what type of advertisement language will be allowed or whether only acknowledgment phrases can be used for certain methods.
- » Revenue would probably not be subject to UBIT, but double-check to avoid unanticipated expenses.

Contracts and Procedures

- » *Contract*: Continuing. One with a specific renewal process.
- » *Procedures*: As a media operation you would use both standard business operations procedures and traffic department operations procedures.

Promotions

- » *General Promotions*: Communication is aimed at the public.

Revenue Method: General—Sponsorship: Furniture

Features	Advantages	Benefits
Prominence	Simple	Efficient memorialization

- » *Targeted Promotions*: Communication is aimed at businesses or foundations.

Revenue Method: Targeted—Sponsorship: Furniture

Features	Advantages	Benefits
Prominence	Simple	Shows support of community
Used in multiple organization announcements	High number of impressions	Builds brand recognition

Moves Management Model

» *Discovery*: Use a media audit as well as personal contacts to find active local advertisers. Arrange an introduction.

» *Cultivation*: Come back and talk about what they want to do and how you can help them.

» *Solicitation*: Your proposal. Include a gift ladder that might involve value-added promotions.

» *Stewardship*: Have a publicity angle ready for them. Acknowledge their support and deliver on what you promised. Stay connected.

First Steps

High start-up costs might be involved if you consider buying new furniture first, but they should be low if you're keeping the current furniture (e.g., a legal reference work table) or waiting until you have funding for purchases. Then it's a matter of the labor involved to develop and pitch the sponsorships and the physical signage involved.

Others steps:

» Investigate the statutory restrictions on all government and oversight levels.

» Confirm that organization's policies for awarding rights are clear enough to avoid controversy.

» Develop a price based on your estimate of the construction costs, as well as the CPM and your market value estimates, as indicated above in the Value section. If the furniture already exists, then costs can obviously be taken out of the equation.

» Put together a proposal outlining the costs + value + intangibles (such as the sponsor's image) that you can use to start shopping the sponsorships around.

Try not to accept in-kind one-for-one dollar exchanges, because the vendor often charges full retail. Unless you are seriously in need of furniture replacement and no other donor can be found, you should avoid this.

Real-World Examples

The Fort Worth library system knows the value of specific definitions when it comes to naming rights. Their page on this subject breaks down naming and sponsorship opportunities into five categories (1) building, (2) section of a building, (3) outdoor feature, (4) collection, and (5) furnishings and equipment, noting for each the minimum and maximum contribution levels and time span the rights will last for. Contribution levels are $5,000 for individuals and $10,000 for corporations. For contributions exceeding those levels, a special mention is made in a prominent place in the library. If contributions are under those amounts, a plaque or book plate is created. Rights last for the life of the purchased item (City of Fort Worth 2015).

Exercises

Determine value using the following methods:

» *CPM*: The method of objectively determining how many impressions of a message will be seen, and what every thousand impressions costs (use the location exercise as a model).
» *Product value*: Estimate the cost of labor and materials. Then it's up to the organization to calculate the profit it would like to earn and set the price accordingly.
» *Market value*: What your local competition is charging.
» *Work with relevant stakeholders*: Successful entrepreneurs always involve others.

METHOD 37

Sponsorship—Materials

One of the more widespread revenue-producing tools libraries use. Buying best sellers or specialty books (or DVDs, Playaways, laptops) and including an acknowledgment of the person or business that purchases it. The source of revenue would be from the public, businesses, and foundations, and should generate a high amount of income.

Establishing Value

Use

» CPM to determine objectively how many impressions of a message will be seen, and what every thousand impressions costs.
» Public motivation, a subjective value composed of emotional elements.
» Product value to estimate the cost of labor and materials. Then it's up to the organization to calculate the profit it would like to earn and set the price accordingly.

Board Considerations, Policy Considerations, and Government Involvement

» Specific board considerations usually involve signing off on the terms of large contracts and long commitments such as sponsorships.
» Specific policy considerations involve establishing the parameters of understanding as to how a method will be conducted—for example, what type of advertisement language will be allowed or whether only acknowledgment phrases can be used for certain methods.
» Revenue would probably not be subject to UBIT, but double-check to avoid unanticipated expenses.

Contracts and Procedures

» There are two ways organizations can approach this method: static or dynamic involvement between the sponsor and the organization receiving the sponsored purchase.

» Static purchases are the common purchase approach: for X dollars the sponsor gets their name or brand message on Y amount of material. Like the famous K.I.S.S. (Keep It Simple, Stupid) method, things are kept simple.

» With a more dynamic purchase approach, a library could work out a nurturing plan, where money is donated to replace core items, for example, in crafts or collectibles areas as well as add new ones, perhaps a "five-by-five" plan—for five newly published items, five repurchases of classics or "core" items to replace worn copies. This approach would lend itself well toward enriching the solicitation and stewardship moves in the Moves Management Model.

Contracts and Procedures for the Two Methods

Static

» *Contract*: One time. A simple exchange of a good for a price. No date span or renewability offered.

» *Procedures*: Standard business operations procedures.

Dynamic

» *Contract*: Continuing. One with a specific renewal process.

» *Procedures*: As a media operation you would use both standard business operations procedures and traffic department operations procedures. Traffic operations like inventory and continuity controls would help you keep the new purchases and replacement items non-replicating and balanced.

Promotions

» *General Promotions*: Communication is aimed at the public.

Revenue Method: General—Sponsorship: Materials

Features	Advantages	Benefits
Prominence	Simple	Memorialization/ recognition effort
Used with specific materials	Aimed at a targeted audience	Positive impact on community

» *Targeted Promotions*: Communication is aimed at businesses or foundations.

Revenue Method: Targeted—Sponsorship: Materials

Features	Advantages	Benefits
Prominence	Simple	Shows support of community
Used with specific materials	Aimed at a targeted audience	Brand development

Moves Management Model

» *Discovery*: Use a media audit as well as personal contacts to find active local advertisers. Arrange an introduction.
» *Cultivation*: Come back and talk about what they want to do and how you can help them.
» *Solicitation*: Your proposal. Include a gift ladder that might involve value-added promotions, or a chance to target specific materials to enhance service to their communities.
» *Stewardship*: Have a publicity angle ready for them, like the five-by-five approach mentioned above. Use their preferred channels of communication whenever possible.

First Steps

High start-up costs might be involved if you consider buying materials first, but they should be low if you wait until you have funding for purchases. Then it's a matter of the labor involved developing and pitching the rights and the physical signage involved.

Other steps:

» Investigate the statutory restrictions on all government and oversight levels.
» Insure organization's policies for awarding rights are crystal clear to avoid controversy.
» Develop a price based on what you estimate will be the material purchases cost, CPM, and your product value estimates, as indicated above in the Value section. If the material already exists that cost can obviously be taken out of the equation.
» Put together a proposal outlining the costs + value + intangibles (such as enhancing the sponsor's image) that you can use to start shopping the sponsorships around.

Try not to accept in-kind one-for-one dollar exchanges, because the vendor often charges full retail. Unless you are seriously in need of material replacement and no other donor can be found, avoid this.

Real-World Examples

The Fort Worth library system knows the value of specific definitions when it comes to naming rights. Their page on this subject breaks down naming and sponsorship opportunities these five categories, noting the minimum and maximum contribution levels and time span the rights will last for: (1) building, (2) section of a building, (3) outdoor feature, (4) collection, and (5) furnishings and equipment. Contribution levels are $5,000 for individuals and $10,000 for corporations; for contributions exceeding those levels a special mention is made in a prominent place in the library. If contributions are under those amounts, a plaque or book plate is created. Rights last for the life of the purchased item (City of Fort Worth 2015).

Exercises

Determine value using the following methods:

» *CPM*: The method of objectively determining how many impressions of a message will be seen, and what every thousand impressions costs (use the location exercise as a model).
» *Product value*: Estimate the cost of labor and materials. Then it's up to the organization to calculate the profit it would like to earn and set the price accordingly.
» *Market value*: What your local competition is charging.
» *Work with relevant stakeholders*: Successful entrepreneurs always involve others.

METHOD 38

Sponsorship—Rooms

Instead of calling a space Meeting Room 1, it can be named for a company or foundation. This has the potential to become one of the highest-value revenue streams, because the sponsor's name can be included in any publicity about activities in the meeting room. If it's a well-used room, that makes the name highly visible not only in your publicity efforts, but also in any publicity from the organizations that use the room. For example, "Tonight, the local auxiliary club will be meeting in the Rossman Auto Dealers Room at Anytown Public Library." The source of revenue would be from businesses and foundations, and should generate a high amount of income.

Establishing Value

Use

» CPM to determine objectively how many impressions of a message will be seen, and what every thousand impressions costs.
» Market value, that is, what your local competition is charging.

Board Considerations, Policy Considerations, and Government Involvement

» Specific board considerations usually involve signing off on the terms of large contracts and long commitments such as sponsorships.
» Specific policy considerations involve establishing the parameters of understanding as to how a method will be conducted—for example, what type of advertisement language will be allowed or whether only acknowledgment phrases can be used for certain methods.
» Revenue would probably not be subject to UBIT, but double-check to avoid unanticipated expenses.

Contracts and Procedures

» *Contract*: Continuing. One with a specific renewal process.
» *Procedures*: Standard business operations procedures.

Promotions

» *Targeted Promotions*: Communication is aimed at businesses or foundations.

Revenue Method: Targeted—Sponsorship: Rooms

Features	Advantages	Benefits
Prominence	Simple	Shows support of community
Used with organization program promotion and publicity	More impressions	Brand development

Moves Management Model

» *Discovery*: Use a media audit as well as personal contacts to find active local advertisers. Arrange an introduction.
» *Cultivation*: Come back and talk about what they want to do and how you can help them.
» *Solicitation*: Your proposal. Include a gift ladder that might involve value-added promotions.
» *Stewardship*: Have a publicity angle ready for them. Acknowledge their support and deliver on what you promised. Stay connected.

First Steps

Obviously, high start-up costs are involved if you consider constructing new rooms as part of the sponsorship expenses. If not, then it's a matter of the labor involved developing and pitching the sponsorship and the physical signage involved.

Other steps:
» Investigate the statutory restrictions on all government and oversight levels.
» Clarify your organization's policies for awarding rights.

» Develop a price based on the CPM and your market value estimates, as indicated above in the Value section.
» Put together a proposal outlining the costs + value + intangibles (such as the enhancing the sponsor's image) that you can use to start shopping the sponsorships around.
» Consider creating a sample naming plaque that you can use to show potential sponsors how their name or brand image can be presented. Could you create one using a 3D printer?

Real-World Examples

Please refer to the Naming Rights for Rooms real world example of method 28's *Memphis Public Library Cloud901 Naming Rights* for a great model of this method.

Exercises

Determine value using the following three methods:
» *CPM:* The method of objectively determining how many impressions of a message will be seen, and what every thousand impressions costs (use the location exercise as a model).
» *Product value:* Estimate the cost of labor and materials. Then it's up to the organization to calculate the profit it would like to earn and set the price accordingly.
» *Market value:* What your local competition is charging.

Work with relevant stakeholders. Successful entrepreneurs always involve others.

METHOD 39

Third-Party Products and Services

This revenue stream involves distributing products created by someone else through the library's website, display cases, computer centers, circulation desks, or other channels, including services such as the operation of coffee shops and the "mall concept," which uses physical or virtual single-purpose kiosks or full-fledged multi-product stores. The source of revenue would be from the public and businesses, and should generate a low to moderate amount of income. (The third party needs to make a profit, and they take on the bulk of the staffing and risk concerns.) Products can be library promotional items like coffee cups, specialized stationary, local artwork, and coupon books—anything that a library can earn money on through commissions. You may be able to get away with not paying UBIT fees for revenue from library promotional items, but will need to pay it for community coupon books or anything else without the library's name on it.

Positioned properly, it should be clear that the patron is supporting your organization as well as getting a good deal on whatever they purchase. You have to be ready to do some publicity, but should also arrange to be listed as a distributor in the third party's promotional material. For everyone involved, it should be a win-win.

Establishing Value

» *Use market value*, that is, what your local competition is charging.

Board Considerations, Policy Considerations, and Government Involvement

» Specific board considerations usually involve signing off on the terms of large contracts and long commitments such as offering space for a gift shop.
» Specific policy considerations involve establishing the parameters of understanding as to how a method will be conducted—for example, what type of advertisement language will be allowed or whether only acknowledgment phrases can be used for certain methods.
» Revenue would probably be subject to UBIT, but double-check to avoid unneeded expense calculations.

Contracts and Procedures

» *Contract*: Continuing. One with a specific renewal process. Set up a trial period of one year to determine seasonal demand and actual work required of library staff, then when renegotiating the next year's contract, consider an increase based on CPI plus a higher proportion of earnings for the library. Or, perhaps drop the vendor if its merchandise isn't moving, as you would with weeding books.
» *Procedures*: Standard business operations procedures.

Promotions

» *General Promotions*: Communication is aimed at the public.

Revenue Method: General—Third-Party Products and Services

Features	Advantages	Benefits
On premises	See what you're getting, as opposed to online shopping	No surprises
Features library brand	Shows support of organization	Shows your support
Variety of items	Multiple choices for all ages and interests	Something of value for everyone, encourages their library "habit."

» *Targeted Promotions*: Communication is aimed at businesses or foundations.

Revenue Method: Targeted—Third-Party Products and Services

Features	Advantages	Benefits
Local	Local promotion	More impressions
Usually cause-oriented; if not, a library partner	Inclusion in event publicity about cause and/or libraries	Brand recognition • "Smaller target, bigger bull's-eye"

Moves Management Model

- » *Discovery*: Target Friends groups, existing partners, patrons, and non-patrons (perhaps through flyers placed at locations outside of the library, for example, at coffee shops, grocery stores, etc.) who would take advantage of the cost-effectiveness and convenience of your facility.
- » *Cultivation*: Tap into your Friends groups, existing partners, patrons, and non-patrons for their input into the development and design of the methods used to achieve maximum exposure and usage.
- » *Solicitation*: Your proposal. Include a rate chart and/or incentives that might increase use and purchases.
- » *Stewardship*: Run periodic status checks, inspect inventory churn (determine what and how quickly items are moving), follow through with figures on attendance and dollars generated, thanks in part to everyone's help. Insure both parties' contractual obligations are being met, and that they know doing business with you helps the wider community.

First Steps

Because this method uses a third party, start-up costs will be low, especially if conducted online. Decide if the third party will be online or physically present.

If physically present in your organizations premises, do you need to build out space for them? Will they assume that cost?

If online, there are considerations that are less expensive but equally important to your revenue. Café Press is a vendor that tries to make the online selling experience as easy as possible for you. Their suggested steps include:

- » Create a simple design and/or brand statement that can be applied to various products.
- » Pick the products you wish to sell (they currently offer a product-match search engine that you could use to make decisions).
- » Publicize!
- » Earn money! They provide a base price for a product, you add your markup, then that markup will be your profit. Based on amount sold based on the base price, they provide bonuses on a sliding scale (Café Press, Inc. 2015).

Real-World Examples

A recent article in *Library Journal* presented seven case studies of various successful library gift shops. The examples were frequently run through Friends organizations, but the article also featured a section on Library Square, a group of private vendors and non-profit organizations situated in a mall-like setting under the auspices of the Salt Lake City Public Library System (Peet 2015). Library patrons can enjoy good food, buy plants, get a haircut, and build their writing skills at locations inside and immediately outside the Main Library (www.slcpl.lib.ut.us/shops) This is a unique concept an organization should consider when designing, constructing, or renovating buildings (Peet 2015).

Exercises

» *Determine value*: Base this on the CPM method, the method of objectively determining how many impressions of a message will be seen, and what every thousand impressions costs. Use the location exercise as a model. Also use the techniques that establish product and market values.
» *Analyze the competition*: Capture the intellectual retail high ground.
» *Work with relevant stakeholders*: Successful entrepreneurs always involve others.

METHOD 40

Tutoring

"Tutoring" is a generic term to describe one-on-one specialized instruction, usually in a subject that overwhelms students, or in which they are underachieving. The source of revenue would be from the public and businesses, and should generate a low amount of income.

Most libraries can't currently afford a "book a librarian" service (i.e., personalized research instruction). However, with proper marketing, families, businesses, and senior citizens might be willing to pay for extra individual instruction for their homework, career research, test preparation, or consumer research. e-media instruction and job research may be beyond the resources of even those libraries that are most desperate for funds. In those cases, do you really want to charge someone to learn how to, for example, download material on a Kindle, conduct a job search, or sign up for a necessary government program? Probably not.

But what about one-one-one bibliographic and research instruction—for example, helping find ten possible cars for sale, complete with consumer reports information, location, and within a specified cost range? It may take a patron five hours to accomplish what it could take a reference librarian one hour to do. Using a specific rate chart and questionnaires prior to research or instruction would help make the process very efficient and transparent. Calculating a value based on prevailing wages and hours will help you set a baseline, and from there you can build in whatever additional percentage you think your market will bear. Some libraries regularly offer ACT prep courses and sample tests, which usually are offered for free and have long waiting lists. Based on factors such as municipal guidelines and relationships with schools, charging a small "participation and materials fee" that goes toward defraying library costs might be feasible, especially if a long waiting list is involved.

Some people may be upset, but most will accept it. Many public libraries have recently started charging for tax forms because the government no longer issues as many paper forms as in the past. It's the way our world is going. To sustain the library's educational mission, some educational expenses down the line will need to be paid for by the end-user.

Establishing Value

» Use market value, that is, what your local competition is charging.

Board Considerations, Policy Considerations, and Government Involvement

» There are no special board and policy considerations except approval of the concept.
» Revenue would probably not be subject to UBIT, but double-check to avoid unanticipated expenses.

Contracts and Procedures

This method would use a onetime contract. As good stewards of the library's resources, it may be useful to discourage frivolous requests by asking for cash in advance, perhaps 50 percent at the start of the project and 50 percent upon completion.

» *Procedures*: Standard business operations procedures.

Promotions

» *General Promotions*: Communication is aimed at the public.

Revenue Method: Tutoring

Features	Advantages	Benefits
Specific subject or research target	Address learning in multiple ways— books, video, online and in-person	Better grades; efficiency in advancing in the learning curve

Moves Management Model

» *Discovery*: Target Friends groups, existing partners, patrons, and non-patrons (perhaps through flyers placed at locations outside of the library—for example, at coffee shops, grocery stores, and other places patronized by those who would take advantage of tutoring services.

» *Cultivation*: Tap into those groups for their input. This will help to develop and design a tutoring program that will achieve maximum exposure and usage.
» *Solicitation*: Your proposal. Include a rate chart and services offered.
» *Stewardship*: This is where you deliver on what you promised. Provide a feedback loop to insure client satisfaction.

First Steps

Start-up expenses should be low. Some libraries have been adding homework centers and tutoring areas into their building plans for new and renovated buildings, but it isn't necessarily useful to count those into the equation of starting up a tutoring service because those spaces could also be used for non-revenue-generating services.

To develop a revenue-generating service, you should:

» Do a statutory check on requirements to be a tutor.
» Consider your relationship with nearby schools.
» Confirm that there is a need for this service.
» Scan your community's other tutoring services to determine their rates, goals, grade levels serviced.
» Determine your range of services and hours; some may include:
  – Test preparation (finding study materials)
  – Government interface training (finding IRS forms, accessing the Affordable Care Act platform, copyright or trademark research)
  – Online school course management systems (how to download material and upload assignments)
  – Consumer research

Create a rate structure and contract for these services. Make sure you screen it with your legal experts.

Real-World Examples

The New York Public Library offers research services on a sliding scale of charges based on time spent searching and deadline requirements (New York Public Library 2015). Their request form is a great model of an online reference interview. In addition to basic contact information, they ask about the nature of the research (e.g., years to be covered); what type of preliminary work has been done (to avoid wasting time); restrictions on the amount of time that can be devoted to a project (to prevent expectations that complicated research can be completed in a couple of hours); any deadlines; and preferred delivery methods.

Although this isn't identical to a tutoring service, the concepts of specifying what needs to be covered and the hours contracted could be cross-pollinated into a tutoring program.

Exercises

» Analyze the competition for pricing and organizational tips. Don't needlessly reinvent the wheel.
» Do stakeholder development. Tap into your Friends groups, etc., for their input. Successful entrepreneurs always involve others.

METHOD 41

Vending Machines

Patrons always need peripheral school and office supplies, not to mention coffee. This method covers items that can be distributed via machines. Once set up, the service pays for itself, is a perk for patrons, and the only library staff that should be involved are those in bookkeeping, although some customer-service training and policies may have to be set up to handle refunds.

The source of revenue would be from the public, and should generate a low amount of income.

Like some of the services already discussed, this could be an easy source of revenue once the start-up process and remuneration details are resolved.

There are at least three possibilities:

1. ATMs
2. Food and beverage machines
3. Office or school supplies

There will probably be more options in the near future as technology develops.

Establishing Value

» Most of the companies in this field require very little in terms of you providing anything other than the space.
» *Use market value*, that is, what other local companies are receiving for vending machine placements.

Board Considerations, Policy Considerations, and Government Involvement

» Specific board considerations usually only involve signing off on the terms of contracts and long commitments.
» There are no special policy considerations, unless your staff and board feel the need to restrict food consumption to certain areas.
» Revenue would probably not be subject to UBIT, because it is a convenience for the public, but double-check to avoid unanticipated expenses.

Contracts and Procedures

» *Continuing*: All the standard contractual elements, including a defined time period, and built-in renewability options. Every vending machine company will have some type of continuing contract service agreement and standards as to what they will accept. These usually deal with the stocking options including timing, and tracking and paying out revenue.

» *Procedures*: Standard business operations procedures. These might include them having access to certain areas.

Promotions

» *General Promotions*: Communication is aimed at the public.

Revenue Method: Vending Machines

Features	Advantages	Benefits
Various food and products offered	Convenience having food and forgotten supplies available	Creates supportive environment for using services

Moves Management Model

» *Discovery*: Do an environmental scan for competing vending or food and product services.

» *Cultivation*: Standard meeting to discover vendors needs and charges.

» *Solicitation*: Your specific offer. Make sure they know doing business with you helps the wider community. They also share being associated with a community asset.

» *Stewardship*: Run periodic status checks to insure both parties' contractual obligations are being met.

First Steps

If you already have a place that can handle the footprint and electrical needs of the machines, start-up costs should be low, but they'll be relatively high if the vending area requires new construction—walls knocked out, new wiring, etc. Other considerations include:

» Will there be public outcries if eating and drinking is allowable? Be prepared with the features and benefits of the new services.

» Is there enough space? Is construction needed for the machine's footprints or electrical needs?

» Is there enough traffic to warrant the placement of the machines? For a staff room, vendors often require staffs of forty or more for placement of beverage machines, and seventy-five or more for placement of food machines. They are concerned not enough traffic will lead to product spoilage. (Vending Solutions 2015).

» Do your due diligence; ask for references and check with them on machine maintenance, restocking, and refund concerns.

Consider an in-house solution using the honor system, especially for staff rooms. It will be a bit more labor-intensive in terms of stocking and cash handling, but chances are you'll be able to provide snacks and bottled water at a much lower cost than machines, and still make a profit that can go to the general fund or toward a specific goal.

Real-World Examples

As mentioned above, due to the revenue being generated by providing a convenience to your employees and the public, UBIT should not be a concern. Nevertheless, library decorum will always be a concern. If you offer these to the public, it's best to have a designated area where people can properly use them. Office supply machines could be located near computer centers, with tables and chairs near food machines.

Exercises

» Will you be using an outside or in-house service?
» If in-house, establish product value: Estimate the cost of labor and materials. Then it's up to the organization to calculate the profit it would like to earn and set the price accordingly.
» If using a vendor, consider the local market value: What are other organizations charging for the goods in their machines?
» Analyze the competition for pricing and organizational tips. Don't needlessly reinvent the wheel.
» Do stakeholder development. Tap into your Friends groups, etc., for their input. Successful entrepreneurs always involve others.

METHOD 42

Vendor Shows

These are essentially events geared toward product education, where the library can invite related vendors such as medical, wedding, or green services into a room, sell table space and/or other equipment, and have exhibitors pay a percentage of promotional costs as well as doing their own advertising for the event. The source of revenue would probably be from the public and businesses, and should generate a moderate amount of income. Some shows are unique enough that you might be able to also charge the public a ticket fee.

You need to prepare for a weather calamity that cancels the event or causes a steep drop in attendance. That should be planned through your contract by determining alternate dates and net refunds based on up-front (not start-up, but annual) costs. There may be high start-up costs with the first one, in terms of vendor review and selection, booth set-up and tear down logistics, event marketing and publicity, concession and entertainment options, and, of course, billing and accounting.

Consider starting with a low-cost event to get the logistics down, like a twenty-table Christmas craft fair that runs for five hours in one of your meeting rooms. Figure the cost for the room if it had been booked by someone else that day, add 10 percent, round up if you have to, throw in maintenance and promotional costs, divide that by the number of tables, and use that as your table registration fee. In my library, a room for a social event goes for $40 an hour. An event that runs for five hours costs $200, plus 10 percent is $220. Add an hour or so of maintenance set-up and tear-down at $15 an hour and $20 in publicity costs, and the total is $255. 255 divided by 20 is $12.75. Round it up to $15 for the registration fee, and at $15 x 20 you've got an event that brings in $300 to the general fund—and who knows how many extra people into the library that day—plus an invaluable learning experience.

After you have the logistics down, you can target not just local craftspersons, but other businesses seeking to expand their sales, brand, etc., in the community; they are used to paying much more for this type of event.

Establishing Value

Use

> » CPM, the method of objectively determining how many impressions of a message will be seen, and what every thousand impressions costs. Be careful not to promise actual numbers for an event until you've hosted a few events and can set up a baseline. Promising numbers can affect tax benefits—and also paint you into a corner if they fall short. You can, however, tell attendees how many times they could be mentioned in the publicity efforts that are under your control, such as web page mentions, newsletter ads for the event, etc.
> » Market value, that is, what your local competition is charging for similar events.

Board Considerations, Policy Considerations, and Government Involvement

> » Specific board considerations usually just involve approval of major events like this.
> » Specific policy considerations involve establishing the parameters of understanding as to how a method will be conducted—for example, you might have a policy that restricts companies from selling goods out of your public meeting rooms; those might need to be adjusted for sales within your organization's running of an event.
> » Revenue would probably not be subject to UBIT, but double-check to avoid unanticipated expenses.

Contracts and Procedures

» *Contracts:* This method would probably use a onetime contract, especially for new business clients or a onetime only presence like a touring play, circus, cultural exhibit or an industrial brand. This method could also use a Seasonal contract for established sponsors. This would be a modified version of a continuing contact, specifying an annual event and right of first refusal in case the business climate changes.

» *Procedures:* Standard business operations procedures.

Promotions

» *General Promotions:* Communication is aimed at the public.

Revenue Method: General—Vendor Shows

Features	Advantages	Benefits
On premises	See what you're getting, as opposed to online shopping; usually local	No surprises
Variety of items	Multiple choices for all ages and interests	Selective shopping opportunity

» *Targeted Promotions:* Communication is aimed at businesses or foundations.

Revenue Method: Targeted—Vendor Shows

Features	Advantages	Benefits
Local event	Local promotion	More impressions
Usually cause-oriented	Inclusion in event publicity about cause	Brand connection with cause • "Smaller target, bigger bull's-eye"

Moves Management Model

» *Discovery:* Use a media audit as well as personal contacts to find active local vendors in the community. Arrange an introduction.

» *Cultivation:* Come back and talk about what they want to do and how you can help them.

» *Solicitation:* Your proposal. Include a gift ladder that might involve value-added promotions or better prominence in the show.

» *Stewardship:* Have a publicity angle ready for them. Insure both parties' contractual obligations are being met, and that they know doing business with you helps the wider community. Make their day by having them feel they're part of the effort, which they are! Others would like their alliance. Strive to keep it.

First Steps

To have a great vendor show, you need to pursue a typical project management plan that you're probably already doing for a special operation already. Create a committee; pick a specific theme, location, date, and timetable of activities. Plan a media and promotional announcement schedule. Find other similar vendor shows online and look at their FAQ's. See what you can learn from others.

» Check your event insurance coverage. Does it cover damage or theft of items?

» What venue can you use? This will probably determine if this will be a low cost or high cost start-up. If in-house, will you have to relocate other programs?

» How will you generate revenue? Vendor registrations? Ticket sales to the show? Commission on sales? All of the above?

» What will be your costs in terms of staff time, special logistical purchases or rentals, or an opening-night celebration? Considering all these will help determine your break-even point.

» What are your objectives? What's your goal past the break-even point? Do you want to convert new library visitors into Friends or have them return to attend another program oriented toward a related theme? Do you want to build up a database of contacts? Offer a contest to gather contact information?

» How much staff or volunteer time will be needed?

» Would participants be interested in participating in your organization's "online mall"? See the Gift Shop and Third Party mini-chapters for more on this concept.

Real-World Examples

In September, 2015, a Comic Convention in Fort Collins, Colorado, raised over $15,000, with over 2,000 attendees and 140 vendors participating. A wide variety of activities and contests took place on a Saturday, and over 180 volunteers were also involved (Coloradoan.com 2015).

Exercises

Determine value via the following:

» *CPM*: The method of objectively determining how many impressions of a message will be seen, and what every thousand impressions costs. Use the location exercise as a model.

» *Product value*: Estimate the cost of labor and materials. Then it's up to the organization to calculate the profit it would like to earn and set the price accordingly.

» *Market value*: What your local competition is charging. Analyze the competition for pricing and organizational tips. Don't needlessly reinvent the wheel.

» *Do stakeholder development*: Tap into your Friends groups, etc., for their input. Successful entrepreneurs always involve others.

❧

All of the methods described will benefit from good documentation. A look at positives and negatives will not only help you tweak your procedures and planning, but, more importantly, will teach you how to gain more value from your efforts by constantly growing them.

Whenever you do something new, documenting it through an activity log will help you process the next attempt more efficiently and profitably. Everything that's a surprise, lucky break or problem, positive or negative, should be documented. For example, in doing a vendor show, maybe you discover you want to stage this event over two days to insure a bigger crowd because the weather the one day you picked was bad, but the next day beautiful, in which case you have to plan for overnight storage of the vendor's display products.

Documenting everything and debriefing as many people as possible post-event will help you to carry on this revenue stream. Use this method to log metrics, new ideas and unforeseen complications, as described above in running vendor shows; do it with every new revenue-generating method tried from part II. Good documentation nurtures those efforts.

References

Airwave Management. 2015. "Cell Tower Income." www.cell-phone-towers.com/Cell-Tower-Income.html.

American Libraries. 2013. "Libraries Weigh Accepting Paid Ads to Keep Afloat," *American Libraries*, August 12. http://americanlibrariesmagazine.org/2013/08/12/libraries-weigh-accepting-paid-ads-to-keep-afloat/.

American Library Association. 2015. "Gale Cengage Learning Financial Development Award." www.ala.org/awardsgrants/gale-cengage-learning-financial-development-award.

ALA-Workman. 2015. *Book Lover's Calendar.* www.ala.org/united/sites/ala.org.united/files/content/friendszone/specialoffers/bookloversorderform2015.pdf.

American Society of Bookplate Collectors and Designers. 2015. www.bookplate.org.

Association for Library Services to Children. 2015. "Publicity, Programming and Promotion—Arrange an Author Visit." www.ala.org/alsc/issuesadv/kidscampaign/authorvisits.

Bakija, M. 2015. "Annual Bike the Branches Library-Hopping Event." http://fortgreenefocus.com/blog/2015/04/07/mark-your-calendar-annual-bike-the-branches-library-hopping-event-is-saturday-may-9/.

Book Sale Finder. 2015. http://booksalefinder.com.

Booksalemanager.com. 2015. "How to Run a Non-Profit Book Sale." www.booksalemanager.com/nonprofit-used-book-sale-guide.aspx.

Burton, T. 2008. *Naming Rights: Legacy Gifts and Corporate Money.* Hoboken, NJ: John Wiley and Sons, Inc.

Café Press, Inc. 2015. "Ways to Make Money." www.cafepress.com/cp/info/sell/index.aspx?area=intro_money&page=intro_money.

CEP-Center for Electrosmog Prevention. 2012. "How Much Revenue is Gained with Cell Tower Leases?" www.electrosmogprevention.org/public-health-alert/cell-towers-health-alerts/q-how-much-revenue-is-gained-w-cell-tower-leases/.

City of Fort Worth. 2015. "Naming/Recognition Policy." http://fortworthtexas.gov/library/about/namingrecognition-policy.html.

Collins, K. 2014, July 16. "Naming Rights Proposed for Library Capital Campaign." www.keepmecurrent.com/current/news/naming-rights-proposed-for-library-capital-campaign/article_6597412e-0cec-11e4-b80e-0019bb2963f4.html.

Coloradoan.com. 2015. "Letter: Comic Con Raises $15,000 for Library," September 24. www.coloradoan.com/story/opinion/2015/09/24/letter-comic-con-raises-library/72769858/.

Community Toolbox Initiative. 2015. Chapter 46, Section 9: Obtaining Corporate Resources. http://ctb.ku.edu/en/table-of-contents/sustain/long-term-sustainability/obtain-corporate-resources/main.

Cuyahoga County Public Library. 2013. "Passport Centers." www.cuyahogalibrary.org/Services/Passport-Centers.aspx.

Eisler, M. 2015. "How to Organize Your First Race." www.active.com/running/articles/how-to-organize-your-first-race.

Gill, L. 2014. "Behind the Scenes at the Friends of the Library Book Sale," *Memphis Flyer*, May 15. www.memphisflyer.com/memphis/behind-the-scenes-at-the-friends-of-the-library-book-sale/Content?oid=3669743.

Gray and Company, Publishers. nd. "Speakers Bureau." www.grayco.com/speakers/index.shtml.

Great Nonprofit.org Blog. 2015. *Corporate Matching Gifts Programs: Billions Not Received by Charities.* http://greatnonprofits.org/nonprofitnews/corporate-matching-ift-programs-money-unused/.

Halsema, L. 2014. "I Love My Library Card FAQ." Syrsi Dynix, www.sirsidynix.com/blog/2014/11/13/i-love-my-library-card-faq.

Harrison Public Library. 2015. "A Taste of Harrison." www.harrisonpl.org/a-taste-of-harrison.php.

Haverford Township Free Library. 2014. "Get the Business Bucks: Creating a Sponsorship Program on a Shoestring." Presentation material from PaLa Annual Conference, September 28.

Jacksonville Public Library. 2015, August 4. "Conference Center: Meeting and Event Guidelines". http://jaxpubliclibrary.org/ConferenceCenter/main.html.

Kelvin Smith Library. 2015. *Multimedia Equipment: Borrowing, Renewals, Fines and Fees.* http://library.case.edu/ksl/services/circulation/borrowing/multimediaequipment/.

Knowhownonprofit.org. nd. "Setting Up a Charity Shop." http://knowhownonprofit.org/funding/trading/charityshops/setup.

LarMar Enterprises Inc. nd. "50–50 Raffle Fundraiser." www.fund-raising-ideas.org/DIY/50–50.htm.

LaVista, S. 2015. "Testimonial, Susan LaVista, Director, Hampton Bays Public Library." www.ebscoppg.com.

Lekocevic, M. 2014. "Library Offers a Taste of Art," June 2. www.columbiagreenemedia.com/greene_county_news/news/article_3a107e60-ea8e-11e3–9964–001a4bcf887a.html.

Lexington Public Library. 2015. "Library Cable Channel 20." www.lexpublib.org/
library-cable-channel.

Library Hotline. 2014, "Queens Library Considers Vending App." *Library Hotline* 43
(47).

Madison Public Library. 2015. "Naming of Library Buildings." www.madisonpublic
library.org/policies/naming-of-library-buildings.

Memphis Library Foundation. nd. "Corporate Knowledge Bowl." www.memphislibrary
foundation.org/corporate-knowledge-bowl/.

Merrimack Journal. 2015 "Kickathon Helps Raise Money for Merrimack
Public Library's Children's Room." www.cabinet.com/merrimackjournal/
merrimacknews/1061556–308/kickathon-helps-raise-money-for-merrimack
-public.html. *Merrimack Journal*, April 17.

Mies, G. 2014. "Which Crowdfunding Platform Is Best for Your Organization?"
http://forums.techsoup.org/cs/community/b/tsblog/archive/2013/09/03/
which-crowdfunding -platform-is-best-for-your-organization.aspx?utm_source
=newsletter&utm_medium=email&utm_term=blog&utm_content
=sep1&utm_campaign=btc.

MLB Advanced Media, LP. 2015. "Scoreboard Messages." http://cleveland.indians
.mlb.com/cle/fan_forum/scoreboard.jsp.

New York Public Library. 2015. "Research Services." www.nypl.org/help/get-what
-you-need/fee-based-research-order-form.

O'Conner, K. P. 2013. "Naming Rights Available at New Tiverton Library." *Herald
News*, July 2. www.heraldnews.com/news/x273428095/Naming-rights-available
-at-new-Tivertonpublic-library.

Peet, L. 2015. "Gifted Libraries." *Library Journal*, March 6. http://lj.libraryjournal.com
/2015/03/managing-libraries/gifted-libraries/#_.

Public Library of Cincinnati and Hamilton County. nd. "The Library Foundation:
Ways to Support-Naming Rights." http://foundation.cincinnatilibrary.org/
WaysToSupport/NamingRights.

Quaal, W. L. and Brown, J. A. 1976. *Broadcast Management: Radio-Television*. New
York: Hastings House Publishers, Inc.

Receipt Media. 2013. *News*. www.receiptmedia.ca/news/.

Rua, R. 2011, February 1. *Running a Passport Acceptance Facility at Your Library*.
http://americanlibrariesmagazine.org/2011/02/01/running-a-passport
-acceptance-facility-at-your-library/.

San Diego Union-Tribune. 2014. "Residents Voice Opposition to Proposed Carmel
Valley Library Cell Tower." *San Diego Union-Tribune*, Jan 30. www.delmartimes
.net/news/2014/jan/30/residents-voice-opposition-to-proposed-carmel/.

Seattle Public Library. 2015. "Podcasts." www.spl.org/library-collection/podcasts.

Shaker Heights Public Library. 2015. "Business Services." http://shakerlibrary.org/
services/business-services/.

Tetanish, R. 2015. "Library Foundation to Kick Off Fundraising Campaign."
Truro Daily, July 17. www.trurodaily.com/News/Local/2015–07–17/
article-4217953/Library-foundation-to-kick-off-fundraising-campaign/1.

Vending Solutions. 2013. "Frequently Asked Questions." www.vendingsolutions.com/
    faq/.

Urban Libraries Council. nd. "Recycling. Memphis Public Library." www.urban
    libraries.org/recycling-innovation-191.php?page_id=42.

Williamson Public Library. 2014, October 2. "Bullets and Bayonets Book Release
    Party." https://wcpltn.wordpress.com/tag/academy-park-press/.

CONCLUSION

AS WE END, ONCE AGAIN I'D LIKE TO FRAME THE TOPIC in the context of the for-profit world. We've been reviewing new revenue sources, also known as revenue streams. In the article I mentioned in the introduction of this book, Inc.com's definition of the term is revenue streams = income = sales. The article states that it's less crass for people to use the phrase "revenue streams," but essentially it means sales. I've heard library directors use the term "commercialization" in the same tactful way to an audience of librarians, some of whom seem to seethe at hearing the word "sales" mentioned in the same sentence with "library."

The Inc.com article says that the quest for revenue streams is stimulated by change, either negative or positive. Change creates opportunities. Public broadcasting, once funded totally by the government, was forced by negative change to develop fund-raising skills. This they've done, and they still have not lost track of their mission, which is similar to the library's mission: to provide access to programming and entertainment not found via commercial outlets. By being both real pros and uplifters when using an advertising model, they have helped their operations thrive, and continue to enrich their communities, as every NP seeks to do.

In the 1980s, I went to Ohio University for my Master's in Communications, specializing in broadcasting. I worked at the university's telecommunications center, a complex that housed the studios of a combination of public radio, TV, and cable stations that provided quality programming to the foothills of the Appalachians, an area ranging for hundreds of miles not serviced by commercial broadcasting.

Although not quite the same concept in practice, these days, thanks to the internet and new technology, any library or nonprofit can become its own telecommunications center. Even without broadcast frequencies, they can still build their own channels for video and aural delivery of programs aligned with their missions. They can be accessible to all, 24/7, and have staffs ready to provide assistance or follow through in real life. We are entering into an exciting golden age of service and communications, with vision and resources the only roadblocks.

The key ingredient to succeed in developing vision and resources is an entrepreneurial spirit, which requires keeping your eyes open to opportunities, and developing the discipline and skill to turn ideas into saleable products or services. This book, I believe, has shown how easy that can be. Use the Money Matrix table as a springboard for productive group discussions and brainstorming with staff and stakeholders, to grow your services and prepare for rainy days.

Reference

Inc.com. "Revenue Streams." *Encyclopedia of Business Terms.* www.inc.com/encyclopedia/revenue-streams.html.

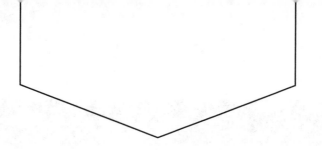

APPENDIX A
THE MONEY MATRIX TABLE

Annual revenue amount:

» Low = >$1K
» Moderate = $1–10K
» High = $10–25K;
» Significant = <$25K

Start-up costs include design, construction, and initial operational costs.
Policy requirements: G = covered by generic existing policies; S = Specific rules.

REVENUE METHOD	SOURCE	AMOUNT	HIGH START-UP COSTS	PUBLIC RELATIONS EFFORT	BOARD INVOLVE-MENT	POLICY REQUIRE-MENTS	GOVERNMENT INVOLVEMENT	RENEW-ABLE	CATEGORY
	Public, Business, Foundation	Low, Moderate, High, Significant	Yes/No	General, Targeted	General, Specific	General, Specific	Taxes, None	One-time, Continuing, Seasonal, Legacy	Advertising, Sponsorship, Facility, Product
Art Show–Sales	P/B	M	Y	G/T	G	G	N	O	P
Athletic Competitions	P/B	M	Y	G/T	G	G	N	S/O	S
Author Sales	P	L	N	G/T	G	G	N	O	P
Advertising–Newsletter	B	M	Y	T	G	S	T	C	A
Advertising–Podcast	B	M	Y	T	G	S	T	C	A
Advertising–Program Rebroadcast and Cable Streaming	B	L-M	Y	T	G	S	T	O/C	A
Advertising–Website	B	M	N	T	G	S	T	C	A
Advertising in Calendars and Special Publications	P/B	M	Y	G/T	G	S	T	O/C	A
Advertising Screens	B	M	Y/N	T	G	S	T	C	A
Book/Resource Templates	P/B/F	M	Y/N	G/T	G	G	N	O/C	S

REVENUE METHOD	SOURCE	AMOUNT	HIGH START-UP COSTS	PUBLIC RELATIONS EFFORT	BOARD INVOLVE-MENT	POLICY REQUIRE-MENTS	GOVERNMENT INVOLVEMENT	RENEW-ABLE	CATEGORY
	Public, Business, Foundation	Low, Moderate, High, Significant	Yes/No	General, Targeted	General, Specific	General, Specific	Taxes, None	One-time, Continuing, Seasonal, Legacy	Advertising, Sponsorship, Facility, Product
Book Sales—Community	P	H	N	G	G	G	N	S	P
Book Sales—Third Party	P/B	M	N	G	S	S	N	C	P
Cell Tower Lease	B	H	Y	T	S	G	T	C	F
Charging Stations	B	L	N	G/T	S/G	G	N	C	P
Crowdfunding	P	M	N	G	S	S	N	O	S
Equipment Rental	P/B	L	Y	G	S	S	T	O	F
Event Sponsorship	B/F	H/S	N	T	S	S	N	O/S	S
Facility Rental	P/B	M	N	G/T	G	S	T	O	F
50-50 Raffles	P	M	N	G	S	S	T	O	P
Gift Shops	P	M	Y	G	S	S	T	C	P
Matching Grants/ Donations Challenges	P/B/F	S	N/Y	G/T	G	G	G	O	S
Medical Services Partnerships	P/B	M	N	G/T	S	G	N	O	F
Meeting Services	P/B	L	Y	G/T	G	G	N	O/C	F
Naming Rights (NR)— Building	P/B/F	S	Y	G/T	S	S	N	L	S/F
NR—Collection Areas	P/B/F	S	N	G/T	S	S	N	L	S/F
NR—Furniture	"	H	Y/N	"	S	S	N	L	S/F
NR—Materials	"	M	Y/N	"	S	S	N	L	S/F
NR—Rooms	"	H	N	"	S	S	N	L	S/F
NR—Own a Day	P/B	M	N	"	S	S	N	O	A/F

REVENUE METHOD	SOURCE	AMOUNT	HIGH START-UP COSTS	PUBLIC RELATIONS EFFORT	BOARD INVOLVE- MENT	POLICY REQUIRE- MENTS	GOVERNMENT INVOLVEMENT	RENEW- ABLE	CATEGORY
	Public, Business, Foundation	Low, Moderate, High, Significant	Yes/No	General, Targeted	General, Specific	General, Specific	Taxes, None	One-time, Continuing, Seasonal, Legacy	Advertising, Sponsorship, Facility, Product
Passports	P	H	Y	G	G	G	N	C/O	P
Publishing	P	M	N	T/G	S	S	N	C/O	P
Receipts—Date Due	B/F	H	N	T	S	S	N	C	A
Recycling	P/B	L	N	G	S	S	N	C	F
Software Apps	P/B	L	H	G/T	G	G	N	O	P
Sponsorship (SP)— Collection Areas	P/B/F	H	N	G/T	S	S	N	C	S/F
SP—Furniture	"	H	N	G/T	S	S	N	C	S/F
SP—Materials	"	H	N	G/T	S	S	N	C	S/F
SP—Rooms	"	H	N	G/T	S	S	N	C	S/F
Third-Party Products and Services	P/B	L-M	N	G/T	S	S	T	C	P
Tutoring	P/B	L	N	G	G	G	N	O	P
Vending Machines	P	L	N-Y Area develop- ment	G	S	G	N	C	P
Vendor Shows	B/P	M	Y-N	G/T	S	S	N	S/O	F

APPENDIX B
SPONSORSHIP LADDER

	$50 ENHANCED	$100 COPPER	$250 BRONZE	$500 SILVER	$1,000 GOLD	$2,500 PLATINUM	$5,000 DIAMOND
Enhanced listing on the Online Community Business & Organization Directory (including business name, type, phone, and link to website)	✓	✓	✓	✓	✓	✓	✓
Your organization promoted as a sponsor on the Library's website and HTFL connection for 1 year (108,000+ impressions annually anticipated)		✓	✓	✓	✓	✓	✓
HTFL Sponsor Badge for your website		✓	✓	✓	✓	✓	✓
Your organization listed in promotional materials and recognition at major Library events throughout the year			✓	✓	✓	✓	✓
Your organization featured in the HTFL Connection eNewsletter and website in "Spotlight on Local Business" (1 two-week period during the year, 2,500 impressions anticipated)			✓	✓	✓	✓	✓
Complimentary tickets to the Friends of HTFL Garden Tour			2	2	2	2	2
Listing including your organization's logo on promotional materials for major library events				✓	✓	✓	✓
Complimentary tickets to the HTFL Gala and Silent Auction					2	4	6	8

INDEX